Realism and Tinsel

Also available in the Cinema and Society series
(Series editor: Jeffrey Richards, *Department of History, University of Lancaster*)

The Age of the Dream Palace
Cinema and Society in Britain 1930–1939
Jeffrey Richards

The Epic Film
Myth and History
Derek Elley

The British Labour Movement and Film 1918–1939
Stephen G. Jones

Mass-Observation at the Movies
Edited by Jeffrey Richards and Dorothy Sheridan

Cinema, Censorship and Sexuality, 1909–1925
Annette Kuhn

Film and the Working Class
Peter Stead

The Hidden Cinema
British Film Censorship in Action, 1913–1972
James C. Robertson

Film and Reform
John Grierson and the Documentary Film Movement
Ian Aitken

Realism and Tinsel

Cinema and society in Britain 1939–1949

Robert Murphy

London and New York

First published 1989
by Routledge
First published in paperback 1992
by Routledge
11 New Fetter Lane, London EC4P 4EE
29 West 35th Street, New York, NY 10001

© *1989, 1992 Robert Murphy*

Transferred to Digital Printing 2003
Printed and bound by Antony Rowe Ltd, Eastbourne

Disc conversion by Columns Typesetters of Reading

British Library Cataloguing in Publication Data
Murphy, Robert
    Realism and tinsel: cinema and society in
    Britain 1939–1949. – (Cinema and society)
    I. Title   II. Series
    306.485

Library of Congress Cataloging in Publication Data
Murphy, Robert
    Realism and tinsel: cinema and society
    in Britain, 1939–1949/Robert Murphy.
        p.   cm.
    Bibliography: p.
    Includes index.
    1. Motion pictures—Great Britain—History. 2. Motion pictures—
    Social aspects—Great Britain.   I. Title.
PN1993.5.G7M87 1989
791.43'0941—dc19

ISBN 0 415 07684 6

For Clare and Sophie

Contents

List of Illustrations

General Editor's Preface

The pre-eminent popular art form of the first half of the twentieth century has been the cinema. Both in Europe and America from the turn of the century to the 1950s cinema-going has been a regular habit and film-making a major industry. The cinema combined all the other art forms – painting, sculpture, music, the word, the dance – and added a new dimension – an illusion of life. Living, breathing people enacted dramas before the gaze of the audience and not, as in the theatre, bounded by the stage, but with the world as their backdrop. Success at the box office was to be obtained by giving the people something to which they could relate and which therefore reflected themselves. Like the other popular art forms, the cinema has much to tell us about people and their beliefs, their assumptions and their attitudes, their hopes and fears and dreams.

This series of books will examine the connection between films and the societies which produced them. Film as straight historical evidence; film as an unconscious reflection of national preoccupations; film as escapist entertainment; film as a weapon of propaganda – these are the aspects of the question that will concern us. We shall seek to examine and delineate individual film *genres*, the cinematic images of particular nations and the work of key directors who have mirrored national concerns and ideals. For we believe that the rich and multifarious products of the cinema constitute a still largely untapped source of knowledge about the ways in which our world and the people in it have changed since the first flickering images were projected on to the silver screen.

Jeffrey Richards

Acknowledgements

Thanks are due to Richard Collins and Vincent Porter who introduced me to forties British cinema; Olga Kenyon, Mary Wood, and Jim Cook who allowed me to explore my ideas by teaching courses on the subject, and to my students who acted as unwitting guinea pigs. Innumerable people have helped me during the long gestation period of this book, but I am particularly indebted to Paul Kerr, Julian Petley, Helen Gray, Robin Cross, Dudley Baines, Tise Vahimagi, Claire Blakeway, Chris Voisey, Victor Dalton, Adeline North, Steve Neale, Allen Eyles, Paul Taylor, David Walters, Sheila Johnston, Gillian Swanson, Ben Churchill, Colin Sorenson, Linda Wood, Kathy Garsten, Maureen Humphries, John Offord, Ian Aitken, and Sarah Street. Pete Todd, Michael Jackson, Sue Harper, Tracey Scoffield, and my father Roland Murphy read parts of the book, and if their criticisms were not always appreciated at the time, I thank them now for trying to put me on the straight and narrow. I would also like to express my gratitude to the staff of the BFI Library and to Elaine Burrows, Jackie Morris, and Tim Cotter of the National Film Archive for their help. Finally, I am deeply grateful for the patience and erudition of my editor, Jeffrey Richards, the support and advice of Richard Dacre, and the endurance of Clare Noel who read each section of the manuscript and helped ameliorate my worst excesses.

Film stills appear by courtesy of Flashbacks and the Stills Division of the National Film Archive.

Introduction

The forties are considered the golden age of the British film industry, though that reputation rests on a very small sample of films: *The Way Ahead, San Demetrio–London, In Which We Serve, Fires Were Started, Millions Like Us, Henry V, The Way to the Stars, Brief Encounter, Passport to Pimlico, Kind Hearts and Coronets, Whisky Galore*, and *The Third Man*. At the time these films and a few more like them were enthusiastically adopted by the film critics as evidence that at last the British film industry had come of age and could produce films of which to be proud. Their defining characteristics (with the exception of *The Third Man*) were a concentration on authentically British subjects, and a realistic approach which owed a debt to the British documentary movement of the thirties. Dilys Powell in her influential pamphlet, *Films Since 1939*, wrote in praise of 'the new movement in the British cinema: the movement towards documentary truth in the entertainment film',[1] and along with other enthusiasts for the new realism, such as Sidney Bernstein, Michael Balcon, Richard Winnington, and Roger Manvell, she welcomed these films as a progressive force which would wean people away from their dependence on unhealthy fantasies and help them to become more worthy and responsible citizens.

Unfortunately this laudable concern for a more democratic society became entangled with an impatient elitism which had no time for the vulgarities and crudities of popular culture, and, as the democratic impulse withered with the forties, what was left was a concern for art in the cinema, a quality which British film-makers seemed ill-fitted to supply. There then followed a long period in which the British cinema was ignored or disparaged as anaemic, parochial, unstylish, shallow, lacking both the vitality of Hollywood and the artistic seriousness of European cinema. Thus it is not altogether surprising that the current generation of up-and-coming film-makers appears to be totally ignorant of the history and traditions of the industry they work in. Mike Radford (*Another Time, Another Place*, 1984) quotes with approval Truffaut's famous dictum 'isn't there a certain incompatibility between the terms "cinema" and "Britain"?', and Neil Jordan (*Angel, Company of Wolves, Mona Lisa*) moving from Irish literature, dominated by the ghosts of Yeats, Joyce, and O'Casey, to British film-making, was attracted by 'the freedom he feels from any sense of tradition'.[2] The limited revival of interest in British cinema which has occurred in the past five years has failed to change the prevailing view that there is little beyond Ealing and the realist classics. Significantly, when the BBC decided to broadcast a history of British cinema in 1987, they turned to the venerable Dilys Powell to present it.

Once one delves into the history of British cinema, it becomes obvious that the realist films are a small, and in box-office terms insignificant, minority, and that many of the films dismissed by the critics have qualities over and above their curiosity value. Films like *The Man in Grey*, *The Seventh Veil*, *So Evil My Love*, *They Made Me a Fugitive*, utterly contradict the idea that British cinema is anything less than full-blooded; and seen in their proper context 'realist' films like *Brief Encounter* and *The Small Back Room*, with their threatening shadows and angst-ridden protagonists, belong more properly to a rich tradition of melodrama.

If one begins to look at films less as timeless art objects and more as manifestations of that popular tradition activated by Charles Dickens, Victor Hugo, and D.W. Griffith to explore the struggle for survival, the fight for love and dignity in urban industrial society, then perhaps a more suitable framework can be built for the study of cinema in Britain.

The book is in two parts. The first four chapters deal with the war period and are roughly chronological. There are now quite a number of studies on British cinema during the war and I have merely tried to widen the field and put the films in a social context. The second and much longer part is organized in a different way. There were a lot more films made between 1945 and 1950 than there were during the war and they are much less well-known. I have attempted to map out the field with five cycles of films – costume pictures, contemporary melodramas, British gangster films, morbid thrillers, and comedies – which I think deserve attention. Though these chapters deal predominantly with the late forties, there is some attempt to reach back into the war years, particularly in the comedy chapter.

To some extent my categories are arbitrary – it would be easy enough to talk about *It Always Rains on Sunday* (a spiv film), *Holiday Camp* (a comedy), and *Temptation Harbour* (a morbid thriller) as realist films; or to classify many of the films dealt with in the chapters 'Exotic Dreams' and 'Passionate Friends?' as women's pictures. Some films which don't fit comfortably into any of my categories such as *Scott of the Antarctic* (technically a costume film but worlds apart from *Caravan*, *Blanche Fury*, or even *Saraband for Dead Lovers*) or *The Fallen Idol* (which has a *Brief Encounter*-like sub-plot but is primarily concerned with the relationship between a lonely boy and his surrogate father) have been left out. This is unfortunate but inevitable in a book which tries to impose a coherent pattern on events rather than simply cataloguing them.

I also regret that in my concern with thematic patterns I have had little space to devote to directors. In some ways, though, this is not a bad thing –

most of the major directors have been paid due attention in earlier histories and monographs and those lesser figures like Lance Comfort, Lawrence Huntington, John Paddy Carstairs, David Macdonald, Brian Desmond Hurst, Leslie Arliss, Marcel Varnel, and John E. Blakeley have at least been introduced here. Perhaps a more important neglect is of producers like Ted Black and Filippo del Giudice; cameramen like Robert Krasker, Guy Green, Jack Cardiff, Arthur Crabtree, Stephen Dade, Otto Heller; art directors like John Bryan, Alex Vetchinsky, Oliver Messel. . . . But this is merely the tip of an iceberg of talent. Hopefully someone else will have the time and resources to carry out the necessary oral history which will record their contribution to British cinema.

1   Britain Alone

Not since the 1924–26 studio slump has the British film been confronted with the disagreeable prospect of temporary extinction, and to prophesy the state of home production a year from now would be as hazardous as any other wartime prediction. Only the optimism of craziness foresees a revival in the worth-while sense, and the task of keeping up a supply of product may necessitate a complete revolution in our methods of promotion and finance. (*Kinematograph Weekly*, December 1939)[1]

Uncertain beginnings

When war was declared on Sunday 3 September 1939 it looked as if the film industry would be the first casualty. A few weeks earlier, cinema managers had received a Home Office circular warning them that 'during the initial stages of a war all theatres, music halls, cinemas and other places of entertainment shall be closed throughout the country'.[2] A radio announcement following Chamberlain's broadcast confirmed the order. On Monday, cinema staffs, uncertain of their future, set about spring-cleaning and carrying out black-out precautions; by the end of the week they were fearful for their jobs.

In Wardour Street, the heart of the film industry, several of the major film distributors, optimistic that the war or the closure of cinemas could not last for long, but mindful of their own safety, set out for unfamiliar green pastures: MGM to Rickmansworth, Grand National to Cheltenham, General Film Distributors to Newbury, Columbia to Wadhurst Castle, Sussex.

In the studios there was confusion. Later reports complained of studio staffs being laid off and productions abandoned. But the industry had not fully recovered from a serious slump. Shepperton had been used for very few feature films since the end of 1937, Pinewood had been closed since the end of 1938, and the big new Amalgamated studios at Elstree had been snapped up by its competitors and leased to the government as a warehouse.

When no bombs fell exhibitors and their audiences began to get restive. Britain had approximately 4,800 cinemas and the Cinema Exhibitors

Association (CEA) had considerable political clout. Delegations were dispatched to Whitehall and the *Kinematograph Weekly* persuasively argued that:

> If intoxication is becoming a public scandal, if public houses have sold out of beer by 8 p.m. just because the people will insist upon being with a crowd of their fellows and there is nowhere else to go, then the time for re-opening the kinema – and the theatres and the music halls – has become an urgent public necessity.[3]

The government was forced to agree. Evacuees, rushed out of the conurbations in the first few days, were drifting back to their homes; plans to disperse government ministries were suspended; the film distribution companies were returning to Wardour Street from their country retreats. Within two weeks of war being declared most cinemas were open again. They were to stay open even when the Blitz did come.

There remained the problem of what was to be shown in the re-opened cinemas. Though the technicians union, the ACT, and a few of the more articulate employers like Sidney Bernstein and Michael Balcon, argued that the production of British feature films was essential for wartime morale, all they were able to achieve was a halt to the requisitioning of studios. Government policy was dilatory and contradictory with the Board of Trade inclined to abandon film production in Britain and rely on Hollywood to supply what entertainment might be necessary, and the Treasury keen to foster production as a means of reducing the outflow of foreign exchange (Hollywood films cost at least forty million dollars a year). There was some doubt, though, whether film production could survive in Britain.[4]

The British film industry was never a very sturdy plant and financial sources tended to dry up at the first sign of trouble. With studios requisitioned and the future of cinema-going uncertain it was hardly surprising that independent producers who had to raise money on a film-by-film basis were forced to shut up shop, but the pessimistic climate also affected much larger companies. ABPC, a major conglomerate with a cinema circuit of over four hundred halls, was insufficiently committed to production to prevent its big Elstree studio from being requisitioned, though a second studio at Welwyn was kept open for the production of low-budget supporting features.

The American companies were required by law to handle a certain percentage of British films, which they either acquired from British producers or made themselves. Initially they reduced their activities to a bare minimum, but once British producers showed it was feasible and even profitable to make films in wartime Britain, Warner Brothers re-opened their Teddington studios (and kept them open until they suffered a direct hit by a V1 rocket in the autumn of 1944), MGM and Twentieth Century-

Fox commissioned a number of films from Gainsborough (including Carol Reed's *Kipps* and *The Young Mr Pitt*), and Columbia and RKO set up their own small production units.

Alexander Korda, the most prestigious producer working in Britain, was in the middle of a lavish re-make of *The Thief of Bagdad* when war broke out. Production was suspended and Korda detailed three directors (Michael Powell, Adrian Brunel, and Brian Desmond Hurst) to work on a flag-waving propaganda piece, *The Lion Has Wings*. The film was completed and in the cinemas before Christmas, but it had no successors, and Korda went to Hollywood to finish *The Thief of Bagdad*.[5]

In the early months of the war the only production companies to continue operating on a regular basis were those of Ealing, British National, and Gainsborough, all of whom had wealthy, patriotic backers, and Butchers, a small production/distribution company which had the unique distinction of having survived the First World War. Butchers was the first company to resume normal production: a prison comedy, *Jailbirds*, was made at their old Walton-on-Thames studio in October and was followed by a succession of appropriately topical subjects, such as *Pack Up Your Troubles*, *Garrison Follies*, *Somewhere in England*, and *Sailors Don't Care*.

Michael Balcon had only recently been appointed head of production at Ealing, but he had managed to pull the company out of the doldrums and had the backing of the Courtauld family, who were the major shareholders, to go ahead with the production of *The Proud Valley*, an off-beat story about a black seaman – Paul Robeson – whose fine singing voice makes him welcome in a Welsh mining community. The planned ending, however, which was to have shown the miners forming a co-operative to run the mine themselves after being let down by the inefficient and short-sighted management, was changed to show miners and management working together to re-open the mine and fuel the war effort.

Gainsborough was a subsidiary of the Gaumont-British Picture Corporation, which was controlled by the Jewish financier Isidore Ostrer. Like Balcon's Ealing it was an efficient, well-run set-up, and, with contracts to produce films for MGM and Twentieth Century-Fox, operations were moved from Gainsborough's Islington home to larger studios at Shepherd's Bush where work was resumed on an Arthur Askey comedy, *Band Waggon*.

British National had been founded by flour millionaire J. Arthur Rank and jute millionairess Lady Yule back in 1933, but had drifted into the doldrums after Rank departed for more ambitious ventures. Early in 1939 the company had been joined by John Baxter, a young director responsible for unusual low-budget films like *Doss House*, *Song of the Plough*, *Say it with Flowers*, *Music Hall*, and *Hearts of Humanity*. Baxter's presence and the outbreak of war seemed to galvanize British National into action and an ambitious production programme was embarked upon. After sharing Walton-on-Thames with Butchers they were allowed to re-open Denham for Powell and Pressburger's *Contraband* in December, and shortly afterwards took over the large Rock studio at Elstree which had seen little production activity since 1937.

Phoney war films

The period between September 1939 and April 1940 is often referred to as the 'phoney war', and there is a light-headed quality about many of the films made then. Of the fifty-one British feature films released in 1940, nearly half were comedies or comedy thrillers. They tended to be characterized by a zany euphoria which went beyond mere complacency. *Let George Do It*, made at Ealing in March 1940 when Chamberlain was suggesting that Hitler had 'missed the bus' and released in August when the Battle of Britain was raging overhead, was one of the most popular films of the year. Directed by Gainsborough's comedy specialist Marcel Varnel, it employed the usual formula of Formby getting himself into a situation he was supremely ill-fitted to handle and with the help of his ukulele, a pretty girl, and his crazy humour, somehow coming out on top, but it skilfully exploited the possibilities for adventure opened up by the war. George, a member of the Dinky Doos concert party, loses the fellow members of his troupe in the black-out at Dover and instead of catching a train to Blackpool finds himself on a boat to Bergen, a replacement for the murdered ukulele player in a dance band. The band-leader is working for the Germans – sending musically encoded messages to U-Boats to guide their attacks on neutral shipping. George discovers the code and after several adventures finds himself re-united with the pretty British agent who has inspired his bravery, on the decks of a British destroyer.

There are some marvellous slapstick sequences and the supporting cast – Garry Marsh as the villain, Phyllis Calvert as the heroine – are excellent. But what most excited audiences was a brief dream sequence: George drifts in a balloon from England to Germany and finds himself floating over a huge Nazi rally being addressed by Hitler. 'Hey you! Hey windbag, Adolf – put a sock in it!' he shouts, and descending on to the platform he proceeds to give Hitler a good hiding. The stormtroopers, far from coming to the Führer's aid, erupt into jubilant cheering. Chaos ensues and George finds himself back in his room struggling with the bedclothes.[6]

Gasbags, made at Gainsborough early in 1940, operated on similar lines. The Crazy Gang, given charge of a barrage balloon in Hyde Park, turn it into a well-patronized fish-and-chip stall ('no coupons required'), and when discovered by their commanding officer, cut themselves loose and soon find themselves drifting over Europe. Inadvertently descending, they fall in line with a platoon of French soldiers and discover too late that these are prisoners being marched to a concentration camp. The film then becomes even more bizarre. The other inmates include Moore Marriott's Jerry Harbottle, an aged eccentric who had featured in the Will Hay films of the thirties, as well as an army of Hitler look-alikes who are being punished for their refusal to undertake the dangerous work of impersonating the Führer on occasions when he is likely to be assassinated. Eventually the gang escape, employing a secret tunnelling weapon to burrow their way back to London – and their commander's office.

Despite the fact that Norway had fallen and Britain was desperately fighting off invasion when *Let George Do It* and *Gasbags* reached the cinemas, audiences welcomed their madcap optimism. According to Tom Harrisson – whose Mass Observation network made some attempt to gauge the public mood – blatantly absurd comedy was often more acceptable than earnest exhortation and false heroics, and he pointed out that:

> Part of good morale, *the ability to endure in any circumstance*, is the ability to switch yourself off completely. It was a very necessary quality which a great many British people were and still are very good at anyway.[7]

Films like *Gasbags* and *Let George Do It* ensured that the switching-off process was a pleasurable one and inaugurated a strain of fantasy in British films which was to survive and flourish during the war years. But there was also a determined attempt to deal realistically with the problems and dilemmas, situations and experiences thrown up by the war.

The Lion Has Wings, Alexander Korda's contribution to the war effort, was released in November 1939, only six weeks after war had been declared. Initially it was well received by the Press, though critics later derided its stilted acting and portentous commentary. Ostensibly an attempt to instil confidence in Britain's air defences, it was hampered by the unwillingness of the RAF to allow Korda's unit shooting facilities. Though there was a reconstruction of the Kiel Canal bombing raid, producer Ian Dalrymple relied mainly on documentary and newsreel footage, filling it out with a patriotic exhortation from Queen Elizabeth (Flora Robson) cut in from an earlier Korda film, *Fire Over England*, and a weakly dramatized coda with Ralph Richardson and Merle Oberon.

In the circumstances the film was something of an achievement. As Dalrymple recalled: 'At the beginning of the war we all suffered from hush-hush, the worst-has-happened, and any-minute-now. . . . We were naturally embarrassed in the construction of the film by not knowing what disaster might not have occurred before its exhibition.'[8] Dalrymple tried to give some durability to the film by concentrating on the virtues of the

English character and the achievements of democracy: 'I opened our film with the suggestion that there was a British ideology arising from our national character; that it was valuable to the world; and that it should not be lost.'[9] Though the war at sea allowed for a certain amount of action to be brought to the screen in films like *Convoy* and *For Freedom*, it was this celebration of 'a British ideology' which was to provide the most fertile ground for film-makers who wanted to deal seriously with the war.

The reality underlying comic discoveries of spies, fifth columnists and saboteurs was that the Second World War was not a simple conflict between nations:

> If there were elements in Britain which would collaborate with Hitler, and large elements in Germany who had opposed him and (wishfully it was thought) were still opposing him, the first were enemies, the latter natural allies. The internationalist, ecumenical Bishop of Chichester suggested, echoing many others, that this was 'a war of faiths in which the nations themselves are divided'. Tom Wintringham, inspirer of the Home Guard, called it 'a People's War', and whoever originated it, this was a phrase which stuck.[10]

Thus there was a persistent attempt to discriminate between Nazis and 'good Germans', and, despite the hasty internment of Italians and Germans settled in England, there was no recurrence of the xenophobic chauvinism which had characterized the 1914–18 War.

Pastor Hall, Ernst Toller's play about a South German priest whose outspoken criticism of the Nazi regime landed him in a concentration camp, had proved popular enough to arouse interest in Hollywood. In the event it was two young English film-makers – John and Roy Boulting, hitherto responsible for only a couple of low-budget thrillers (*Trunk Crime* and *Inquest*) – who persuaded the American-backed distribution company Grand National to let them make it. For the part of the pastor, the Boultings chose Wilfrid Lawson, hitherto best known for his portrayal of sinister criminal masterminds in *The Terror* and *The Gaunt Stranger* and the outspoken dustman, Doolittle, in *Pygmalion*. He handles the role with great sensitivity and restraint and turns what might have been sentimental propaganda into a moving testament to human dignity and bravery.

The film was well received in Britain but in America the depiction of concentration camp horrors was regarded with suspicion. According to a report in the *Documentary Newsletter*:

> the film has been admired for certain intrinsic production qualities, but it is observed that concentration camps and other European cruelties create only a sense of distance in the native mind and a feeling of 'Thank God we emigrated from Europe to a decent country'. . . . Jewish

maltreatment, concentration camps, sadistic lashings are, one is afraid, old stuff, alien, slightly discredited and do not command people's deepest attention.[11]

The Germans had been shown running concentration camps in Gainsborough's *Gasbags* and *Night Train to Munich*, but perhaps because of this sort of reaction, they appeared infrequently in later war films.

The most attractive of the early war films is Powell and Pressburger's stylish thriller *Contraband*, made for British National as a follow-up to *The Spy in Black*, a great popular success of the first autumn of the war. Shooting was started at Walton but in December Korda transferred production of *The Thief of Bagdad* to Hollywood, and left Denham empty. British National moved in and Powell was able to commandeer the services of the great German art director Alfred Junge for *Contraband*. The film re-unites Valerie Hobson and Conrad Veidt, the stars of *The Spy in Black*; Veidt – an anti-Nazi German who had become a British citizen – was cast in the sympathetic role of a Danish sea captain delayed by British Contraband Control and caught up with a secret agent (Hobson) in a Hitchcockian world of mystery and danger in blacked-out London. Although rather late in celebrating the benevolent neutrality of the Scandinavians – Norway and Denmark were firmly under German control when the film came out – Powell and Pressburger were more prescient about coming political changes. Having escaped the clutches of a German spy-ring, Captain Andersen and the beautiful Mrs Sorenson briefly take shelter in a warehouse filled with dusty, unsold busts of Neville Chamberlain, which are shot-up in the ensuing gunfight. A telling metaphor for the dustbin of history!

Britain alone

Britain had not been totally unprepared for war in September 1939. Re-armament had begun back in 1936 and the Munich crisis had brought to hurried fruition plans for wartime dispersal of people, government, and industry. A Ministry of Information had been planned and its personnel informed of their intended positions – if not what they were supposed to do. Unfortunately, the combination of weak political leadership and confusion about how the war would develop led to an unhappy state of inaction and discontent. As A.J.P. Taylor put it: 'The war machine resembled an expensive motor car, beautifully polished, complete in every detail, except that there was no petrol in the tank.'[12]

The MOI seemed particularly afflicted by political ineptitude and the Minister himself, Lord Macmillan, sadly ill-suited for the task of building and maintaining morale. After Christmas he was replaced by the former General

Manager of the BBC, Sir John Reith, an able administrator who established a degree of order and consistency before he resigned in May 1940, appalled at the prospect of having to work with 'that horrid fellow' Churchill.[13]

Though plans to keep the cinemas closed had retarded its development, the MOI had a Films Division, entrusted with the production of film propaganda. This was headed by Sir Joseph Ball, who had been Director of the Research Department at Conservative Party Central Office throughout the thirties. It was a politically insensitive appointment, but Ball was someone who was thought to understand film propaganda and could be relied upon to get things moving. Ball despised the artistic pretensions of the documentary movement (and distrusted their left-wing tendencies) and turned to advertising, newsreel, and commercial film-makers to get across the government's message. But in the early stages of the war, nobody but the documentary-makers appeared both willing and able to make propaganda films, and Ball's period in office proved to be an extremely barren one. Reith soon saw him off and replaced him with Sir Kenneth Clark, who had made a name for himself as a dynamic Director of the National Gallery.

Clark reversed his predecessor's policy and brought the documentarists into the fold. Before war had been declared, the GPO Film Unit, headed by the Brazilian Alberto Cavalcanti, had been commissioned to make a film instructing people what to do in the event of air raids and gas attacks, but the resulting film, *If War Should Come*, was considered bad for morale when war did come and was shelved and then released in truncated form as *Do It Now*. Taking as its theme Chamberlain's speech – 'It is the evil things that we shall be fighting against – brute force, bad faith, injustice, oppression and persecution – and against them I am certain the right will prevail' – it is a sensible and effective little film: demonstrating how to put up an Anderson shelter, warning that a lot of the noise during an air raid would come from our own guns, but once it was completed, the unit was left to cool its heels. As director Harry Watt recalled:

It was then that Cavalcanti, magnificent old Cav, the alien, whom some Blimps always suspected, took the law into his own hands, and sent us all into the streets to film anything we saw that was new and different. Cav realised that history was being made all around us, and a tremendous opportunity to record it for posterity was being lost, so six small units went out with all our film stock and filmed the extraordinary scenes of a nation amateurishly preparing its capital for a new kind of war. We filmed the frantic sandbag filling, the new balloons rising up in the oddest places, the endless drilling in the parks, the new auxiliary policeman – I remember I got a chap in plus-fours and monocle directing traffic at Piccadilly Circus – anything that was different from the normal peacetime way of life.[14]

Though Watt claimed 'it wasn't a good film', *The First Days* is the first manifestation of that stoical, underplayed, poetic spirit which was to prove so potent a force in British propaganda. In contrast to aggressive German militarism, the British, it was argued, were fighting because they had to, more in sorrow than in anger:

> A generation of young men, born in the last war and brought up in contempt of militarism ... went into uniform, willingly and with clear understanding, because they found they had grown up in a world where there was no peace.

This was not yet the official line and the film was put out by a commercial company, Pathé, and ignored by the MOI.

Things changed with the arrival of Kenneth Clark. He had been a member of the Empire Marketing Board, the first official body to sponsor documentaries, and was welcomed by the documentarists as an ally. There were momentary tremors when Churchill began a purge of the Chamberlainites in May 1940 and Clark was promoted to become Controller of Home Propaganda, but his replacement, Jack Beddington, who had been responsible for enlightened publicity at Shell, was even more closely aligned with the documentary movement.

With Beddington, government policy began to assume clear lines. The GPO Film Unit was renamed the Crown Film Unit and allowed generous studio facilities, first at Denham, and then at Pinewood. A large 'non-theatrical' section was established with seventy-six cinema vans touring the country showing programmes of documentaries and instructional films to specialized audiences. But the commercial industry was mobilized too. Nearly two thousand government films were made during the war, and this required the assistance not only of the wide spread of independent documentary companies which flourished during the war, but also feature film companies like Ealing and Gainsborough.[15]

The potentially embarrassing situation of having a Brazilian as head of the official government film unit was avoided when Michael Balcon invited Cavalcanti to Ealing – where he was to exercise an influence almost as great as that of Balcon himself. His replacement as head of the Crown Film Unit was Ian Dalrymple who had pursued a successful career in the mainstream industry but had become interested in documentaries after producing *The Lion Has Wings*.

In August 1940 the MOI came under severe attack from a House of Commons Select Committee on National Expenditure. The Films Division was praised for its 'five-minute films' – short snappy films like Harry Watt's *Dover – The Front Line* and Brian Desmond Hurst's *Miss Grant Goes to the Door* – but condemned for its ambitious non-theatrical programme, which was considered not effective enough in reaching large numbers of people, and heavily criticized for its investment in feature films. This was a policy initiated by Kenneth Clark and had resulted in a £60,000 investment in Powell and Pressburger's *49th Parallel*. By this time, though, the Ministry was beginning to acquire a degree of political adroitness. Beddington promised to cut back on those areas criticized by the Committee, but by 1942 there were one-hundred-and-thirty film units on the road instead of seventy-six, and investment in feature films continued surreptitiously throughout the war.

Beddington was helped by the fact that he now had a formidable team working with him and results were becoming increasingly impressive. Sidney Bernstein, the socialist businessman who controlled the Granada cinema circuit, was brought in as a special adviser to liaise with Wardour Street. He was to prove very effective in getting wide exposure for the MOI's films in Britain and America. Arthur Elton, a respected member of the documentary community who had some knowledge of the commercial industry having begun his career at Gainsborough, was recruited to supervise production.

During the early days of the Blitz, the Crown Film Unit set about making a record of the endurance and resilience of the British people under fire. *London Can Take It* proved to be one of the most successful documentaries made during the war. Simply depicting twenty-four hours in the life of London during the Blitz, it managed to convey an extraordinary impression of stoical British heroism. Designed primarily for an American audience, the commentary was spoken by *Colliers Magazine* reporter Quentin Reynolds. Earlier in the year Alfred Hitchcock, perhaps stung by accusations that he was one of those who had 'gone with the wind up', had made a Hollywood film called *Foreign Correspondent* with Joel McCrea as a journalist caught in Europe by the gathering clouds of war. At the film's climax he broadcasts to America from blacked-out London in the middle of a bombing raid:

'Hello, America. I've been watching a part of the world being blown to pieces. A part of the world as nice as Vermont and Ohio and Virginia and California and Illinois lies ripped up, bleeding like a steer in a slaughterhouse . . . I can't read the rest of this speech because the lights have gone out so I'll just have to talk off the cuff. All that noise you hear isn't static, it's death coming to London. Yes, they're coming here now, you can hear the bombs falling on the streets and the homes. Don't tune me out, hang on a while, this is a big story and you're part of it. It's too late to do anything here now except stand in the dark and let them come, as if the lights are all out everywhere except in America. Keep those lights burning, cover them with steel, ring them in with guns, build a canopy of battleships and bombing planes around them and, hello America, hang on to your lights, they're the only lights left in the world.'

The film's combination of intrigue, romance, and political relevance made it deservedly popular in Britain and America, but its picture of London in the Blitz was necessarily impressionistic. *London Can Take It* showed more graphic detail with its resonant images of huge fires, flattened streets, and a battered but still cheerful populace. As if to still any doubts that if London's lights were out, the spirit and courage of the British people remained undaunted, Reynolds concludes:

'I am a neutral reporter, I have watched the people of London live and die ever since death in its most ghastly garb began to come here as a nightly visitor five weeks ago. I have watched them stand by their homes. I have seen them made homeless. I have seen them move to new homes. And I can assure you that there is no panic, no fear, no despair in London town; there is nothing but determination, confidence and high courage among the people of Churchill's island.'

The film's director, Harry Watt, quickly followed up *London Can Take It*'s success with another film narrated by Quentin Reynolds, *Christmas Under Fire*. Neither man wanted to make the film and according to Watt 'we decided, very much tongue in cheek, to make a weepy. Our private motto was "Not a dry eye in the house".'[16] None the less, considering the opportunities for sentimentality afforded by its subject, the film appears sober and restrained.

Watt was happier with his next film, the feature-length *Target for Tonight* which, despite its tiny budget, was a big commercial success. Made in the spring and summer of 1941 when, with set-backs in North Africa, the war seemed to be going badly, the film provided a timely boost to morale. As Watt modestly admitted:

I can say that while the film was honest and well-made, it was no cinematic revolution, but an understated and unemotional account of an average air raid. To give the real reason for its success one must realise the emotions of the people of this country at the moment it came out. All propaganda had been geared to encourage us to bear up, to stay cheerful and optimistic under bombs, mines, torpedoes, rationing and cold, while a constant stream of success stories came from the other side. There was no sign of cracking, but I believe, away back in many people's minds, there had arisen the doubt that we could ever win, although I am sure we would have fought to the end. Then came this film, actually showing how we were taking the war into the heart of the enemy, and doing it in a very British, casual, brave way. It was a glimmer of hope, and the public rose to it.[17]

This was the first time that a documentary had competed successfully with entertainment feature films, and Watt, now something of a celebrity, was recruited by RKO to make a film about the American airmen who had volunteered for service with the RAF. The 'Eagle Squadron', however, was only twenty-four strong and their high casualty rate played havoc with continuity. After several months Watt gave up and the project was made – with actors – in Hollywood.

Hands across the ocean

The question of American support was a crucial one, and films were seen as a weapon whereby American public opinion might be swayed in Britain's favour. But until Pearl Harbor brought America into the war, the isolationist lobby remained powerful. There was a sizeable British colony in Hollywood, made up of actors like Ronald Colman, Cary Grant, David Niven, C. Aubrey Smith, and Cedric Hardwicke, and directors such as James Whale, Victor Saville, and Alfred Hitchcock, most of whom were anxious to do their bit. Herbert Wilcox and Laurence Olivier – and their wives Anna Neagle and Vivien Leigh – chose to return, though before they went Wilcox helped organize *Forever and a Day* to which a wide range of expatriate talents lent their services; and Vivien Leigh and Laurence Olivier starred in Korda's *Lady Hamilton*, which Churchill valued highly as pro-British propaganda.

Jewish magnates like Louis B. Mayer and the Warner Brothers had their own reasons for opposing Fascism and had tried to alert America to its danger with films like *The Mortal Storm* and *Confessions of a Nazi Spy*. With Hitchcock's *Foreign Correspondent*, Chaplin's *The Great Dictator*, and other pro-British films such as *Eagle Squadron*, *This Above All*, *Desperate Journey*, and Fritz Lang's *Man Hunt* in the pipeline, it was with some justification that the isolationists accused Hollywood of an anti-German bias.

Films made in Britain, on the other hand, were rather less effective propaganda. According to a report from America in the *Documentary Newsletter*:

> The films sent over here have been scattered, odd, unequal, and have built up no single or solid impression. The millions spent in creating a British film industry have produced no dividend of influence in England's hour of need.[18]

Documentaries like *London Can Take It* marked a turn for the better. Bernstein was able to get the enthusiastic support of Harry Warner for the film and it was shown in twelve thousand cinemas to an estimated sixty million viewers.[19] In August 1941 he went to America with *Target for Tonight* to see if he could negotiate a similar deal. Though the studio executives were sympathetic, their reaction to the film was unenthusiastic. Watt's film-making ability was unquestioned – his adeptness at capturing

mood and atmosphere, his skill at combining documentary and fiction –
but American audiences had trouble enough with the accents of English
actors, they would find these brave but awfully posh young men of the
RAF incomprehensible. A compromise was reached whereby the American
companies agreed to give widespread distribution to *Target for Tonight*
and other British films, but on condition they could cut and dub them to
suit the requirements of the American market.

In the prevailing pro-British climate Bernstein did manage to persuade
the Americans to find screen time for British feature films:

> When I went to America for the government I knew we could only get
> worthwhile commercial presentation of British features through the
> eight major American companies. I am glad to say that, after some
> negotiations, they agreed to give commercial distribution to eight
> British features and eight shorts a year even though they knew it meant
> that these films would displace their own.[20]

His task was made easier by the fact that British films were getting
better. *49th Parallel*, the film backed by the MOI, emerged as the top box-
office picture of the year in Britain. It was well up to Hollywood standards
of professionalism and its story was less parochial than most British war
films.

After sinking merchant ships in Canadian waters, a U-Boat is trapped
and sunk in the Gulf of St Lawrence. Six survivors try to reach safety in
neutral America. In their long trek they have a number of encounters:
with Eskimos and a French Canadian trapper (Laurence Olivier); with a
German Hutterite community (presided over by Anton Walbrook); with a
dilettantish writer (Leslie Howard); with a disgruntled but none the less
patriotic Canadian soldier (Raymond Massey). There was criticism at the
time that the Germans, particularly their zealous and resourceful leader
(Eric Portman), were allowed too much sympathy, and they are certainly
allowed a level of intelligence and a degree of success normally denied
screen Nazis. But Powell and Pressburger cleverly load the dice against
them. Though technically the pursued, the hunted, the Nazis appear as
violators, as incongruous 'as cobras in a Surrey garden' as critic William
Whitebait put it, among the peace-loving, democratic Canadians.[21]

49th Parallel represented a more sophisticated attitude to the war and
propaganda, and, though it was a better film than most of its
contemporaries, the film industry generally was becoming more adept at
dealing with the war. There was a slight decrease in the number of British
films released in 1941 but they were notably more successful than they
had been the previous year. Ealing enjoyed some success with the stagey,
old-fashioned *Ships with Wings*, and there were two very popular films
dealing with the air war – *Target for Tonight* and *Dangerous Moonlight*
(directed by Brian Desmond Hurst for RKO British).[22] The approach of the

two films could not have been more different. In contrast to Harry Watt's modest heroes – most of whom were dead by the end of the war – Anton Walbrook's Stefan Radetsky plays the Warsaw Concerto among the ruins of Warsaw, falls in love with beautiful heiress Sally Gray, survives the fall of Poland, raises money for the cause by giving concerts in America, and miraculously escapes death in the Battle of Britain. As C.A. Lejeune explains in 'A Filmgoer's Diary':

> It was the general experience of managers, in the bad years, that the public couldn't sit through the ordinary talkie-talkie-tea-table picture. We wanted action, movement, colour, music, comedy – some sort of proxy release from our pent-up emotions.[23]

Hence the full-blooded fantasy of *Dangerous Moonlight* was as acceptable as the casual realism of *Target for Tonight*. Significantly, though, the two most popular war films of 1941 were *49th Parallel* and *Pimpernel Smith*.

Both films concentrated on showing the moral superiority of the quietly decent Englishman and his allies to the ruthless, humourless, machine-like Nazis. In both films Leslie Howard – the foppish writer in *49th Parallel*, the absent-minded professor who is master-minding the escape of victims of Nazi persecution in *Pimpernel Smith* – plays a key role. Through his film performances and his numerous radio broadcasts, Howard became a sort of icon, a popular hero representing everything that was best about the British character – gentleness, humour, unassuming courage – an incarnation of British traditions, but at the same time a standard bearer of a new sort of British society, distinctly different from the pre-war period.[24]

The film industry was quick to recognize and adapt to this new culture. In the middle of 1940, George King, a sharply commercial producer who had survived the thirties making 'quota quickies', announced that the low-budget 'programme picture' was dead; he was forming a production company with Leslie Howard – British Aviation – to make war films. Their first production was a lavish biography of the inventor of the Spitfire, R.J. Mitchell, *The First of the Few*. Other commercially acute producers followed the same line. Warner Brothers at Teddington switched from low-budget thrillers and farces to a much smaller number of quality productions, and at Butchers there was a conscious attempt to mould their comedies to wartime needs. Their veteran managing director, Francis Baker, explaining the popularity of Elsie and Doris Waters' comic characters Gert and Daisy, pointed out that:

> Gert and Daisy pictures are topical as well as funny. In the first one [*Gert and Daisy's Weekend*] the public is now exercising its laughing faculties for the good of war-time morale over the comediennes'

adventures with mischievous evacuee children; in the second one [*Gert and Daisy Clean Up*], the lively pair will be hilariously implicated in affairs of the Merchant Navy, the black market, a salvage drive and a war-time Christmas party'.[25]

Though its operations remained on a relatively modest scale, the British film industry now seemed fully mobilized for war.

2 War Culture

It needs some very great disaster, such as prolonged subjugation by a foreign enemy, to destroy a national culture. The Stock Exchange will be pulled down, the horse plough will give way to the tractor, the country houses will be turned into children's holiday camps, the Eton and Harrow match will be forgotten, but England will still be England, an everlasting animal stretching into the future and the past, and, like all living things, having the power to change out of recognition and yet remain the same. (George Orwell, *The Lion and the Unicorn*, 1941)[1]

Resistance films

It was important for the British, in their belief that they were fighting a just war against a tyrannical power, to believe that occupied Europe was only waiting for a signal to rise up and overthrow its oppressors. Adventure, secrecy, the threat of torture and death, dare-devil missions, the prevalence of beautiful and mysterious women, made the resistance an ideal subject for film-makers. A resistance cycle followed on naturally from those phoney war films concerned with rooting out spies and rescuing eminent scientists and scholars from the clutches of the Nazis. Dilys Powell, writing in 1947, remembered that:

> From the Continent, across the Channel, travellers came back with stories beyond the invention of men; a dark curtain of secrecy had been lowered, but the British knew that beyond it a great war of sacrifice and desperation was being fought.[2]

The first of these films, Anthony Asquith's *Freedom Radio* (1941), has a Viennese throat specialist (Clive Brook) teaming up with a radio ham 'to tell the people the truth about their rulers', but most of the resistance films of 1942 and 1943 forsook the Czechs, Austrians, and 'good Germans' for Western Europe.

One of Our Aircraft is Missing follows the fortunes of a British bomber crew grounded in Holland. *The Day Will Dawn* is largely set in Norway and centres on the attempt by patriotic Norwegians and a British agent to blow up a German U-Boat base. *Uncensored* concerns a group of Belgian patriots who run an anti-Nazi newspaper, *La Libre Belgique*. *Secret Mission* has four British agents parachuted into France to work with the French underground movement in destroying ammunition dumps. The more grittily realistic *Tomorrow We Live*, directed by George King, was made with the co-operation of the Free French and dispenses with bold British heroes. The resistance fighters are successful in blowing up an ammunition train but the Germans retaliate by shooting fifty hostages, and there is a strong sense of the strains and tensions – for both sides – of life in an occupied country.

Though none of these films was very successful at the box-office a further wave followed in 1943: *The Silver Fleet* (Holland), *Undercover* (Yugoslavia), *Escape to Danger* (Denmark), *Flemish Farm* (Belgium), *The Adventures of Tartu* (Czechoslovakia), and *The Night Invader* (Holland), after which the cycle came to an abrupt halt. *The Adventures of Tartu*, with Robert Donat and Valerie Hobson, made with Hollywood slickness for MGM British, succeeds as a comedy thriller but its setting looks more like Ruritania than Czechoslovakia. *The Silver Fleet*, made for Powell and Pressburger's production company The Archers, has Ralph Richardson as a Dutch Scarlet Pimpernel, a shipyard owner who collaborates with the Nazis as a cover for organizing sabotage, and is very competently directed by Vernon Sewell. But it is very much a *Boy's Own* adventure story and lacks the resonance of Powell and Pressburger's own contribution to the cycle, *One of Our Aircraft is Missing*.

'One of our aircraft is missing' was the laconic phrase often heard on the radio after a raid. Powell and Pressburger imaginatively reconstruct what might have happened to that missing aircraft. In a dramatic prologue we see the plane smashing spectacularly into a pylon. Fortunately, as is now revealed, the crew have all bailed out safely and the film concerns their exploits in escaping from German-occupied Holland. It is interesting for three reasons. First, its heterogeneous bomber crew looks forward to films like *In Which We Serve*, *San Demetrio–London*, and *The Way Ahead*, which show a cross section of the nation pulling together to win the war. Second, it depicts the Dutch underground as led by strong, resourceful women. Third, it strongly endorses Britain's bombing policy. During a bombing raid Googie Withers explains to the Englishmen:

'You see, that's what you're doing for us. Can you hear them running for shelter, can you understand what that means to all the occupied countries, to enslaved people having it drummed into their ears that the Germans are masters of the earth, seeing those masters running for shelter, seeing them crouching under tables and hearing that steady hum, night after night, that noise which is oil for the burning fire in our hearts.'

In reality, British bombing of occupied countries was soon seen as counter-productive, and there was a growing awareness that the resistance movements were powerless unless backed up by invasion.

Dissenting voices

Popular commitment to the war was wholehearted but not uncritical; even after the departure of the 'Old Gang' the government was not immune from criticism. The *Daily Mirror*, the first daily paper to aim itself unashamedly at a working class audience, built up a huge readership with its mildly salacious strip cartoon 'Jane', its polemical contributions from the columnist Cassandra (William Connors) and its demagogic insistence on a more vigorous prosecution of the war. With the Labour party fully involved in Churchill's government, it was left to outsiders like J.B. Priestley – 'a plump prophet with a cosy Bradford accent and a big pipe', whose radio broadcasts rivalled Churchill's in popularity – to offer a different and radical perspective on events.[3] The publication of the Beveridge Report – the blueprint for a Welfare State – in December 1942, helped launch a new political party, Common Wealth, which enjoyed considerable success in by-elections before being overtaken by the revived Labour party in 1945.

One might have expected little of this radicalism to come through in films. During the thirties there had been strict moral and political censorship by the British Board of Film Censors and during the war this was supplemented by MOI controls. As Sidney Bernstein recalled:

> the Ministry both advised the producers on the suitability of subjects which they had suggested, and proposed subjects which we thought would do good overseas. Whenever the Ministry had approved a subject, we gave every help to the producer in obtaining facilities to make the film. For instance, we helped them get artists out of the Services, we aided them to secure raw-stock, travel priorities and so on.[4]

But the liberal intelligentsia who increasingly dominated the MOI had more robust sensibilities than the BBFC censors and were generally sympathetic to film-makers who wished to make films which were meaningful and relevant. According to Paul Rotha, the MOI Films Officer Jack Beddington set up an informal 'ideas committee'.

> 'This consisted of a number of writers and directors from feature films and a number of directors and others from documentary, who met round a table over beer and rather lousy sandwiches, once every fortnight. . . . We would talk backwards and forwards across the table for a couple of

hours and then we'd go down to the theatre and see some films, and this was a very healthy and excellent thing. It broke down the barrier which had existed between feature and documentary.'[5]

A questioning of what the war was being fought for was implicit in *The Lion Has Wings*, but English decency was regarded as too vague a war aim by more radical spirits and it was not long before their voices were being heard in films. In 1941 the Boulting Brothers made a short film for the MOI called *The Dawn Guard*.

It begins almost as a parody of an English pastoral, with two English Home Guardsmen making a desultory round of the countryside in the early hours of the morning. Veteran character actor Percy Walsh complains about the Nazis 'upsetting the ways and wrecking the lives of millions of people'. It seems as if we are in for another celebration of traditional English values, but then his companion, played by Bernard Miles, speaks up. Miles was at that time virtually unknown, though he had played a small role in *Pastor Hall* and his appearances in *One of Our Aircraft is Missing* and *In Which We Serve* were soon to make him famous. An odd, uncomfortable figure, he would have been eligible only as a villain or a buffoon in thirties films, but during the war his eccentricity made him all the more English and his sincerity and seriousness made him an ideal spokesman for the new England of the future. 'That's all right Bert', he tells his ageing companion,

> 'But that isn't enough. We've been doing some hard thinking lately and we haven't got to stop when this job's finished. We've made a fine big war effort and when it's all over we've got to see to it we make a fine big peace effort. There's no two ways about it. We can't go back now we've made a start. Look at that Dunkirk: there wasn't no unemployed there. Every man had a job to do and he done it and that's what we got to see they has in peacetime – a job.
>
> There'll be work enough when this lot's over, building up something new and better than what's been destroyed. There mustn't be no more dirty filthy back streets and no more half-starved kids with no room to play in. We got to pack all them up and get moving into the brightness of the sun. Fresh air and sunshine don't cost nothing. We can't go back to the old ways of living, leastways not all of it, that's gorn forever and the sooner we all make up our minds about that the better. We gotta all pull together.'

When he begins speaking the scene changes to men and women working busily in factories, and as his voice becomes more indignant, to slumland streets, a squalor which is then contrasted with the new model flats and images of children playing, familiar from *The Lion Has Wings*, as evidence of Britain's achievements in the thirties. It is a simple, even a crude film, but very moving in its exposition of the desire for change.

The Boultings, who had already made their mark with *Pastor Hall*, went on to make *Thunder Rock*, a strange film about an investigative journalist (Michael Redgrave) who, after trying in vain to warn Britain that the spread of Fascism in Europe posed a grave danger, retreats to a lighthouse in Lake Michigan. There he conjures up a shipload of ghosts who had been wrecked there ninety years earlier, and in re-creating their life stories – all of them had left Europe after losing their battle against bigotry and ignorance there – he realizes that he too, in running away, has given up the battle too soon, and prepares to emerge from his isolation.

Redgrave's lighthouse-keeper could be seen as a metaphor for America, which after the 1914–18 war had tried to wash its hands of Europe and its problems but was now being remorselessly drawn back into the conflict, but *Thunder Rock* has a less abstract message. Redgrave is shown as arrogant and impatient, with little sympathy for the problems and preoccupations of the people who fail to heed his message of doom. Initially the lives of the ghosts he re-creates are shallow and superficial – like characters in a bad British film – and it is only in trying to understand their motives and to tolerate their human weakness and fallibility that he is able to come to terms with himself. It is here that the film, in its stress on the need for harmony and tolerance if civilization is to triumph, becomes sincere and convincing.[6]

A similar sort of radical humanism was being propagated by John Baxter at British National. *Love on the Dole*, Walter Greenwood's grim tale of life in the Salford slums, had been one of the best-sellers of the thirties. It had quickly been adapted for the stage, but attempts to film it had been vetoed by the BBFC. By 1940, however, unemployment was no longer a problem and British National was at last given the go-ahead.

Its relevance now rather limited, one might have expected the film to flop. In fact it generated considerable interest and at least a measure of box-office success.[7] Though Baxter kept faithfully to the story and mood of Greenwood's book, he was able to infuse it with a powerful political message. Unemployment in Britain's traditional great industries – coal, steel, cotton, and shipbuilding – had been severe, and the plight of skilled men denied work through no fault of their own had aroused considerable sympathy. As Bernard Miles' country soldier had intimated, in the all-out war effort of 1940–41 there was a determination that if the war was won a new society must be built where such injustices would not be tolerated.

Love on the Dole is a working-class tragedy set in the worst years of the Depression. The Hardcastles, a typical northern working-class family, have their happiness blighted and their lives thrown into confusion by unemployment and its consequences. Baxter had clearly defined views and was not hesitant about ramming them home. The film starts with an omen. Mrs Hardcastle tries to draw her fire with a newspaper, but, distracted, allows it to catch fire and the cheery announcement that the economy is on the mend goes up in flames. So begins the remorseless decline of the family's fortunes. Mr Hardcastle is put on short-time working and then laid-off completely. Young Harry, proud to have at last reached eighteen and ready to earn a man's wage, finds himself thrown on the dole, his job given to a younger and cheaper school-leaver. A lucky win on the horses allows him a week's idyllic holiday in Blackpool, but he returns with a pregnant girlfriend to demoralizing poverty. Sally, the remaining member of the family, retains her job but finds her dreams of happiness shattered when Larry, the man she loves, is sacked for trying to improve the lot of his fellow-workers and then killed during a demonstration. Bitter and cynical, she agrees to become the 'housekeeper' of a wealthy bookie, Sam Grundy. The film ends with her return, in a car and fine clothes, to face her morally outraged father and tell him that through her

1 Sally (Deborah Kerr) looks sceptically on as her mother (Mary Merrall) and the local gossips (Marie Ault, Iris Vandeleur, Marjorie Rhodes, and Maire O'Neill) discuss her future. *Love On the Dole* (1941).

influential contacts she has found him and her brother jobs with the local bus company.

Some sequences of the film – the utopian visions of Larry the Labour party activist for example – have not worn very well, and a crudely drawn communist agitator is introduced to excuse the workers and the police responsibility for the riot in which Larry is killed. Most of the acting though, particularly Deborah Kerr as Sally and George Carney and Mary Merrall as her worn-out, beaten-down parents, is superb, and the film recreates the claustrophobia of working-class life with its small, over-crowded rooms, pawn shops, and ever-present neighbours very effectively. 'Honest' Sam Grundy (Frank Cellier) in his big car and check suit looks more like a teddy bear than a repulsive villain, but Deborah Kerr's Sally is no whiter-than-white heroine: she repeatedly points out that the tragedy lies less in her selling herself than in the impossibility of a happy life in Hankey Park. In this she shares a stoical solidarity with Mrs Bull (Marjorie Rhodes) who makes a meagre living laying out the dead. 'Always been respectable?', she retorts to the gaggle of black-coated gossips who comment like a Greek chorus on the unravelling tragedy. 'Yes, so have I, but only because I've had no chance to be anything else . . . I wouldn't worry about a fat belly as long as it had a gold chain on it.' Sally is tough enough to know when she's well off, but sensitive enough to convey a weary depression at the wastefulness of it all.

'One day we'll all be wanted,' Mrs Hardcastle tells her distraught husband at the end of Love on the Dole, and Baxter's subsequent films indicated what a new and better society should concern itself with. British National, he promised, would deliver:

> Pictures with a promise of the better times that are to come, pictures that will show them just what we are fighting for, pictures with a glimpse of the better world we all envisage after these sacrifices and hardships are through, pictures that will spur them on to fresh effort and endeavour because they hold out hope and compensation for all they have suffered – and what better propaganda could you have than that?[8]

He followed up the success of Love on the Dole with The Common Touch, about a public schoolboy (Geoffrey Hibbert, last seen in more straitened circumstances as Harry Hardcastle) who inherits a property company and sets out to discover the truth about a lodging house for down-and-outs which his managers want to demolish. Though considerably more sentimental than George Orwell's explorations of the lower depths in Down and Out in Paris and London and The Road to Wigan Pier – people lean out of windows and listen in silent wonder to itinerant pianists playing Rachmaninov – The Common Touch is still a fascinating film. The young hero comes to respect and care for these battered but cheerful wrecks of humanity and exposes the plot which his managing director has instituted to deprive them of their haven. Taking control of his own business, he asserts his belief in the importance of 'using power to benefit the whole community' and determines to incorporate a bright new shelter with modern facilities for the down-and-outs in the building project.

War culture

Baxter's films expressed the sort of concern for 'the deeper things in the lives of ordinary people' which J.B. Priestley was propagating through his broadcasts and journalism. As Priestley had scripted films in the thirties it was almost inevitable that these two like minds would eventually come together. This they did in 1942 with *Let the People Sing*, the story of a second-rate music hall comic (Edward Rigby) and a mid-European refugee (Alastair Sim) mobilizing the populace of a small town to save their last venue for live performances from the clutches of industrialists and killjoys.

The film was only mildly popular at the box-office and the critics hated it. William Whitebait in the *New Statesman*, for example, complained that:

> the dialogue is flat, the photography dull to the point of ugliness; and the whole thing shows that ingenuous, happy-go-lucky mediocrity which' used to be the glum hall-mark of English films.[9]

Baxter is erratic rather than mediocre, brilliantly executed sequences being followed by others of disconcerting banality. But forty-five years on, imperfections in technique seem less important than the film's atmosphere of infectious enthusiasm. *Let the People Sing* may be a very shaky monument to wartime populism, but it is a monument nevertheless.

Soon after *Let the People Sing*, Priestley was involved in another patchy attempt to capture the spirit of the times. *Battle for Music*, directed by documentary-maker Donald Taylor, told the story of the survival, against the odds, of the London Philharmonic Orchestra, which had been abandoned by its financial backers at the beginning of the war. Priestley had encouraged them to issue a 'musical manifesto' which managed to attract enough public subscriptions for them to keep going until classical music acquired a popular appeal and they began touring the variety halls. He had also approached Oscar Deutsch, founder of the Odeon cinema circuit, with the idea of making a film about the LPO's struggle, but plans had been shelved when Deutsch died in 1941, and the project was eventually made by Strand, an independent documentary company, with backing from British National. Compared with the best of the Crown Film Unit feature documentaries – *Target for Tonight, Fires Were Started, Western Approaches* – *Battle for Music* is clumsy and stilted. Worthy though they are, the viola player, trombonist and french horn players who steer the orchestra to a glorious and democratic future, have little charisma and less acting ability and the film labours heavily to get across its point about bringing good music to the people.

A more precise and effective analysis of the role of music and other sounds in the life of the nation had been made in 1941 by Humphrey Jennings in his short documentary *Listen to Britain*. Jennings, a product of Cambridge in the thirties, dabbled in painting, literature, and the theatre, as well as film. He helped organize the International Surrealist Exhibition in 1936 and the following year set up Mass Observation with Charles Madge and Tom Harrisson. In his first significant film, *Spare Time*, he put the principles of Mass Observation into practice with a cool, unromanticized look at the leisure habits of working-class people in Bolton, Sheffield, and South Wales.

Like many British film-makers, the war had a radicalizing effect on Jennings. The common danger, the shared intensity of experience, seemed for a moment to fuse Britain into a harmoniously classless society, and Jennings' letters to his wife in America are filled with exhilarated admiration for the heroism of ordinary people. In October 1940 he wrote:

'Some of the damage in London is pretty heart-breaking but what an effect it has had on the people! What warmth – what courage! what determination. People sternly encouraging each other by explaining that when you hear a bomb whistle it means it has missed you! People in the north singing in public shelters: "One man went to mow – went to mow a meadow." WVS girls serving hot drinks to firefighters during raids explaining that really they are "terribly afraid all the time!" . . . Maybe by the time you get this one or two more 18th cent. churches will be smashed up in London: some civilians killed: some personal loves and treasures wrecked – but it means nothing; a curious kind of unselfishness is developing which can stand all that and more. We have found ourselves on the right side and on the right track at last!'[10]

In collaboration with the editor Stewart McAllister, Jennings evolved a screen poetry which celebrated this new found harmony. The more robust and forthright documentaries of Harry Watt and Paul Rotha were preferred by contemporary critics, but Jennings' work has better stood the test of time.

In *Listen To Britain* he takes the simple idea of exploring the sounds most characteristic of wartime England: tanks blundering surreally through a leafy English village; Dame Myra Hess playing in the denuded National Gallery; Flanagan and Allen performing in a vast canteen and almost drowned by the whistling of the workers. Obvious choices these may have been, but they now seem intensely evocative of the reality of a 'people's war'.

A distinct war culture – populist, strident, sentimental, its insistence on having immediate answers to the big questions of life tempered by an awareness of the absurdity of sudden death – had evolved remarkably quickly, and the film industry wasted no time in recruiting the popular heroes of this new world. Columbia, after poaching George Formby from Ealing, was encouraged to sign up 'forces sweetheart' Vera Lynn for two films – *We'll Meet Again* and *One Exciting Night*. Strand, the company which had made *Battle for Music*, put out three issues of *The Brains Trust* with Julian Huxley, C.E.M. Joad, and Commander Campbell answering questions on anything from the identity of the Loch Ness monster to whether women should bear arms. With the break-up of the Crazy Gang, Flanagan and Allen deserted Gainsborough for British National and their place was filled by Bebe Daniels, Ben Lyon, and Vic Oliver whose radio show *Hi Gang!* had a considerable following, and by Tommy Handley and the *ITMA* team.

ITMA (It's That Man Again) was the most popular radio show ever put out by the BBC but it transferred badly to the screen. According to the director Walter Forde, the film version of *ITMA* was:

'A very poor film, because I had such a poor script. It was never finished – I had to extemporise all the way through it. I had so many characters going that you lost track of them. There was no straight line in the film. And I made it in three weeks.'[11]

Forde had an excellent sense of comic timing and had coaxed hilarious performances from the likes of Jack Hulbert and Gordon Harker. But *ITMA* never properly integrates the catch phrases and stock characters, so popular on the wireless, into its backstage musical story. 'Dust my dickie with a dishcloth', 'slap me on the jetty with a jellyfish', and the unpredictable appearances of Mrs Mopp, Funf, and the Diver may have been very funny in the radio fantasy world of Foaming-at-the-Mouth, but, as Ted Kavanagh the scriptwriter of the radio shows pointed out, 'the ITMA characters, unlike good children, were designed to be heard and not seen'.[12]

MGM did rather better with another popular radio show, *Happidrome*. Two of its three stars – Harry Korris and Robbie Vincent – had already been teamed with the greatest of the northern music hall comedians, Frank Randle, in the low-budget *Somewhere* series. Freed from Randle's anarchic presence, Korris was able to exert his own larger-than-life personality as an old-school tragedian with a fur-lined dressing gown and a bloodshot voice. The story is not of great significance and tends to peter out completely towards the end, but in its affectionate nostalgia for a dying theatrical tradition, the film is very appealing. With the backing of a wealthy, stage-struck, and talentless young woman, Bunty Mossup (Bunty Meadows), Korris puts on a show which goes disastrously wrong.

'I gave them the best I had and they just laughed me off the stage', he laments before realizing that the situation can be turned to advantage. Then, with his less-than-competent lieutenants Enoch (Robbie Vincent), Ramsbottom (Cecil Frederick), and the irrepressible Bunty, he abandons 'culture' for popular entertainment and creates his 'Happidrome'.

Wartime populism

A.J.P. Taylor argues that by 1941 the direction and control of the economy had 'turned Great Britain into a country more fully socialist than anything achieved by the conscious planners of Soviet Russia'.[13] Although class barriers remained, they became more negotiable, and the *them* and *us* attitude of the phoney war period began to dissolve. Patriotism became less a matter of King and Country than an appeal to a tradition, a common set of values which all classes could share.

The first film which tried to articulate this tradition in fictional terms was David Macdonald's *This England* (released as *Our Heritage* in Scotland) made for British National late in 1940. Macdonald had run a rubber plantation in Malaya before beginning his film career in Hollywood in 1929 as an assistant to Cecil B. De Mille. In 1936 he returned to England and survived by making 'quota quickies' before attracting attention directing Emlyn Williams in *Dead Men Tell No Tales* for British National in its 'B' movie days. By the time he returned to the company in 1940 he had two modest box-office successes – *This Man Is News* and *This Man in Paris* – and a documentary, *Men of the Lightship*, under his belt. After making *This England* he joined the Army Film Unit where he was responsible for the documentary compilation films, *Desert Victory* and *Burma Victory*.

This England, a historical pageant, follows the fortunes of the Rookeby family of yeoman farmers (all played by John Clements) and the Appleyard family of farm labourers (all played by Emlyn Williams) over an eight-hundred-and-fifty-year period – concentrating on 1086, 1588, 1804, 1918, and the present day of 1940. An American journalist (Constance Cummings), visiting the village of Clavely Down during an air-raid, is impressed by the coolness of the villagers under fire, and Rookeby and Appleyard take her through a number of historical crises which their ancestors have faced.

In the first episode the Norman Lord, despite repeated warnings that 'the British must not be roused', insists on provoking them and pays with his life. His young son, an upholder of liberty and justice, is installed in his place and Rookeby and Appleyard are left to farm the land in peace. The second episode, set during the approach of the Armada, looks forward to the Gainsborough melodramas which were soon to prove so popular.

Rookeby is tempted from his allegiance to the land by a shipwrecked gypsy (Constance Cummings), whom the villagers suspect of both witchcraft and collusion with the Spaniards. In a gloomily spectacular climax she leaps to her death from a cliff, Appleyard is debased into becoming a murderer, and Rookeby returns, defeated, to the drudgery of his responsibilities. The eighteenth-century episode presents a hardly more appetizing picture of England's past. Rookeby is now a piano-playing fop, Appleyard a sturdy beggar, and Lord Clavely, descendant of the Norman Baron, has to sell out to a blunt northern industrialist, to cover his gambling losses. Fortunately the industrialist has a beautiful daughter (Constance Cummings) whom Rookeby can marry and thus save his farm. But it is with much lamentation about 'this sticky, clinging, damnable creeper of an English past', that he returns to his responsibilities.

These three episodes represent virtually a feudal view of society, with the land determining a man's place in the scheme of things and a rigidly hierarchical system being balanced by harsh and heavy responsibilities for those who hold power and the land. The final episode, set at the end of the First World War, with its neatly composed montage sequences and restrained, realistic acting, is stylistically very different – a reminder of Macdonald's documentary interests – but it has a similar sombre and downbeat atmosphere. Rookeby, a blind officer, Appleyard, a disillusioned private, and Constance Cummings, an unmarried mother whose boyfriend has been killed at Vimy Ridge, share a tentative solidarity against the boisterous, jingoistic crowd celebrating the end of the war, and together they walk away from the warm, well-lit pub out into the misty night.

Though not a very well-made film – the *Monthly Film Bulletin* pompously declared 'It has been conceived theatrically and without a proper understanding of the limitations and possibilities of the medium' – *This England* is interesting in its view of the past as a burden and its stress on the responsiblities of those who own and work the land. It was made at a time when invasion still seemed a possibility, and the film has an urgency and a harshness which later films celebrating 'this England' lacked.

Certainly, everything is sweetness and light in MGM's contribution to the cycle, the hugely popular, Oscar-adorned *Mrs Miniver*. In New York in 1942, Sidney Bernstein had been approached by an alarmed Lord Lothian with the news that MGM had made a film which was a horrific caricature of Britain at war, and must be stopped at all costs. Bernstein, with his showman's instincts, saw the film and realized it conveyed the sort of idealized view of England which would attract audiences on both sides of the Atlantic. He was right, but the film had its detractors. Harry Ashbrook in the *Sunday Pictorial* indignantly enquired:

Why resurrect this useless baggage, Mrs Miniver, from the comfortable court page of *The Times* to represent the nation at war? What sort of people do Hollywood directors think we are?[14]

But audiences were familiar with the conventions of Hollywood's England, and were happy to watch Greer Garson doing her bit at the village flower show and Walter Pidgeon bringing the British Army home from Dunkirk. Like *Dangerous Moonlight*, and *Gone With the Wind* which played to packed houses in the West End throughout the war, its lush romanticism appealed to audiences whose lives were plagued with the dreariness of war.

The entry of Russia into the war, in June 1941, ended Britain's isolation. The scale of the fighting and the extent of Russian sacrifices made Britain's campaign in North Africa look little more than a sideshow, and an unlikely alliance of Lord Beaverbrook and the British Communist party pushed vigorously for a second front to be opened up in Western Europe. Churchill was reluctant to change his tactics, but the pro-Russian enthusiasm which swept the country was good for morale – and for industrial productivity with Communist shop stewards eager to support the war effort – and Mrs Churchill spearheaded fund-raising schemes to aid the Russians. The only feature film to explore this now forgotten component of war culture was *The Demi-Paradise*, an upper-class comedy directed by Anthony Asquith.

Asquith, as the son of a prime minister, was quite at home in the garden party world of Mrs Miniver, and if anything 'Barchester', the idyllic English community of *The Demi-Paradise*, is even more of a caricature with its nightingales singing in the moonlight and Margaret Rutherford and Joyce Grenfell organizing the village pageant. But *The Demi-Paradise* has as its hero a Soviet engineer. Ivan Koutznetsoff (Laurence Olivier) comes to England in 1939 to supervise the production of an icebreaker for which he has designed an exceptionally powerful propellor. The England we see through his eyes is unfriendly, wet, and eccentric to the point of madness. After an unresolved love affair with the shipbuilder's grand-daughter (Penelope Dudley Ward), he goes back to Russia none the wiser. Returning a year later, though, he finds the situation utterly changed. These toytown eccentrics have now mobilized themselves for war, and when Russia is invaded, any vestige of reserve is swept away and Ivan is welcomed into the community. As with many of Asquith's films it is permeated with a fey sentimentality which blunts any radical edge. But Olivier's superbly consistent comic performance makes the glum, self-righteous Russian very endearing, and a genuine feeling of fellowship between Britain and Russia comes across.[15]

Though popular support for Russia remained a significant factor, the invasion of Britain by large numbers of American servicemen had a more direct impact on the social and cultural life of the country. From January

1942 there was a steady build-up of GI's en route for the continental battlegrounds and American airforcemen stationed in Britain as a base for bombing raids on Germany. Powell and Pressburger's *A Canterbury Tale* (1944) is one of the first films to acknowledge the American presence, weaving the question of Anglo-American relations into its weird celebration of the English countryside. US Army Sergeant Bob Johnson (played with emphatic realism by US Army Sergeant John Sweet), trying to spend his last few days' leave in Canterbury, finds himself stranded in the Kentish village of 'Chillingbourne', where he teams up with a land-girl, Alison (Sheila Sim), and a cynical British officer, Peter (Dennis Price), to unmask the local JP (Eric Portman) as the 'glue man' who has plagued the district with his mysterious attacks. But behind the facade of this simple whodunnit, the film unravels much deeper mysteries.

Thomas Colpeper JP is no ordinary psychopath – his glue attacks are motivated by an altruistic desire to disrupt normal patterns of boy-meets-girl behaviour and channel the interests of the large number of servicemen in the area away from land-girls and milk-maids into a mystical communion with the Kentish landscape, with the timeless England of Chaucer. It was not the sort of thing the critics approved of. C.A. Lejeune, the crabbed doyenne of British film journalism, tartly told Observer readers:

> *A Canterbury Tale* is about a Kentish J.P. who believes so deeply in the message of his native soil that he pours glue on girls' heads in the blackout lest they distract the local soldiery from his archaeological lectures. That's the theme, and to my mind, nothing will make it a pleasant one. This fellow may be a mystagogue, with the love of England in his blood, but he is also plainly a crackpot of a rather unpleasant type with bees in the bonnet and blue-bottles in the belfrey. Only a psychiatrist, I imagine, would be deeply interested in his behaviour.[16]

Though *A Canterbury Tale* is generally regarded as a commercial failure, Josh Billings in the *Kinematograph Weekly* mentions it as one of the few popular British films of 1944 and audiences may have been more in tune with this obscure mystical interpretation of English history than has been assumed.

The disruptions of wartime provided ample opportunities for transient relationships between men and women and, despite the misgivings of Thomas Colpeper, they were not always sordid. Perhaps because both sides had something to give to one another, there does seem to have been a refreshing equality about relations between Americans and Englishwomen, which *A Canterbury Tale* represents in the relationship between Alison and Bob Johnson.[17] It is a relaxed comradeship which characterizes their feelings for each other though, and Alison's luminous sensuality shines to more significant effect on Thomas Colpeper, shifting his misogyny and renewing his faith in people. In return he grants each of the latter-day pilgrims a miracle. When they finally arrive in Canterbury, where troops are gathering for a pre-D-Day blessing in the Cathedral, Alison and Bob Johnson find their lost loves and Peter finds his lost faith.

3   Realism and Tinsel

The real world is made up of people and things, and ideas about people and things. All these can be made exciting and attractive without building fantasies to cloak their true nature.

The way in which we make the real world seem exciting does not matter – it may be by slick montage, clever stories, lots of colour, pretty people, in films, radio or television, in music or painting, in ballet or sculpture.

But whatever method is used it must be to the point that men and women welcome the idea of living in a real world. It is only by knowing it truly and honestly, that they can work and play in it happily. With knowledge of that real world they can have such a full life that all of man's heaven from Mount Olympus to Hollywood Calif. will seem as less than the dreary emptiness of a ballroom in the morning sunlight. (*Documentary Newsletter*, May 1943)[1]

Since the beginning of the war, producers had debated whether the public wanted films which offered them an escape from the reality of war or whether they wanted to see their wartime experiences reflected on the screen. The realist position was naturally espoused by the documentarists but it also found a vociferous champion in Michael Balcon, who promised that at Ealing he would 'grasp with both hands the opportunity of putting every phase of the war on the screen'.[2] Maurice Ostrer, in charge of production at Gainsborough, was equally resolute in his support of escapism. He described himself as 'no great believer in the serious, patriotic war setting, which an increasing number of the public must find "too near home" for complete enjoyment', and declared 'Good themes and good laughs – that is what audiences want, and that is certainly my production policy'.[3]

Nevertheless, both men were shrewd and pragmatic producers, and in the early years of the war both studios relied heavily on comedies with a war background. Gainsborough's Arthur Askey films (*Band Waggon, The Ghost Train, I Thank You, Back Room Boy, King Arthur Was a Gentleman*) might just as easily have been made at Ealing, while Ealing's serious war films (*Convoy* and *Ships with Wings*) were hardly more realistic that Gainborough's *For Freedom* and *Night Train to Munich*. The Ealing and Shepherd's Bush studios were roughly the same size –

each had five stages, Shepherd's Bush with a total of 30,785 square feet, Ealing with 28,437 square feet – and until the old Islington studio re-opened in 1942, giving Gainsborough another two stages, their output was roughly equal. Though often seen as representing different traditions of British film-making – Ealing realism and social responsibility, Gains-borough fantasy and commercial exploitation – their histories are curiously intertwined.

Ealing and the Realist tradition

Michael Balcon had entered the film industry in 1923, leasing a converted power station in Islington from Paramount-British and going into production with a Birmingham colleague, Victor Saville. His company, Gainsborough Pictures, enjoyed some success at a time when British film production was at a low ebb and in 1927, when the Gaumont British Picture Corporation was set up by Isidore Ostrer and his brothers, Gainsborough was taken over and Balcon appointed head of production at the new combine.

After 1931 when the re-built Gaumont studios were opened, Balcon based himself at Shepherd's Bush, delegating responsibility for Islington to Maurice Ostrer and Edward Black, a young producer with a show-business family background whose brother George ran the London Palladium. Gainsborough/Gaumont-British produced a regular supply of films to feed the large chain of Gaumont cinemas – a more consistent and higher quality output than any other British studio in the thirties. But the search for international success led to serious over-expansion and by the end of 1936 production had to be abandoned at Shepherd's Bush. Balcon had already been approached by MGM to head a production unit which would make Anglo-American films with an appeal to both sides of the Atlantic. Though Balcon's contribution to the cycle, *A Yank at Oxford*, was a huge commercial success, he had been used to being his own boss and found it impossible to work with Louis B. Mayer and his minions. By the end of 1937 he was working as an independent producer in association with Ealing and in mid-1938 he took over from Basil Dean as head of production.

Balcon's bad experience with MGM seems to have killed for ever his desire to make 'international' films, and for the next thirty years he was to be the prime exponent of modestly budgeted films which were distinctly British in their style and subject matter. Though most of the young men who made their directing debuts at Ealing – Charles Frend, Charles Crichton, Robert Hamer, Henry Cornelius – had worked in the thirties as feature film editors, and others such as Thorold Dickinson, Sergei Nolbandov, and Basil Dearden, who worked at Ealing during the war

years, had served similarly commercial apprenticeships, Balcon's two
recruits from documentary, Cavalcanti and Harry Watt, exercised a
considerable influence at Ealing. As Monja Danischewsky put it, 'if Mick
was the father figure, Cavalcanti was the Nanny who brought us up'.[4]

Cavalcanti had come to Europe in the early twenties to study
architecture, but he became involved in French avant-garde film-making
and established an international reputation with his 'city symphony', *Rien
Que Les Heures* (1926). He moved into commercial film-making, directing
a number of feature films before falling out with his employers and joining
John Grierson's GPO Film Unit in England. With the outbreak of war his
position as an alien made his presence at the head of a government film
unit anomalous and he moved to Ealing to handle their war documentaries.
The narrowing gap between documentaries and features soon gave him
the opportunity to develop more adventurous projects.

In 1941 he produced *The Big Blockade*, a feature-length propaganda film
dramatizing the activities of the Ministry of Economic Warfare (MEW). It
is a peculiar film and by no means wholly successful, mixing stylized
reconstructions of life in Europe, newsreel, and a barrage of information
on the vital importance of MEW. Crude, noisy, and unrealistic, it was not a
film that the British critical establishment took to its bosom, and the box-
office appeal of economic warfare left much to be desired. But in its
vigorous and experimental way, *The Big Blockade* represents an
interesting alternative to the mainstream of quiet, realistic, underplayed
British documentaries.

For their next film, *The Foreman Went to France*, Cavalcanti and
director Charles Frend dispensed entirely with a documentary framework.
The story (by J.B. Priestley) was based on real events but it is told in
conventional fictional terms. There is no overt propaganda, no commentary,
and the acting – including that of comedian Tommy Trinder – is
naturalistic. Made in 1942, it begins by showing its foreman hero (Clifford
Evans) running an arms factory before flashing back to 1940 and the fall
of France. Like the MEW officials of *The Big Blockade*, the foreman is
concerned with economic warfare – rescuing a vital piece of machinery
from a factory in France – but Priestley's story has a more radical edge:
the authorities are not above criticism ('the trouble is the people at the top
think they're fighting the last war all over again'), and it is two ordinary
British soldiers (Tommy Trinder and Gordon Jackson) who help the
foreman fulfil his mission when the charming upper-class officer turns out
to be a spy. It was Ealing's most successful film of the year (a respectable
third at the box-office to John Ford's *How Green Was My Valley* and Cecil
B. de Mille's *Reap the Wild Wind* when it was released in June 1942) and
appeared to vindicate Balcon's policy of 'reflecting each phase of the war'.

The Foreman Went to France represented a step forward for Ealing into
a mature, confident blending of documentary sincerity with simple, well-

told stories featuring 'ordinary' lower-class characters, often with clearly defined regional accents (Evans was Welsh, Jackson Scots, and Trinder a Cockney). It was followed by a series of films – *The Next of Kin*, *Went the Day Well?*, *Nine Men*, *The Bells Go Down*, *Undercover*, *San Demetrio –London*, and *For Those in Peril* – which use the same formula.

The Next of Kin started life as a twenty-five minute army-training film on the dangers of careless talk, but Balcon thought it worthwhile to supplement the £20,000 which the army was prepared to spend and turn it into a commercial feature film. The director, Thorold Dickinson, was something of a maverick, and not part of the regular Ealing team. An intellectual with left-wing sympathies (which nearly got him vetoed by the army as a 'premature anti-fascist'), he had worked on low-budget commercial feature films rather than joining the documentary movement and proved his abilities as a director with an adaptation of Patrick Hamilton's melodrama *Gaslight* for British National in 1940. None the less, *The Next of Kin* is almost a textbook example of British war realism.

Like *Target for Tonight* the film deals with an attack on the enemy – a raid on a German submarine base on the French coast – but here the emphasis is less on the preparation and execution of the raid than on German efforts to penetrate British security and find out the date and destination of the operation. In Britain it was well received by the government, the army, the critics, and the public, but the Americans were less impressed. David Selznick viewed the film with Nunnally Johnson and Ernst Lubitsch and strongly advised Bernstein against releasing the film in America:

> All the English officers are portrayed as stupid, careless and derelict. . . .
> Calculated to increase the fears of Americans and mothers especially that the British are simply muddling along, and that their sons will die because of British incompetence. This is aggravated by contrast with portrayal of brilliance and complete efficiency of German intelligence. . . . The latter point is felt so strongly that all here believe the film could be more profitably run in Germany for home consumption and for building German morale. . . . Perhaps even worse is the portrayal of so many British civilians as informers and spies, giving the impression that England is overrun by traitors.[5]

The film was eventually released in America, but shorn of thirty minutes of what was considered morale-damaging footage.

The Americans' viewpoint is understandable enough, but the film's success depends on making the German agents realistically anonymous and their unwitting helpers no more careless and irresponsible than most people. As the security officer says ruefully after being given directions and allowed entrance to an army camp without being asked for any form of identification: 'Nice friendly people, tell you anything you want to know. . .'. It is a measure of how far the MOI had progressed towards a confident and assured propaganda policy that the Germans and fifth columnists are portrayed as shrewd, ruthless, and resourceful. Four of the agents are caught or killed but the fifth discovers enough about the raid to make it a hazardous and costly affair. This fifth agent is played by Mervyn Johns – the solid, dependable mainstay of so many Ealing films – and the film is chillingly effective in spreading the message that even the most innocent-seeming acquaintance should not be trusted.

Cavalcanti's first directorial assignment at Ealing, *Went the Day Well?* has a similarly disturbing quality. In a quiet English churchyard a pipe-smoking grave-digger (Mervyn Johns) points us towards a black cross marking the grave of a contingent of German soldiers and proceeds to tell us their story. One might have expected the film to be set in the dark days of 1940 when Britain was seriously threatened by invasion but our narrator, looking back from somewhere in the future, tells us the incident occurred during Whitsun 1942 – around the time the film was made. The story, by Graham Greene, tells how German paratroopers move into an English village disguised as a British army unit on manoeuvres, but then blow their cover by crossing their sevens and eating Viennese chokolade. With the help of the treacherous local squire (Leslie Banks), the village is sealed off and the villagers rounded up and imprisoned in the church. A Cockney evacuee (Harry Fowler), helped by the local poacher (Edward Rigby), manages to escape and raise the alarm, and army forces join the villagers who have broken out of the church in wiping out the invaders.

It is a remarkably savage film, the idyllic English village in which it is set – so similar to those model communities of *Mrs Miniver* and *The Demi-Paradise* – making the violence seem all the more shocking. The venerable old clergyman (C. V. France), like Pastor Hall, refuses to kow-tow to Nazi bullying: 'You ask me to bow down before the forces of evil, here in this House of God?', he asks the German Commandant. 'I am a Minister of the Christian faith, I will take no orders from the enemies and oppressors of mankind', and with that he begins ringing the church bell which will warn the outside world of the invasion. He is unceremoniously shot. In the woods one of the village Home Guards thinks he hears the bell, but his companions laugh and tell him he is imagining things. They cycle home, whistling merrily, and in a quiet country lane they are mown down by German machine-gunners. The villagers repay savagery with savagery. The kindly postmistress (Muriel George) makes her German escort feel at home, throws pepper in his face and kills him with an axe. The clergyman's daughter (Valerie Taylor), who has had amorous intentions towards the squire, confronts him with his treachery and shoots him. Cavalcanti's view of war is an uncomfortably bleak one and the film was not notably popular with audiences or critics, but with its imaginative realism and its clever dissection of rural English society, *Went the Day Well?* can now be seen as the best of the Ealing war films.[6]

Some time in 1943, Michael Balcon gave a talk to the Film Workers Association in Brighton which was later published as a pamphlet, 'Realism and Tinsel'. He spoke of the 'happy marriage' effected between the documentary movement and progressive producers like himself, and the new sort of realist cinema it had produced in films such as *One of Our Aircraft is Missing*, *The First of the Few*, and *In Which We Serve* as well as in Ealing's own films, and contrasted it with the artificiality of films which derived their ideas from stage plays and cheap romances. *San Demetrio–London*, then in the final stages of production at Ealing, was considered by Balcon:

> to be the best example of the final departure from tinsel which the film industry can make without any misgivings on the part of the shareholders. We took an actual incident of this war, the shelling and setting on fire of the tanker 'San Demetrio' and of the crew, or what remained of the crew, subduing the fire and bringing the tanker home to port. The scenario of the film follows faithfully the official account of the incident. The characters are named by their proper names and in casting we tried to find actors who most nearly approximated the actual men. Even a great deal of the dialogue is authentic, inasmuch as Chief Engineer Charles Pollard of the 'San Demetrio' was able to recall much of it during constant questioning by the script-writers. Yet the film is in no sense a documentary as was, for example, *Target for Tonight*. All the technical tricks of a film studio are employed to give authenticity without either going outside the studio to obtain it, or using the actual people whom the story portrays.[7]

No doubt shareholders would not sanction a film crew sitting in the North Sea for months on end, shooting in rare and expensive Technicolor and using a cast of non-actors as Pat Jackson was able to do a year or so later for the Crown Film Unit's *Western Approaches*. *San Demetrio*'s antics in the studio tank suffer by comparison but the film has qualities beyond its faded surface realism which make it memorable. The story – of a band of sailors who, after two days adrift in a lifeboat, come across the oil tanker they have abandoned and are so cold and desperate that they re-board her, put the fires out, and sail her to England – is much stronger than that of either *Western Approaches* or *In Which We Serve*. The ship itself is something of a *tour de force* by the art director Duncan Sutherland: a sinister, smouldering, volcano-like wreck which constantly threatens to sink or explode. And the underplayed heroism of the men – which doesn't depend on officers for inspiration – turns the film into a sincere and convincing homage to the courage and endurance of ordinary seamen.[8]

San Demetrio–London, released a year after *In Which We Serve* and a year before *Western Approaches*, won the praise of the critics and modest success at the box-office. *The Bells Go Down* had the misfortune to be released within weeks of Humphrey Jennings' *Fires Were Started*, to which it was unflatteringly compared, and it was unenthusiastically received by the public. Subsequently it has fallen into neglect. Like later, more celebrated Ealing films such as *Hue and Cry*, *It Always Rains on Sunday*, and *Passport to Pimlico*, it is rooted in a cheery London community where private problems, rivalries, and jealousies are not entirely subsumed under the war effort. As the narrator tells us at the beginning of the film:

'Down beside the docks, in the East End of London, they say that London isn't a town, it's a collection of villages. This is the story of one of those villages, a community bounded by a few streets, with its own market place, its shops, its church, its police station and its fire brigade.'

Tommy Turk (Trinder) joins the Auxiliary Fire Service (AFS) and strikes up a friendship with a petty crook (Mervyn Johns), who has realized the advantage a fireman's uniform gives him for nocturnal raids on London's docks, a wet-behind-the-ears newly-wed (Philip Friend), and a dour veteran (William Hartnell) who has fought with the International Brigade in the Spanish Civil War. Despite Trinder's clashes with authority and Mervyn Johns' running battle with the police, they come together effectively as a team.

Fires Were Started, made by Humphrey Jennings for the Crown Film Unit, is remarkably similar in theme, atmosphere, and subject matter. Jennings' film has a middle-class recruit (the writer William Sansom) join an AFS unit just as Trinder does in *The Bells Go Down*. There is much less in the way of plot – no romantic interest, no set-piece rivalries – and at times one misses the cheery eventfulness of the Ealing film. Jennings uses real firemen and real fires – kindled among the blitzed warehouses of London's dockland – but his aim is something more than documentary realism. It is the epic quality of the firemen's struggle that excites him and there are moments when his celebration of ordinary people working together in the shadow of disaster is very impressive. But if Jennings' concentration on the mythological aspect of the war effort gives his film a magic lacking in more mundane efforts, a film like *The Bells Go Down* with its very human, fallible heroes, is a useful reminder that for most people the war was lived on a less exalted level.[9]

The different qualities of the two films can be seen most clearly in their endings, both of which involve the death of a fireman. In *Fires Were Started*, Jacko, a phlegmatic little Cockney tobacconist, is cut off by the flames and dies heroically. The film ends with his companions solemnly bearing his coffin to the graveyard while the munitions ship which Jacko and the others have preserved from the fire sails safely away down the Thames.

In *The Bells Go Down* it is Tommy, the nearest the film gets to a hero, who dies. Throughout the film he is continually caught out by the veteran fire chief, McFarlane (Finlay Currie), for smoking on the job. Attempting to save the local hospital from going up in flames, McFarlane is cut off and Tommy goes to his rescue. The old man is trapped under a wooden beam but Tommy manages to free him just before the floor falls in. Marooned on a ledge, Tommy jovially remarks, 'Well I reckon that puts us off duty', and takes out his fags. McFarlane smiles and accepts one, but just as Tommy lights up a huge wall collapses and they are plunged into a fiery inferno. It is a shocking moment in a film which until then has been essentially light-hearted and it drains the film of any sentimentality. Tommy's death serves no useful purpose – he saves McFarlane's life only to die with him moments later – but it expresses the spirit of community, of pulling together with people one doesn't necessarily like, which is so clearly articulated in the film.

Whereas Jennings' film is concerned with the nation, with a national myth, the Ealing film is much more parochial. *The Bells Go Down* ends not with Tommy's funeral but with the christening of the baby born to the newly-weds on the night Tommy and McFarlane die. The camera pulls back from the christening service in a burnt-out church to reveal the shopkeepers and stall-holders still busily carrying on their business despite the battering their little community has suffered. It is a more clichéd, less ambitious image, but not without its grandeur.

By 1944, despite the success of *San Demetrio–London*, Balcon was prepared to admit the possibility that the public was getting sick of war films. They were certainly getting sick of the war. Discontent with the coalition government had led Richard Acland and J.B. Priestley to launch a new political party, Common Wealth, in July 1942, and its policy of common ownership of land and industrial resources, 'vital democracy', and a new morality in politics, attracted considerable support at by-elections. The entry of America into the war and Montgomery's victory at El Alamein in November 1942 raised hopes for an invasion of France and an end to the war in 1943. But caution prevailed and the Allied commanders decided to strike at Hitler's 'soft underbelly' by invading Italy. In July 1943 Allied forces captured Sicily, but progress was slow. Italian resistance quickly collapsed, but the Germans made full use of Italy's mountainous terrain to fight a determined rearguard action.[10]

In Britain a mood of jittery cynicism prevailed, exacerbated by the presence of large numbers of American servicemen. Until the middle of 1943 good industrial relations had made possible enormous increases in productivity, but in the long lead-up to the D-Day landings of June 1944 there were as many strikes as in the worst period of the 1914–18 War.[11] There was an echo of this discontent in many of the films made during this final period of the war. Sober realism tended to be jettisoned in favour of subjects with an element of the exotic and the bizarre. Ealing made two modest drama documentaries, *For Those In Peril* and *Painted Boats* (both directed by Charles Crichton), but put most of its resources into two films dealing with the supernatural – *The Halfway House* and *Dead of Night* – and two costume pictures, Cavalcanti's musical, *Champagne Charlie* and Robert Hamer's melodrama, *Pink String and Sealing Wax*.[12]

Balcon's position on 'realism' and 'tinsel' was keenly endorsed by the *Sunday Times* critic Dilys Powell. In *Films Since 1939* she spoke out harshly against 'a group of cheaply romantic costume pictures . . . films on trivial conventional themes trivially handled . . . undeserving of the popular success they have won'.[13] These blots on the realist landscape were the Gainsborough melodramas.

The Gainsborough melodramas

Though Gainsborough had been implicated in the financial problems of its parent company, Ted Black's reputation as an efficient producer of comedies, thrillers, and low-budget musicals enabled him to keep his Islington team intact. Because of the workings of the 1927 Quota act, film distributors which handled American films were also required to offer for hire a percentage of British films and both MGM and Twentieth Century-Fox agreed to let Gainsborough supply them with British films to make up their quota requirements. When war broke out Black and his team moved to Shepherd's Bush to allow them to continue production away from the vulnerably sited Islington studio with its tall power-station chimney.

For the first three years of the war Gainsborough enjoyed modest success with its Arthur Askey comedies and the more prestigious period films such as *Kipps* and *The Young Mr Pitt* it made for Twentieth Century-Fox. At the end of 1941 the whole of the Gaumont-British empire was taken over by J. Arthur Rank, but Gainsborough was allowed to continue its semi-autonomous existence and the following year the studio seemed to get into its stride. Six films were released in 1943 – *Miss London Ltd, ITMA, We Dive at Dawn, Dear Octopus, Millions Like Us*, and *The Man in Grey*. The two which might have seemed the safest bet, the Arthur Askey vehicle *Miss London Ltd* and *ITMA* were the least successful; *We Dive at Dawn*, Anthony Asquith's drama about the exploits of a British submarine in the Baltic, and *Dear Octopus*, a tasteful adaptation of a play by Dodie Smith – typical Gainsborough projects – were modestly successful; *Millions Like Us*, jointly directed by Frank Launder and Sidney Gilliat, and *The Man in Grey* were two of the most popular films of the year.

Success with a balanced programme of films had been what Gainsborough producer Ted Black had been working towards. Black, one of the unsung heroes of the British film industry, held the studio together during its most difficult period, backed Launder and Gilliat in establishing a strong scriptwriting department, retained the services of some of the best cameramen in the business, and put under contract a number of promising actors. *The Man in Grey* launched James Mason, Stewart Granger, Margaret Lockwood, and Phyllis Calvert as major British stars, but the film's huge success upset the delicate balance of power at the studio. Though Black was in practical control of Gainsborough's production policy Maurice Ostrer, a major shareholder in the company, was nominally in charge of production. Until 1943 he had spent little time at the studio – according to Rank's biographer Alan Wood, Black would cheerfully direct inquiries after the elusive Ostrer to Newmarket racecourse – but *The Man in Grey* epitomized perfectly the sort of film Ostrer thought the public wanted and its success prompted him to play a larger part in the running of the studio.[14]

Black wanted to continue his balanced programme of comedies, serious dramas, war films, costume pictures, and anything else that his team of writers and directors came up with; Ostrer was determined to exploit the formula for box-office success which *The Man in Grey* seemed to have revealed and was increasingly intolerant of Black's eclectic approach. According to Sidney Gilliat the crunch came over *Waterloo Road*, his follow-up film to *Millions Like Us*:

> 'Ostrer thought it an absurd venture and I suspect had no wish to see me, or Frank [Launder], established as directors after *Millions Like Us*. The rift between Ostrer and Black grew into a chasm – the tension between the two men had been growing for a long time. Black was not backed by Rank, who had just taken over the group, and he resigned towards the end of the production. But he never let me know during the filming that the picture and myself were a direct cause. He was a man to go tiger-shooting with.'[15]

Though Black had been appointed a director of Gainsborough in May 1943, Ostrer's support was essential to Rank in the delicate negotiations with Twentieth Century-Fox over the structure and control of Gaumont-British, and Black was allowed to slip away to join Alexander Korda who had returned to Britain in 1943. He died of cancer in 1948 while working on the ill-fated epic *Bonnie Prince Charlie*.

Ostrer ran the studio from the end of 1943 until mid-1946, appointing the actor Harold Huth and the newspaper editor R.J. Minney as joint producers to take Black's place. His policy of concentrating on melodramas was vindicated by their huge box-office success, but production became increasingly attenuated as talent drained away from the studio.

Seven films were released by Gainsborough in 1944: *Bees in Paradise*, the last of the Arthur Askey films; *Time Flies*, with Tommy Handley; *Give*

Us the Moon, a futurist comedy starring Margaret Lockwood and Vic Oliver; *2,000 Women*, Frank Launder's female prisoner-of-war camp comedy-drama; and three melodramas – *Fanny by Gaslight*, *Love Story* and *Madonna of the Seven Moons*. Though much maligned by the critics, the three melodramas were big box-office successes, but none of the other films did very well. In 1945, *Waterloo Road* was finally released, along with a ghost story, *A Place of One's Own*, and a period musical, *I'll Be Your Sweetheart*. They were all modestly successful though once again the big money-makers were melodramas, *They Were Sisters* and *The Wicked Lady*. In 1946 only two films were released, *The Magic Bow* and *Caravan*, and though both were box-office successes Rank brought in Sydney Box as a new head of production. In an industry not renowned for its commercial acumen the achievements of the Ostrer/Minney/Huth regime at Gainsborough deserve more credit than they have received, but one can still regret the departure of Ted Black, Frank Launder, and Sidney Gilliat who might have given the studio a resilience and adaptability which would have ensured its survival.

There had been a certain vogue for period films during the war. After the patriotic shenanigans of *This England*, attempts were made to explore England's glorious heritage in *The Prime Minister*, *The Young Mr Pitt*, and *The Great Mr Handel*, and homage was paid to America in *Penn of Pennsylvania* and *Atlantic Ferry*. *The Man in Grey*, deliberately escapist, deliberately salacious, makes an altogether deeper and more subtle use of history.

Killing time while on leave, Phyllis Calvert (a WREN) and Stewart Granger (a white Jamaican airforce pilot) meet at an auction and become fascinated by the portrait of 'The Man in Grey', Lord Rohan. Calvert is his descendant and through her we enter into his dark and dangerous past. Clarissa (Calvert) is a woman who has everything: wealth, beauty, happiness; at finishing school she strikes up a friendship with unhappy, poor, and restlessly ambitious Hesther (Margaret Lockwood). Hesther elopes with a young ensign and Clarissa marries the Marquis of Rohan (James Mason), a sneeringly cynical aristocrat who treats her with contemptuous indifference. A few years later, their lives ruined by marriage, the two women meet again. Hesther becomes Rohan's mistress and Clarissa falls in love with Swinton Rokeby (Stewart Granger), Hesther's partner in a down-at-heel acting troupe, who is in fact a dispossessed Jamaican landowner. Rokeby proposes to elope with Clarissa but is determined to claim back his Jamaican inheritance first. While he is away Hesther causes the death of the feverishly unhappy Clarissa, leaving the way clear for her to marry Rohan. But although Rohan cares nothing for his wife, her murder besmirches his family honour and he beats Hesther to death.

In *The Man in Grey* there is a balance between the good and bad

2 Amy Veness, Gainsborough's favourite housekeeper, fails to reassure Phyllis
Calvert about the pleasures of marriage to the bad Lord Rohan. *The Man in
Grey* (1943).

characters which doesn't survive into the later melodramas. Rohan is the
magnetic centre of the film but the main relationship is between Clarissa
and Rokeby – strong positive characters whose goodness is something vital
and active rather than mere absence of malice. Rohan and Hesther too are
something more than cardboard villains. Rohan is unhappily imprisoned
in rigid codes of honour and manliness which allow no room for pleasure
beyond the grim sadism of punishing others' transgressions. Hesther, who
from her first rebuff of Clarissa's generosity – 'I don't care for sugary
things' – refuses to be grateful, also refuses the right of those who 'have
everything' to enjoy a happy untrammelled life. Her evil has a motive, it
stems from her refusal to accept her lowly position in life. The tragic
denouement of Clarissa and Rokeby's romance ('we've only had one
summer, it's not much in a lifetime') brings no happiness to Hesther and
Rohan, and when we return to the gloomy auction room in war-torn
London the past seems a sombre and disturbing place instead of the cosy
depository of good old English traditions usually shown on the screen.

Though Gainsborough's melodramas were to get progressively lighter, they retained this sense of the past as mysterious and dangerous.

Fanny by Gaslight, the last of the melodramas to be produced by Ted Black, was an ideal follow up to *The Man in Grey*. Based on a solid, well-respected novel and directed by experienced craftsman Anthony Asquith, it repeats the successful formula but in a different setting and with a different resolution. Whereas *The Man in Grey* reflects the gloom and uncertainty of war-torn London, with transient romances and the ever-present threat of death, *Fanny*, though hardly light-hearted, is much more optimistic. Mason and Granger play roles almost identical to their characters in *The Man in Grey*, though Mason's Lord Manderstoke and Granger's Harry Somerford are respectively a little blacker and a little whiter than their predecessors. Lord Rohan – for all his misanthropic misogyny – only acts when he considers himself wronged: killing the rash young man who labels him a rat, avenging his wife's death by murdering

3 Intrepid heroine Fanny (Phyllis Calvert) turns to confront her lover's vituperatively snobbish sister (Cathleen Nesbitt). *Fanny by Gaslight* (1944).

4 Star-crossed lovers Lissa and Kit (Margaret Lockwood and Stewart Granger)
part for what they think will be the last time. *Love Story* (1944).

his lover. Lord Manderstoke is actively evil. He kills Fanny's adopted
father in a brawl, drives her real father to suicide, and nearly succeeds in
killing her lover in a duel. In Michael Sadleir's book he is an aristocratic
thug, whose propensity for sex with children puts him beyond the pale.
Mason's Manderstoke is a more developed character, openly sadistic in his
treatment of women but retaining an air of tragic dignity which makes his
hold over the strong, sensual, ambitious women he attracts entirely
understandable.

  Granger's Somerford is much in the mould of bold, cheerful, devil-may-
care Rokeby, but he also has political aspirations. He wants to do away
with class distinctions and proves his adaptability by wooing and winning
Fanny in the hostile proletarian environment of an Islington pub, The
Jolly Bargee. The Lockwood role of the brazen, scheming, unscrupulous
woman who repays sisterly affection with uncompromising malevolence is
here split between Jean Kent's Lucy, a determined good-time girl who
twice brings Fanny into contact with the odious Manderstoke, and
Margaretta Scott's Alicia, on one level a selfish, aristocratic bitch, on

another a strong, independent woman fighting, with humour and irony, to survive in a society where women are chattels or decorative objects.

The central performance, though, is Phyllis Calvert's Fanny. Less sweet, less privileged, less fragile than Clarissa, she comes to represent the average British housewife, turning her hand to any sort of work to survive, slogging her way through death and misfortune and in the face of adversity shedding her reserve and blossoming into a full-blooded woman determined to fight for her share of happiness.

It is a theme shared by Gainsborough's first contemporary melodrama, *Love Story*. Margaret Lockwood plays a successful concert pianist, Lissa, who on volunteering her services to the army discovers she has an incurable disease and not long to live. Determined to enjoy her last few months of life, she goes down to Cornwall and among the human wrecks who are weathering out the war there she discovers an old mining engineer with a heart of gold, Tom (Tom Walls); a chain-smoking theatre director who is putting on an outdoor performance of *The Tempest*, Judy (Pat Roc); and a handsome, healthy-looking fellow who somehow seems to have evaded military service, Kit (Stewart Granger). After she has fallen in love with him, she finds out that he is an RAF pilot who as a result of his gallant action in allowing his crew enough time to bail out before doing so himself, is going blind. Melodramatic conventions drive them apart, Lissa to spend what she thinks are her last few months playing to the troops, Kit to a risky operation which leads to him recovering his sight. In the end they come together and Kit persuades her that they should grasp what happiness they can. He argues:

'Happiness such as we can have is worth grasping, even if it is for just a day, an hour. If you can stand on the highest peak for a moment you've had what most people strive in vain for all their lives . . . we're all living dangerously, there isn't any more certainty. Just today and the possibility of tomorrow.'

Lockwood and Granger both look suspiciously healthy (though Granger had been invalided out of the Black Watch) and the concentration on bright, airy Cornish location photography prevents any build-up of claustrophobic tension. But *Love Story* is a very torrid romance. The characters lead anguished lives full of frustration and longing and are wracked by deep emotional traumas. This sort of intensity had been seen occasionally in war films like *Dangerous Moonlight*, but the favoured British method of arousing pathos was through the representation of a restrained, low-key, underplayed heroism as in *The Bells Go Down* and *In Which We Serve*. *Love Story* deliberately employed a broader technique. According to Gainsborough's publicity department, Leslie Arliss, who directed *Love Story* and *The Man in Grey*, believed:

in subordinating action to emotion. He says that British films and British players are afraid of genuine emotion on the screen and maintains that this is the reason for the supremacy of the Americans in human dramas. Arliss wishes to change this diffidence and to concentrate on allowing his characters to express themselves and their feelings without any embarrassment either to themselves or to their audiences.[16]

This was flying in the face of critical opinion and, not surprisingly, his films provoked strong reaction.

The Man in Grey had been reluctantly accepted because of its novelty and its star performances, *Fanny by Gaslight* because of the respect due to Asquith as a director and Sadleir as a novelist. *Love Story*, scripted by Arliss and Doreen Montgomery from a short story by J. W. Drawbell, had no such redeeming credentials. According to *Time and Tide*:

> *Love Story* is an apt screen version of an old-fashioned novelette. It's simpering, it's mawkish, it makes one squirm in one's fauteuil. Why, I

5 Rosanna (Phyllis Calvert with the seven-moon ear-rings) warns Vittoria (Jean Kent) that her place is in the kitchen, not in Nino's bed. Nino (Stewart Granger) and his mother (Nancy Price) keep a low profile. *Madonna of the Seven Moons* (1944).

ask piteously, did Gainsborough Pictures choose to make it? Why do Eagle-Lion select it for selling in America? We hear a lot about the desirability of putting ordinary English life into films. Can this be the result? Go to *Love Story* and ask yourself whether this is life as you have seen it. Observe that all lower class characters are quaint and ridiculous, that all female characters fight for men, that no single character frames a sentence as you and I hear English sentences framed. If Eagle-Lion have their way these puppets tortured by whimsy will be accepted all over the world as English men and women.[17]

Much of this is merely silly. There are no working-class characters apart from a camp waiter played by Reginald Purdell and the 'fight' between Judy and Lissa for the war-battered Kit is conducted with some dignity and conviction. Some of the dialogue does wobble on the edge of high-flown banality but then the same could be said for *In Which We Serve*. And, like the best of the realist films, *Love Story* appeals because it deals deeply and sympathetically with real emotional issues. Not many romances between the war-wounded would resemble that of Kit and Lissa, but the problems – the morality of grabbing a happiness which might be all too temporary, the humiliating prospect of a life of disability and dependence – would be familiar enough. The sequences wherein Granger attempts to prepare himself for blindness by groping around with his eyes shut and those where Lockwood becomes lost in musical reverie are emotionally satisfying without needing to be realistic. These 'puppets tortured by whimsy' might not have the rounded authenticity of some of the naturalist characters created by Bernard Miles or Rosamund John but they still have a relevance and significance for British society.

Love Story, for all its emotional hyperbole, is solidly situated in wartime Britain. *Madonna of the Seven Moons*, Gainsborough's next melodrama, assumes the war is over (if it ever took place at all), and has its plot triggered off by the return to Italy of a young woman, Angela (Pat Roc), who has just completed a liberal education in England which has encouraged her to wear shorts and consort with men as equals. Her mother Maddalena (Phyllis Calvert), a saintly, retiring woman married to a rich Italian banker, is shocked by her daughter's ideas and jolted into a complete change of identity. After a ball to celebrate Angela's return she goes into a trance, dons gypsy clothes and exotic ear-rings, and buys a one-way ticket to Florence. It appears that, having been raped as a young girl, she suffers from amnesia and leads a double life, alternating saintly respectability with passionate abandon as the lover of a Florentine bandit chief, Nino (Stewart Granger). In this other life where she is known as Rosanna, she is as fiery, headstrong, and sensual as Maddalena is meek, demure, and conventional.

Critical response to this peculiarly convoluted film, unique even among the Gainsborough melodramas, ranged from condescending indulgence towards what was regarded as engaging nonsense, to harsh condemnation of its betrayal of the principles of British realism. William Whitebait in the *New Statesman*, after a laudatory review of *Western Approaches* as an example of the advances made in British film-making since the war, moaned that: 'With *Madonna of the Seven Moons*, we slip back almost as far as it is possible to slip. It is notably bad. . . . Everything in *Madonna of the Seven Moons* is treacly: characters, dialogue, situation.'[18] *Madonna* has an intensity and vitality which makes it anything but treacly, but the sub-plot in which Angela attempts to discover her mother's whereabouts and ends up trapped by a lounge-lizard is irritatingly weak. Pam Cook and Sue Aspinall, recent champions of the Gainsborough melodramas, both consider that Angela offers a significant alternative to the split existence of her mother – a modern woman who can express her sexuality openly and doesn't need to retreat into fantasy.[19] Unfortunately Pat Roc's Angela is silly and superficial, a left-over from some thirties British comedy where an ostensibly independent young woman tries to investigate by herself only to reveal that she is weak and helpless and in need of rescue by a strong man. In contrast Rosanna/Maddalena is a complex and magnetic character, and the fantasy of combining safe domesticity with carefree, sensual independence which is created around her is much more powerful and resonant than the busy modern life represented by Angela.

Madonna of the Seven Moons was directed by Arthur Crabtree, the cameraman responsible for the atmospheric photography of *The Man in Grey* and *Fanny by Gaslight*. *Madonna*, if unsurely directed, is equally stylish visually. *They Were Sisters*, Crabtree's next film as director, provides fewer opportunities for visual pyrotechnics, but the long complex story is handled with much greater assurance. Three sisters, Lucy (Phyllis Calvert), Vera (Anne Crawford), and Charlotte (Dulcie Gray), have varying fortunes with their marriages. Lucy marries a kindly, sympathetic architect, William (Peter Murray Hill, Calvert's real husband), but their happiness is blighted by the death of their only daughter; Vera marries Brian (Barrie Livesey), a rich man she does not love, and uses his wealth to find pleasure with other men; Charlotte marries Geoffrey (James Mason), the ambitious, rather uncouth insurance salesman she adores, but he develops into a domineering bully and makes her life a misery.

Whereas *Madonna of the Seven Moons* and *Love Story*, like the costume pictures, are heady fantasies with larger-than-life characters pursuing passion and excitement in exotic settings, *They Were Sisters* is a much cooler film, an aberrant descendant of those well-made plays like *Quiet Wedding* and *Dear Octopus* which celebrate the joys and agonies of upper-middle-class family life.

After a brief prologue in which each of the sisters finds her husband, the film cuts to 1937 when William and Lucy are celebrating seventeen years of domestic bliss, Vera's marriage to Brian is fatally eroded by her infidelity, and Charlotte is driven to drink and then to suicide by the sadistic, manipulative Geoffrey. As in *The Man in Grey* and *Fanny by Gaslight*, there is a central conflict between Calvert and Mason, though in *They Were Sisters* their class positions are reversed. Geoffrey is a social upstart and there is every indication that Charlotte has married beneath herself. Geoffrey lacks the aristocratic sexual charisma of Lord Rohan and Lord Manderstoke and Lucy's eventual triumph is diminished by the fact that her enemy is unambiguously obnoxious. But there are other factors which compensate for this loss of complexity.

Dulcie Gray's transformation from a delicate, happy girl into an ageing, worn-out woman is very impressive. There is a remarkable sequence where, after being contemptuously dismissed from the marital bed, Charlotte decides to leave home. To prevent her Geoffrey feigns a heart-attack. It is not a very convincing performance but Charlotte, pathetically

6 The sexual enslavement of women in marriage. Geoffrey (James Mason) caresses and torments his wife (Dulcie Gray). *They Were Sisters* (1945).

grateful that she is wanted after all, quickly backs down. Geoffrey is so pleased with the effect of his little charade that he forgets his 'illness' and kisses Charlotte. The way in which he takes her poor, wasted body in his arms and fastens a voluptuous kiss on her lips chillingly captures the sexual enslavement of women embodied in the vampire myth. It is an enslavement Lucy is determined to end.

Hostility between Geoffrey and Lucy is apparent from their first meeting. She tries repeatedly to rescue Charlotte from her husband's clutches but his hold over her is unbreakable. When Vera says that she feels numb about Charlotte's death, Lucy grimly replies, 'Isn't that because the real Charlotte died years ago, on her wedding day?' Ostensibly though, she seems to become more sympathetic towards her brother-in-law after Charlotte's death and she agrees, for the sake of her sister's reputation, to support his claim that their marriage was a happy one and that Charlotte's death was an accident. Once in the witness-box, however, she asks the coroner, 'Isn't a person who by shabby little cruelties kills the life and soul of another a murderer?' and she proceeds with a damning indictment of Charlotte and Geoffrey's marriage:

'My sister was rather a simple woman who just wanted a happy home, a husband and children. Soon he found her dull and too simple. So he set out on a deliberate course of snubbing her – I mean in front of everybody – the tradesmen, servants and even the children. He humiliated her until at last she became the fool he so often said she was and couldn't manage the simplest things. She answered stupidly and was incapable of even shopping properly. She wavered and fumbled and dropped things. You see she was afraid of him, terribly afraid.'

The film ends sunnily enough, with Lucy making a real home for Vera and Charlotte's neglected children and William assuring her that 'God's in his heaven, all's right with the world'. But Mason's seedily sadistic Geoffrey casts a pall over the cosy edifice of family life and it is difficult to regard the 'dear octopus' with quite the same affection again.

The disruption which the war brought to normal family life gave women the opportunity to challenge the unquestioning subservience still expected of them in some quarters. Nella Last, a lower-middle-class Cumberland housewife in her early fifties, found that though war-work exhausted her it was a tonic for her self-confidence. On 1 August 1943 she wrote excitedly in her diary

I suddenly thought tonight, 'I know why a lot of women have gone into pants – its a sign that they are asserting themselves in some way.' I feel pants are more of a sign of the times than I had realised. A growing contempt for man in general creeps over me. For a craftsman, whether a sweep or Prime Minister – 'hats off'. But why this 'Lords of Creation' attitude on men's part? I'm beginning to see I'm a really clever woman in my own line, and not the 'odd' or 'uneducated' woman that I've had dinned into me. . . . I feel that, in the world of tomorrow, marriage will be – will *have* to be – more of a partnership, less of this 'I have spoken' attitude.[20]

William and Lucy's relationship, despite its pre-war setting, would seem to be an ideal example of a marriage of equal partners. There is so much kindness, tolerance, friendliness, and affection between them that one hardly notices the lack of sexual passion. However, its absence sharply distinguishes *They Were Sisters* from the other melodrama Gainsborough released in 1945, *The Wicked Lady*.

In contrast to *The Man in Grey*, where our sympathies are divided between Clarissa and Hesther, *The Wicked Lady* is heavily weighted towards Lockwood's villainous Barbara Worth. The 'good' woman, Caroline (Pat Roc), is insipid, spineless, and rather silly. In the first half of the film she is humiliated and manipulated by Barbara just as Charlotte is by Geoffrey in *They Were Sisters*. Barbara, a poor relation, comes to help Caroline prepare for her wedding and coolly steals the bridegroom, Sir Ralph Skelton (Griffith Jones), from under her nose. The broken-hearted Caroline, who has been trying on her wedding dress, wants to leave at once but Barbara tells her she must stay for the wedding in order to avoid a scandal. Caroline agrees and tearfully offers Barbara her wedding dress. 'Wear that, I wouldn't even be buried in it!', Barbara tells the audience in a contemptuous aside.

On the night of the wedding Barbara meets and falls in love with a young architect, Kit Locksby (Michael Rennie), but she is bustled off to the bridal chamber and despairs of ever seeing him again. The new Lady Skelton soon tires of quiet country life with her worthy, wealthy, but dull husband and seeks excitement in night-time exploits as a highway robber. She shares this side of her life with Captain Jerry Jackson (James Mason), a good-natured, swashbuckling highwayman who admires her boldness but disapproves of her ruthless disregard for human life. Their relationship is explicitly sexual and is contrasted with the chaste affair of Ralph and Caroline. After a scene where Ralph and Caroline declare their love for one another but renounce any possibility of ever being able to consummate it, we see Captain Jackson expressing his satisfaction at an arrangement which gives him 'a partner on the road and an armful of hungry passion for my leisure hours' before making love to Barbara in the moonlight. It is Barbara, however, who is the dominant partner. When she returns to Jackson after a prolonged absence and finds him in bed with another woman she betrays him and he is hanged at Tyburn. He makes a dramatic return from the dead, looming up threateningly in her mirror as she makes herself ready for a night of passion with her re-found Kit. He half

7 Lady Barbara Skelton (Margaret Lockwood). *The Wicked Lady* (1945).

strangles her and forces her to make love to him, but the tables are soon turned and when they meet again he acknowledges that he is no match for her:

> 'You cold-blooded fiend. I've ached to ride and rob with you again, but I've no stomach for your kind of evil. I've finished with you Barbara. And if ever I want another partner, I'll choose a weasel or a viper, something reasonably friendly.'

And as he turns away she shoots him in the back.

The wicked Lady Skelton is made to pay for her sins in the end and conventional morality is satisfied, but there are no doubts about where our sympathies are supposed to lie. All the characters Barbara works her wicked deeds on – goody-goody Caroline; Hogarth, the bible-thumping old retainer who tries to reform the 'sin-sick soul' of his errant mistress; Henrietta, her bitchy sister-in-law, even Ned, the country bumpkin who trustingly tells her about a consignment of gold, seem to ask for punishment. There is a pantomime-like atmosphere which makes Barbara's villainy acceptable and the sentimental sequences between Sir Ralph and Caroline light interludes in a pell-mell farrago of melodramatic action.

There were three more Gainsborough melodramas produced under the Ostrer regime – *The Magic Bow, Caravan*, and *Root of all Evil* – but *The Wicked Lady* represented their peak of popularity. Significantly, J. Arthur Rank, gradually drawing in the reins on his far-flung empire, vetoed Ostrer's plan to make a sequel which would exploit *The Wicked Lady's* box-office success.

The Gainsborough melodramas seem to me valuable because they represent a rich tradition of visceral, garish, flamboyant popular cinema – a bridge between the barnstorming style of the old Tod Slaughter melodramas and the sophisticated atmospherics of Hammer's horror films. Within that melodramatic tradition, though, they are unique in the importance they allow their female characters.

In contrast to Ealing where Googie Withers pursued a lone furrow of feminine action, Gainsborough had a whole stable of female talent – Margaret Lockwood, Phyllis Calvert, Jean Kent, Pat Roc, Anne Crawford, Enid Stamp Taylor, Dulcie Gray – and gave them substantial, if at times banal, parts to play.[21] Writers like Sue Harper, Pam Cook, and Sue Aspinall have argued convincingly that the vaguely historical settings, the concentration on the bizarre and the exotic, allowed an expression of the fears and desires of women which were not allowed to surface in the realist films of the period.[22]

Women and Realism

Women, like the working class, were called upon to play a vital role in winning the war, and there was a frank acknowledgement of the new importance of women in some of the government-backed realist films. The wives and mothers of *In Which We Serve* and *The First of the Few* do little more than sit and wait, but other films provided more positive roles: the Dutch resistance appeared to depend entirely on cool, resourceful women (Joyce Redman, Pamela Brown, Googie Withers) in *One of Our Aircraft is Missing*; Rosamund John's architect-turned-nurse in *The Lamp Still Burns* is as indomitable a heroine as Phyllis Calvert's Fanny, standing up to the dragon-like Matron (Cathleen Nesbitt, the same thin-lipped tyrant Fanny had defied) and renouncing Stewart Granger in the interests of a good nursing service; Anna Neagle gives a powerful performance as pre-war heroine Amy Johnson in *They Flew Alone* and is even more impressive in *The Yellow Canary*, as a secret agent who establishes her credentials with the Nazis by shocking society with her outspokenly pro-German views; and Sheila Sim, despite the depredations of the glueman, remains fiercely independent in *A Canterbury Tale*: treated as an equal by the British and American servicemen she befriends, giving as good as she gets to the village blacksmiths, and finally dissolving the glueman's misogyny with her resolute common sense. The most striking indication of the importance attached to women as useful and productive workers, though, were the two films dealing directly with their contribution to the war effort, *Millions Like Us* and *The Gentle Sex*.

Launder and Gilliat had already proved their ability as screenwriters

8 Celia (Pat Roc) steels herself to become a 'mobile woman'. *Millions Like Us* (1943).

with films like *The Lady Vanishes* and *Night Train to Munich*. *Millions Like Us*, tackling the dangerously amorphous subject of the contribution of women factory workers to the war effort, proved they could direct their own scripts. Initially intended as an MOI documentary, Ted Black allowed them to jointly direct it as a full-scale feature film with extensive location shooting. The story begins with the Crowsons, a prosperous working-class family, setting out for their annual seaside holiday. They, like most people, choose to ignore the gathering clouds of war. 'Alas regardless of their doom, the little victims play', intones a gloomy Cockney pierrot in a summer-show dressing-room. 'No sense have they of ills to come nor cares beyond today.' But when war does come, the Crowsons do their bit. Dad joins the Home Guard, Phyllis, the elder daughter, joins the ATS, and son Jim is soon with the army in Africa.

The film centres on Celia (Pat Roc), the younger daughter who, as a 'mobile woman', is called-up and has her visions of chauffering Generals or nursing wounded heroes shattered when she is sent to work in the huge aircraft factory at Castle Bromwich. Despite the boring work, the factory offers Celia a rich new life. She meets, falls in love with, and marries Fred, a young Scots airman (Gordon Jackson), but shortly after they begin living together, he is killed in a bombing raid over Germany. Celia is a deliberately ordinary heroine, shy and unglamorous, in marked contrast to her restless, flirtatious sister (Joy Shelton). It is Pat Roc's only thoroughly satisfying performance, Launder and Gilliat encouraging her to underact so that the slightly hysterical energy which mars her performances in the melodramas is submerged, and she gives the impression of having reserves of passion and resilience under her placid exterior. The love scenes between her and Gordon Jackson, showing two inarticulate working-class characters attempting to express their feelings for each other, were not to be equalled until the 'kitchen sink' films of the sixties.

Though the romance between Fred and Celia is an important element, it is by no means the sole concern of the film. Apart from the obvious propaganda message ('you can help your country just as much in an overall as you can in a uniform', Celia is told by a harassed civil servant, upset that the saccharine for her tea has 'melted in the overflow'), *Millions Like Us* is preoccupied with social justice and the need for a decent post-war society. En route to the factory-workers' hostel, Celia teams up with a Welsh girl, Gwen Price (Megs Jenkins). They are both working-class girls, but Gwen is from a 'distressed area' – 'you know, lovely damp patches of fungus blossoming on the wallpaper and a bath in a zinc tub in the kitchen Saturday night' – whereas Celia is from the South East where unemployment was much lower. An even greater contrast is evident between two of the other girls sharing a room – the languid, upper class Jennifer (Anne Crawford) and Annie Earnshaw (Terry Randall), a chirpy Lancashire urchin who shocks her room-mate by going to bed in her underclothes. 'What's the point of taking them off, they've only got to go on again in morning', she cogently points out.[23]

Class difference and the need to overcome it, and the concurrent need to build a post-war society where damp patches of fungus don't grow on the walls and everyone has a bath, are themes which are pursued throughout the film. Fred and Celia's romance develops alongside a more turbulent relationship between Jennifer and Charlie, the dour, working-class foreman (Eric Portman) whom she antagonizes through her sloppy attitude to work. 'It's a bit different from dropping lumps of sugar into cups of coffee in a West End canteen', he tells her, and they continue to trade insults throughout the film. Gradually they acknowledge the growing attraction they feel for each other and before the end they discuss their future. On the sort of idyllic hillside from which profound speeches were made so often in British films (*Love on the Dole*, *A Canterbury Tale*, *They Came to a City*, for example), Charlie tells the woman he has come to love that marriage between them is impossible. 'Are you thinking of my parents?' she asks. 'Because I can handle them. Anyway they'd approve of you.' 'Ay but would I approve of them, I doubt it', he retorts and goes on to explain:

'The world's roughly made up of two kinds of people. You're one sort and I'm the other. I know we're together now there's a war on, we need to be What's going to happen when it's over? Shall we go on like this or are we going to slide back? That's what I want to know. I'm not marrying you Jenny till I'm sure. I'm turning you down without even asking you.'

This importance attached to a post-war society which would retain the democratic, caring solidarity found in wartime, is emphasized by the ending. Celia, still grief-stricken by the death of her young husband, goes with Gwen to the huge factory canteen where a band and the singer Bertha Willmott are entertaining the workers. Bombers pass overhead on their way to Germany. Celia stops eating and looks upwards as Bertha Willmott begins singing *Waiting at the Church* which had been sung in happier circumstances at her wedding reception. Gwen smiles at her and gently encourages her to sing, and as we see her, hesitantly at first, join in, her face is framed on the one side by Jenny, on the other by Annie Earnshaw before a cut to the massed workers singing and then to a wave of bombers passing over the factory. Celia's sacrifice, her loss, is just one of many which society must try its best to heal.

The Gentle Sex, directed by Leslie Howard and Maurice Elvey, was released around the same time as *Millions Like Us*. Despite the greater experience of its directors, it is a much less polished film, relying heavily on Howard's commentary to provide links between the sequences. Seven women – a waitress (Joan Gates), a good-time girl (Jean Gillie), a stuck-up teacher (Barbara Waring), a sweet-sucking Scot (Rosamund John), a Czech refugee (Lili Palmer), a sheltered girl who has never been away from home (Joan Greenwood), and a Colonel's daughter (Joyce Howard) – join the army and after basic training become gunners and lorry drivers.

Though the film is less well-made than *Millions Like Us*, Howard's women, particularly Rosamund John's wry, resourceful Maggie, are more unconventional and the emphasis is on the relationships they form among themselves rather than on their relationships with men. These women rapidly prove that they can do 'men's jobs', mending their lorries, working as an efficient team on an ack-ack battery, and they are accepted as friends and equals by the ordinary British tommies (led by Jimmy Hanley) even when their officers remain supercilious. Despite their varying backgrounds, there is none of the class antagonism evident in Launder and Gilliat's film, and hostility is focused on Joan, the teacher, who for no apparent reason is unpleasant to everybody.

The romance, between Ann the Colonel's daughter and David Sheridan, a well-bred young flying officer (John Justin), is a very upper-class affair, and it is indicative of the film's more conservative standpoint that it is this gallant young officer who makes the set-piece speech about being 'sick of a world where people have to die because they don't know how to live' and of the need to fight for a decent peacetime society. But there is an interesting sequence where Ann and her friends encounter the boy's mother. Sipping tea with this old lady (Mary Jerrold) in her country cottage, these brash young women discover with some surprise that their experience of engines and guns is nothing new to their frail hostess, who drove an ambulance in the 1914–18 War. Ann apologizes for their patronizing assumption that they are the first generation of women to achieve anything worthwhile. But Mrs Sheridan reassures her:

> 'Oh my dear you must believe in all those things with all your heart and soul. And you must fight for them, as you are fighting for them. We didn't really know what we wanted but I believe you do. And I believe you'll get it.'

The Gentle Sex and *The Lamp Still Burns* were made by Derrick de Marney's company Concanen for Two Cities which, like Gainsborough, was coming increasingly under the orbit of J. Arthur Rank. Launder and Gilliat, after leaving Gainsborough in 1944, formed their own production company, Individual Films, and under the umbrella of Rank's Independent Producers, joined Powell and Pressburger's The Archers, the David Lean/Ronald Neame/Anthony Havelock-Allan team's Cineguild, and others in making films for the Rank empire. Rank's power and influence seemed ubiquitous by 1944 and deserves to be treated in some depth.

4   The Rank Empire

When I got into this business in all its sides and branches I realised the
great possibilities for making entertainment films with a message that
would not merely please the eye and stimulate the imagination but
would also become a help in the serious matter of the daily lives of film-
goers. If I could relate to you some of my various adventures and
experiences in the larger film world, you would not only be astonished
but it would be as plain to you as it is to me that I was being led by
God. (J. Arthur Rank, *Methodist Recorder*, March 1942)[1]

Joseph Arthur Rank was the third son of a Yorkshire miller, who had
turned his small local business into the largest milling concern in the
country. J. Arthur received a thorough grounding in the milling business
but as it was unlikely that he would inherit the family firm he sought
outlets for his ambitions elsewhere. In 1933 he began to involve himself in
the film industry, starting in a small way by backing the Religious Film
Society and providing a few thousand pounds for a short religious film,
Mastership. A year later he founded British National with Lady Yule, and
in 1935 he joined a group of City of London financiers in putting up the
money for a major new studio – Pinewood – and a film distribution
company, General Film Distributors (GFD).

The slump that hit the industry in 1937 deterred some of his partners,
but Rank was not a man to give up easily. In 1938 he bought up two other
major studios – Denham and Elstree Amalgamated – and began
negotiations for an interest in two of the three biggest cinema circuits,
Odeon and Gaumont-British. In October 1941 he bought the Ostrer
brothers' shares in Gaumont-British; in December he succeeded Oscar
Deutsch as chairman of Odeon. He now controlled more than half the total
studio space, over six hundred cinemas, the largest British distribution
company and over eighty Gaumont-British subsidiaries. He was now the
overwhelmingly dominant figure in the British film industry.

The growth of the Rank empire attracted little comment at the time. He
had kept a low profile, content to be overshadowed by more flamboyant
figures; and his business deals were by no means straightforward. He had
succeeded Deutsch only after a bitter boardroom struggle and his control
over the Gaumont-British empire was as yet uncertain. The other reason

why Rank's empire-building attracted so little attention was that in financial terms the future of the British film industry looked decidedly bleak. In November 1940 the *Economist* had gloomily concluded that 'Probably nothing but the return of peace can put the cinemas on their feet.'[2] Naturally this pessimism found expression in share prices. The Gaumont-British 10/- ordinary shares stood at 6/9d in December 1941, Odeon's once prized 5/- ordinary shares at 7/9d. But over the next five years they were to rise dramatically. By December 1946 the Gaumont-British shares were valued at 28/3d and Odeon's stood at 50/6d. Much of this can be attributed to the steady rise in cinema attendance. The lack of alternative entertainment, the dislocation of social life caused by the war, and the satisfaction of escaping from the danger, boredom, and inconvenience of war into a warm, dark fantasy world, combined to make cinema-going more popular than at any time before or since.[3] Rank's profits rose too, and to avoid them being drained away by Excess Profits Tax, substantial amounts were invested in film production, where any profits that did accrue could be more easily disguised.

Independent producers

Of Rank's studios, Elstree Amalgamated was leased to the government for storage before war broke out and Pinewood was requisitioned. Denham was kept open, occupied in the early days of the war by British National, which Rank had resigned from in 1937. Lady Yule's patriotic production programme was rewarded by success at the box office, particularly with the Powell and Pressburger films *Contraband* and *One of Our Aircraft is Missing*, and Rank decided to follow her example. According to his biographer, Alan Wood, Rank invited Powell and Pressburger to lunch with him at Denham, one day in 1942:

> Rank explained that he was resolved to keeping British production going during the war, however much he had to pay for it. Powell and Pressburger explained that they were full of ideas for films, and that all they needed was someone to pay for them. Would Rank give them the money – not, as was usual, with strings attached and dictation from a distributor, but with full artistic freedom to make the kind of films they wanted? Rank said he would.[4]

The four films Powell and Pressburger had made together – *The Spy in Black, Contraband, 49th Parallel*, and *One of Our Aircraft is Missing* – were well-crafted, eocnomical, commercial, patriotic, and very popular. Their first film for Rank, *The Life and Death of Colonel Blimp*, was a two-and-a-half-hour Technicolor extravaganza created round a cartoon figure meant to epitomize everything that was wrong with British militarism.

Churchill strongly disapproved and tried to prevent its being made. To his credit, Rank resisted this pressure. The film was completed and became a big box-office success.[5] *Colonel Blimp* is typical of Powell and Pressburger's mature work in mounting a critique of modern society while espousing traditional values. Unlike David Low's hide-bound, bigoted cartoon figure, Powell and Pressburger's Colonel Blimp is honourable, lovable, and richly human. Like *This England, The Demi-Paradise*, and *This Happy Breed* the film is a pageant which celebrates aspects of English tradition – here the ethos of the English gentleman-soldier. By the end of the film Blimp is forced to acknowledge that his attitude to war might be outmoded, that 'unfair' tactics might be necessary against a savage and inhuman enemy, but there is no attack on the army hierarchy and no simple message about the need for any radical change in army thinking.[6]

Their next film, *A Canterbury Tale*, attempted to relate the traditional England of Chaucer's pilgrims to an England where tanks roared down country lanes and American GIs mingled with the countryfolk. It looked a safe enough subject on paper but the film itself is bizarre and disturbing and provoked very mixed reactions from critics and audiences. Powell and Pressburger's next four films for Rank – *I Know Where I'm Going* (1945), *A Matter of Life and Death* (1946), *Black Narcissus* (1947), and *The Red Shoes* (1948) – represent a still unsurpassed peak of artistic achievement in British cinema, but their escalating budgets put increasing strain on the relationship with Rank. After *The Red Shoes* – which cost £500,000 though it eventually grossed over $5 million in America – they left to join Alexander Korda.

In 1942 Powell and Pressburger had established their own production company – The Archers – but the financial and managerial business was handled by a Rank company, Independent Producers Ltd.[7] Other, less prestigious production units were already sheltering under the Independent Producer umbrella. Excelsior, which had been set up by Romanian producer Marcel Hellman during the mid-thirties boom, was revived to make two films for Rank, *Secret Mission* (1942 d. Harold French) about British intelligence officers at work in France; and *They Met in the Dark* (1943 d. Karel Lamac), a spy thriller with Tom Walls as a treacherous Blackpool theatrical agent. More in tune with Rank's own views were the four films made by Norman Walker's production company, GHW – *The Man at the Gate* (1941), *Hard Steel* (1942), *The Great Mr Handel* (1942), and *They Knew Mr Knight* (1945).

Walker, like John Baxter, brought a moral seriousness not always matched by cinematic talent to his films. But whereas Baxter's utopian socialist outlook and his success with *Love on the Dole* has attracted some attention, Walker, whose films are permeated with evangelical Christianity, has been ignored even by Rank's biographer. After making *Turn of the Tide* for Rank and Lady Yule in 1935, he turned his hand to acting and then teamed up with fellow Methodist James B. Sloan, Rank's production manager at Pinewood, to form GHW. Their first three films all starred the brilliant but erratic Wilfrid Lawson.

The Great Mr Handel was Rank's first Technicolor film, though with its modest sets and small cast it doesn't look a very extravagant production. The film spans a period of sixteen years but the main stress is upon Handel's years in the wilderness leading up to a long night of the soul and the creation of his 'Messiah'. Lawson's Handel is magnificent: irascible, dishevelled, slightly seedy, but confident of his own worth and incapable of bending his standards and principles to please a stupid, hypocritical, and bigoted aristocracy. Poverty brings him closer to the common people and enables him to shake off the fetters of the world and produce his greatest work. The film has none of the dash and razzmatazz of a Hollywood biopic but its concerns are altogether more spiritual. Handel, like J. Arthur Rank, is led by God and the long sequence wherein he creates the 'Messiah', his Brook Street home awash with hazy Technicolor visions, is truly remarkable.

They Knew Mr Knight is rather different, an offbeat family melodrama comparable to Ealing's *Pink String and Sealing Wax* or Ian Dalrymple and Jack Lee's *The Woman in the Hall*. Tom Blake (Mervyn Johns), a factory manager in a Midland town, is given the chance to buy out the business he works for when he meets Mr Knight (Alfred Drayton), a high-powered financier. Though business is slack he manages to keep the factory going by participating in Mr Knight's dubious financial speculations, but eventually he is caught out. Some shares he has invested in crash, and after making fraudulent statements to the bank he is sentenced to twelve months in Lincoln gaol.

Mrs Blake (Nora Swinburne) returns after visiting him to a dark, unwelcoming house. None of the children have been home, the morning mail is still on the mat. She picks it up and carries it to the mantelpiece, looks up into the mirror and imagines her husband going into his cell to be locked up. 'Oh my darling, what can I do?' she sighs. 'How can I help you when I can't even help myself?' She turns away, wanders distractedly towards the window and slumps into a chair. 'Oh God help us!', she gasps. 'Help me, help me!' There is a cut to a patch of light on the wall and then to the rain-sodden garden. Gradually the rain stops and the sun breaks through. Light floods into the room and Mrs Blake looks up, surprised but happy that her spontaneous prayer has been answered. She is able to carry on with renewed strength, the family rallies round, and finally the day comes for her husband's release. She goes to meet him and from the prison they walk across the road into Lincoln Cathedral. He explains that he is not bitter but he is very sad at the suffering he has caused his family. She reassures him: 'You've been sad long enough. The account's settled. We've lost nothing that mattered', and points out that he will need all the strength and support he can muster: 'Can you face your situation?', she asks. 'Face pity, curiosity, perhaps even contempt? Be willing to take the little job when you've been master? Can you begin again?' And Mervyn Johns, with just the right degree of humble dignity, affirms that he can.

With its industrial setting and ventures into high finance, its answered prayers and repentant sinners, *They Knew Mr Knight* must have been a film after Rank's own heart, but it was not a box-office success and Walker never directed another film for Rank. Though he liked to tell journalists that he was in films because he had been led there by the Holy Spirit, Rank had business sense enough to realize that his stay would be a short one unless his films made profits. According to one colleague:

> Rank himself always took the view that he was a commercial man who had a sense of mission regarding the place of films in the life of the nation, but had no creative ability whatsoever. But he depended on the creative artistry of others and felt compelled to accept their philosophy.[8]

Thus many of the films sponsored by Rank embodied world views very different from his own.

Clive Brook's *On Approval*, for example, a frothy, risqué comedy of manners, can have given the Holy Spirit little satisfaction; and the script for *The Rake's Progress*, Launder and Gilliat's first film for the consortium, aroused the opposition of both Mrs Rank and the Hays Office. Rank's reluctance to interfere meant that it was made with very few changes and Rex Harrison's pleasure-loving cad proceeds along his immoral way, breaking hearts, disrupting business-life, and causing the death of his own father until he is redeemed by heroism in the war. Launder and Gilliat followed up *The Rake's Progress* (1945 d. S. Gilliat) with *I See A Dark Stranger* (1946 d. F. Launder); *Green For Danger* (1946 d. S. Gilliat); *Captain Boycott* (1947 d. F. Launder); *London Belongs to Me* (1948 d. S. Gilliat); and *The Blue Lagoon* (1948 d. F. Launder). As with Powell and Pressburger's *The Red Shoes*, *The Blue Lagoon* was a lavishly budgeted Technicolor film with an unhappy production record. By the time it became apparent that the film was going to be a big commercial success, Launder and Gilliat had been lured from Rank by Alexander Korda.

Rank's sensitivity about films which exceeded their budget was rooted in his unfortunate experience with another of his independent producers, Gabriel Pascal, a charismatic Transylvanian who had captured the affections of George Bernard Shaw and persuaded the Grand Old Man of British drama that his plays should be turned into films. *Pygmalion* (1938), produced by Pascal but directed by Anthony Asquith and Leslie Howard, had been one of the few thirties British films to be well received in America; *Major Barbara* (1941), which Pascal directed himself, had been an expensive flop. None the less, Rank was persuaded to back Pascal's next venture, a Technicolor version of Shaw's *Caesar and Cleopatra*.

Production costs had risen steadily since 1939: *49th Parallel* (1941) had been expected to cost £60,000 but actually cost £120,000; *In Which We Serve* (1942) had been originally budgeted at around £100,000 but cost £240,000; *Henry V* (1944) was allowed the unprecedentedly large budget of £350,000 and cost nearly £500,000. Maurice Ostrer at cost-conscious Gainsborough pointed out that:

Since the war the time taken to produce a film has steadily increased. It is not merely because we are aiming at better pictures; it is because things take longer to do owing largely to staff and raw material difficulties. So studio rentals go on much longer, and they eat up expenditure. The old saying that time is money is desperately true of film production. No planning in the world can prevent a film being more expensive now than it would have been in 1938. That is obvious.[9]

But *Fanny by Gaslight* and *The Man in Grey* had been made on budgets of £90,000, *Love Story* and *Madonna of the Seven Moons* for around £125,000, so their box-office success brought substantial profits. Only international success on the scale of *Gone With the Wind* would be enough to recoup the million pounds that Rank and Pascal spent trying to turn Shaw's *Caesar and Cleopatra* into an epic blockbuster.

Pascal, like Norman Walker, made no more films for Independent Producers. Their places were taken by talented young men who had made their names in the war years. Ian Dalrymple and Jack Lee left the Crown Film Unit to form Wessex, responsible for five films between 1947 and 1950: *The Woman in the Hall* (1947 d. Jack Lee), *Esther Waters* (1948 d. Ian Dalrymple), *Once a Jolly Swagman* (1948 d. Jack Lee), *All Over The Town* (1949 d. Derek Twist), and *Dear Mr Prohack* (1949 d. Thornton Freeland). David Lean, Ronald Neame, and Anthony Havelock-Allan – Noel Coward's production team on *In Which We Serve*, *This Happy Breed*, and *Blithe Spirit* – made seven films for Rank between 1945 and 1950: *Brief Encounter* (1945 d. David Lean), *Great Expectations* (1946 d. David Lean), *Take My Life* (1947 d. Ronald Neame), *Blanche Fury* (1948 d. Marc Allegret), *Oliver Twist* (1948 d. David Lean), *The Passionate Friends* (1949 d. David Lean), and *Madeleine* (1950 d. David Lean). Until branching out on their own, the Cineguild team had been the backbone of the other major beneficiary of Rank's generosity, Filipo del Giudice's Two Cities Films.

A Tale of Two Cities

Giudice had come to England in 1932, a refugee from Mussolini's Italy. A lawyer, he managed to gradually build up a practice specializing in cases involving film contracts. In 1937 he teamed up with another Italian, Mario

Zampi, to establish Two Cities. In 1938 they brought out two films: *Stepping Toes*, a low-budget musical directed by John Baxter; and *Thirteen Men and a Gun*, made in Italy by Zampi. The following year, Two Cities enjoyed more success with an adaptation of Terence Rattigan's *French Without Tears* directed by Anthony Asquith, and signed a distribution contract with Paramount. When war broke out Giudice and Zampi were quick to respond, making one of the best of the comic espionage films, *Spy for a Day* (d. M. Zampi). But by the time their next film was released, *Freedom Radio* (d. A. Asquith), both men had been interned as enemy aliens.

Zampi was kept locked up for the duration of the war, but Giudice had made powerful political friends and was released after four months. Two Cities made a resistance movie, *Unpublished Story* (d. Harold French), for Columbia, but Giudice's next project, *In Which We Serve*, a war film starring Noel Coward, was dismissed as too costly and he had to look elsewhere for financial support. Coward's script was inspired by the experiences of his friend Lord Louis Mountbatten, whose ship, the *HMS Kelly* had been torpedoed during the Battle of Crete. Government support was lukewarm: the Admiralty was dubious about the propaganda value of a film celebrating a lost battle and a sunk ship, and Beddington and Bernstein at the MOI regarded Coward as a highly unsuitable person to portray a Captain in the Royal Navy. Wardour Street was equally unenthusiastic about the film's commercial prospects and Giudice took the unusual step of shooting the film without securing a distribution contract. Money was supplied by Two Cities' genial financial backer, Major A.M. Sassoon, and the film was eventually picked up for distribution by British Lion, then a small company mainly concerned with the distribution of Gene Autry and Roy Rogers Westerns.

Unlike earlier naval dramas such as *Convoy*, *For Freedom*, and *Ships with Wings*, which concern themselves exclusively with officers, the story of Coward's Captain Kinross is intertwined with that of two of his lower-deck shipmates – Chief Petty Officer Walter Hardy (Bernard Miles) and Ordinary Seaman 'Shorty' Blake (John Mills). Social divisions between lower-middle-class Hardy and working class Blake are easily bridged, and the fact that they inhabit a different world from their Captain hardly seems to matter as they cling together to the same life-raft. As one expects with Coward, the dialogue is a mixture of bathos and inspired cliché, but his script is extremely well served by the actors, none of whom, with the exception of Coward himself, was very well known at the time, and the group of young film-makers Giudice recruited for the film – producer Anthony Havelock-Allan, art director David Rawnsley, cinematographer Ronald Neame, and director David Lean. Lean, who shares the director's credit with Coward and who appears to have done most of the work, was considered by many the best editor working in Britain at the time, and he arranges Coward's rather predictable scenes into a complex but highly satisfactory network of interlocking flashbacks.[10] With Celia Johnson as his wife, Coward manages to make the upper-middle classes look convincingly altruistic, considerate, and sincere, and though there were a few critical quibbles about his performance, *In Which We Serve* proved to be the most popular British film of the war – in America as well as Britain – and established Two Cities as a major production company.

Though Rank had declined to finance *In Which We Serve*, it had been made at Denham, and all Two Cities' subsequent films were financed through distribution contracts with Rank's company GFD. In 1943 four films were released – *The Gentle Sex*, a co-production with Derrick de Marney's company Concanen; *The Flemish Farm*, directed by the scriptwriter and novelist Jeffrey Dell; *The Lamp Still Burns*, completed by veteran director Maurice Elvey after Leslie Howard was shot down over the Bay of Biscay; and Anthony Asquith's *The Demi-Paradise*. All of them were commercially successful and Rank was encouraged to back Giudice's more ambitious plans the following year.

Coward triumphantly followed up *In Which We Serve* with *This Happy Breed*, the most successful British film of 1944 despite its nostalgic view of the thirties. It spans the whole of the inter-war period through the lives of Frank and Ethel Gibbons (Robert Newton and Celia Johnson) and their bickering, feuding, lower-middle-class family. The lives of the Gibbons are. marked not only by births, deaths, marriages, and family crises, but by a selection of historical events – the end of the 1914–18 war, the British Empire Exhibition of 1924, the General Strike of 1926, the coming of Al Jolson and the talkies in 1929, the rise to power of Hitler in 1932, the elections of 1931 and 1935, the death of King George V in 1936, and the Munich crisis of 1938.

Though Coward's own lifestyle would have been far beyond the pale for these pillars of respectability, he heartily endorses the complacent self-satisfaction of English suburbia. When Queenie Gibbons (Kay Walsh) rebels against the stifling conformity of Sycamore Road her father tells her angrily:

'We're as we are and that's how we're going to stay. And if you don't like it you can lump it. But one of these days, when you know a bit more, you'll find out that there are worse things than being just ordinary and respectable and living the way you've been brought up to live.'

But she has to learn the hard way, running off to Paris with a married man, and soon finding herself alone and penniless in a foreign land. She survives and prospers, running an English tea shop in one of the Riviera resorts, but she is happy to return to England with sailor Billy Mitchell (John Mills), the boy next door who has always loved her. He marries her and brings her home to Sycamore Road.

Frank Gibbons works as a black-leg bus-driver during the General Strike, is fiercely patriotic, and believes that 'it is up to us ordinary people to keep things steady' – the sort of man one would expect to be a solid supporter of the Conservative party. But Coward carefully distances him from Baldwin, Chamberlain, and their associated sins of unemployment and appeasement. Frank refuses to enthuse about the Tory electoral victories in 1931 and 1935 and when it comes to Munich Frank's moderation gives way to uncharacteristic belligerence:

'I've seen something today that I wouldn't believe could happen in this country. I've seen thousands of people, British people mark you, carrying on like maniacs, shouting and cheering with relief for no other reason than that they've been thoroughly frightened. And it made me sick and that's a fact. And I only hope to goodness that we've got guts

9 Edwards (Alan Wheatley), his own career blocked by class prejudice, shows Vivian (Rex Harrison) how the coffee business works. *The Rake's Progress* (1945).

enough to learn one lesson from this. And we shall never find ourselves in a position again where we have to appease anybody.'

This Happy Breed is a very clever, very moving film but one can feel the bonds holding together its conservative consensus creaking loudly. It makes an interesting contrast to Launder and Gilliat's *The Rake's Progress*, which also spans the whole of the inter-war years.

Its hero, Vivian Kenway (Rex Harrison), is a playboy and a cad but his actions are shown to stem not from any inner rottenness but from the corrupt ethos of the society in which he moves. Sent down from Oxford he secures a good job in the South American coffee business through his father's influence. The embittered manager who shows him the ropes complains, 'I'm sick and tired of teaching their jobs to gilded youth backed by influence and class privilege and then watching them end up with better positions than me own.' But Vivian quickly becomes interested in the business and works hard, only to be told off by his superiors for neglecting his duties at the bridge table and the cricket pitch. Disillusioned, he gets drunk, insults the company chairman, and is sent back to England in disgrace. Rejecting any further attempts by his family to place him in a responsible position, he becomes a playboy, squandering the money left him by a rich uncle.

A montage of events follows showing Vivian at Wimbledon, at Monte Carlo, at St Moritz, at the Derby, and then, as he achieves some success in motor racing, his career is intercut with the rise of Fascism in Europe. With his finances at a low ebb he makes a deal with a young Jewish girl, Rikki (Lilli Palmer), that she should pay off all his debts in return for him marrying her and helping her leave Austria. Here Vivian's hitherto superficial life is disturbed by deep emotions as Rikki falls in love with him at the same time that he falls in love with Jenny Calthorp (Margaret Johnston), his father's secretary. Tragedy ensues and Vivian disappears from polite society to work in a succession of seedy jobs – second-hand car dealer, door-to-door salesman, professional dance hall partner – which show the obverse side to the world of Wimbledon, Epsom, and Monte Carlo. He is rescued by Jenny and after a long night of the soul comes to a proper appreciation of his place in society:

'Looking at it quite unemotionally, the truth is my type's becoming obsolete. Can't compete with the international situation. Not even news any more. The thirties produced us. The champagne's gone flat, and we're going out with the thirties. And nothing to show for it but cirrhosis of the liver and a lot of wasted time.'

But war gives him the chance to redeem himself, and though he dies, he does so bravely and honourably. Jenny, who never consummates her love for him, speaks a fitting epitaph at the end: 'Yes that was Vivian, in peace a misfit, a man who wanted to live dangerously in a world that wanted to play safe. In war a fine soldier.' Whereas *This Happy Breed* looks back on the inter-war years with nostalgia, *The Rake's Progress* waves it a cheerful and unregretful farewell.

As well as *In Which We Serve* and *This Happy Breed*, Two Cities was responsible for three of the other best remembered films of the war period – *The Way Ahead* (1944), *Henry V* (1945), and *The Way to the Stars* (1945). In analysing *In Which We Serve*, Jeffrey Richards talks of the film's 'resounding endorsement of the existing class system' and points out that Coward 'sought not the abolition of class distinction, but a greater sympathy and understanding between classes.'[11] This sort of 'conservative populism' was also a characteristic of Olivier's *Henry V* and Asquith and Rattigan's *The Way to the Stars*. *Henry V*, shot in Technicolor, costing £475,000, and directed by an actor who had never directed a film before was, to say the least, a risky project. In Britain, despite the plaudits of the critics, the film found a mixed reception among audiences, but skilful marketing in America turned it into a major international success.

The Way to the Stars cost much less but with its sub-theme of Anglo-American relations it too was intended to appeal to an international audience. Though extremely moving in its evocation of the bravery and sacrifice of wartime airmen, it offered nothing very new in the way it presented its material. Lindsay Anderson in an early explosion of truculent bile dismissed the film as:

> the epitome of all the popular West End comedy-drama successes of the last ten years – young lovers, comic background characters, misunderstandings, happy endings and all. Certainly the RAF background is well-observed and realistically done; but the story that unrolls before it contains all the ingredients of a romance by Berta Ruck or Ethel M. Dell, and is as expertly contrived.[12]

But like the Lean/Coward films it displays the sort of stiff-upper-lip quality which to the orthodox critics counted as realism. C.A. Lejeune enthusiastically declared:

> Mr Asquith's work is one more proof that the British film has at last attained its majority. It has the great merit, rare in Hollywood pictures these days, of emotional restraint. The intimate scenes between Miss Rosamund John, Mr Redgrave, Mr Montgomery, and Mr John Mills, are beautifully charged with a feeling that never spills over. These people are real people and like real people, they do not make much of their private emotions. Again and again the audience is left to resolve its own tensions: an operation that is painful, unusual, and good for the soul.[13]

The two factors determining Giudice's choice of films were his wish to work closely with the MOI and his insistence on introducing artistic credibilty to British films.[14] But as an Italian anti-fascist with many friends in the British Labour party, he was politically more closely aligned with the egalitarian ethos of Carol Reed's *The Way Ahead* than with Coward, Rattigan, and Olivier's Churchillian patriotism.

Carol Reed, after leaving Gainsborough for the Army Kinematograph Unit, had made a forty-minute training film, *The New Lot*, which had greatly impressed his military superiors. Army morale was low in 1943 – unsurprisingly given the poor pay and conditions and the lack of action – and the success of *In Which We Serve* encouraged the MOI in their belief that a similar film was needed about the army. David Niven, Peter Ustinov, Carol Reed, and Eric Ambler, all of whom were serving in the army, were thrown together to produce a script and Two Cities persuaded to make the film with a distribution contract from Rank.

In Which We Serve had acknowledged the importance of the lower ranks, but not since the 'call-up comedies' in the early days of the war had the ordinary soldier been allowed a prominent role in a British film. *The Way Ahead*, like *The Gentle Sex*, takes a number of individuals from different walks of life and follows their trials and tribulations as they come to terms with army life. Reed achieves his transformation of this bunch of lazy, quarrelsome civilians into a proficient fighting force with a minimum of tub-thumping patriotism. This is very much a 'people's army', David Niven's officer is a car-mechanic not a gentleman and William Hartnell's sergeant-major scourges out class differences with a rigorous application of army discipline.

Two Cities could claim to have a more interesting and successful programme than any other British production company, but costs rose rapidly. *The Way Ahead* netted £183,700 from its release in Britain, a respectable enough figure. But it had cost £252,500 to make and, as it had little appeal for American audiences, it lost money.[15] As a condition of guaranteeing the completion of *Henry V*, Rank joined the Two Cities board and the company became a Rank subsidiary. Three more very successful films were to be made under the Giudice regime – *Blithe Spirit* (1945 d. David Lean), *Odd Man Out* (1947 d. Carol Reed), and Hamlet (1947 d. Laurence Olivier), but there were expensive flops too, and in 1947 Giudice left Rank to set up a new company, Pilgrim Films.

Rank: monopolist or benevolent patron?

In July 1944 the Cinematograph Films Council, a government advisory body, published a report on *Tendencies to Monopoly in the Cinematograph Film Industry*. Known as the Palache Report after its Chairman Albert Palache, it expressed the growing concern of independent producers like Michael Balcon at the dominant position Rank had secured in the industry. Palache surmised that:

The British public are vitally concerned that the British Cinematograph industry should not be allowed to become either a mere reflection of a foreign atmosphere or a channel for disseminating the ideas and aspirations, no matter how worthy in themselves, of one or two dominating personalities in this country.[16]

It is unlikely that the British public, which throughout the twenties and thirties had shown a solid preference for Hollywood films, shared any such concern; and Rank, financing a wide variety of independently-minded film units had much less opportunity for imposing his ideas and aspirations on his films than Balcon had in the cosy but tight ship he ran at Ealing.[17] What was really at risk was a particular type of small-scale producer:

Independent producers, meaning by independent those who are not dependent for finance upon Mr Rank's finance corporation and who prefer to make their own distribution arrangements, have been placed in a very vulnerable position by the combination of Government war-time needs and the tendency towards corporate ownership.[18]

More than half the studio space had been requisitioned and of the remaining thirty stages, fifteen were owned by Rank. Shortage of space was aggravated by the fact that Rank's own films were sometimes produced with a disregard for cost:

It is alleged that the budgeted periods for shooting are often in themselves far in excess of the number of weeks which normal efficient planning would require, that production schedules are frequently inadequately planned and supervised, that the commencing of shooting is often delayed, that pictures continue to occupy floor space for many weeks after the due completion dates. This wasteful occupation of scarce studio space, it is represented, is due as much to an apparent disregard for economy in production costs, engendered by the knowledge that excess costs will in any case merely reduce the Excess Profits Tax liability of particular companies, as to any other cause.[19]

This condemnation of extravagance in the midst of austerity is understandable enough, but the Palache solution was less realistic:

So long as the minimum essential needs of British films for exhibition in the cinemas of this country are not met, first place in the studios should be given to the production of a larger volume of medium-cost feature pictures which are in demand throughout this country, rather than to the smaller number of highly speculative luxury products which may or may not chance to prove acceptable in the United States.[20]

The idea that what British audiences wanted was a staple diet of low-budget, authentically British films was shared by few people involved in production and fewer in exhibition. The perennial argument as to whether the British film industry should concentrate on small, indigenous films which could earn their money back in Britain, or make big-budget films for the world market, was now complicated by the international success of a handful of authentically British pictures – *49th Parallel*, *In Which We Serve*, *Henry V* – which were also extremely costly. If Rank was to continue to back the film-makers who were winning a new prestige for British films and make a profit, he had no choice but to seek a bigger market for their films.

Challenge to Hollywood

In both Britain and America a shortage of films and high cinema attendance figures made big-budget production a much less precarious proposition than it had been in the past. Rank had an organization which was as large and as powerful as the big American companies, and his control over two of the three major circuits which provided the chief outlet for Hollywood films in Britain gave him a powerful lever with which to force the Americans into granting him a share of their home market.[21] A golden opportunity came up in 1943 when Alexander Korda sought to sell his partnership in United Artists. UA already had shares in the Odeon cinema circuit and Rank was the obvious replacement. Negotiations began early in 1944, but Rank tired of the inability of UA's squabbling partners to reach agreement and persuaded the two men sent to negotiate with him to help him set up a new world-wide distribution organization, Eagle-Lion Films Ltd.

Establishing the British branch was simply a matter of hiving off films and personnel from Rank's distribution company GFD. But it was soon realized that the plan to build an entirely new distribution organization in the United States – particularly at a time when property and man-power were in short supply – was unrealistic. In July 1944 a compromise was reached whereby UA would handle all Rank's big-budget pictures for the next two years. They proved to be unsatisfactory partners, inflexible and dilatory in putting Rank's films across to exhibitors. *The Life and Death of Colonel Blimp*, for example, was drastically cut to fit the double feature bill and dumped on an uncomprehending public, and *Henry V* was only handled under duress, the UA salesmen insisting that Shakespeare was box-office poison.

In June 1945 Rank came to America. By the time he left, on July 17, he was able to announce that henceforth all his big pictures would be handled by Universal. Back in 1936 Rank and his City of London partners had bought a twenty-five per cent share in the company, thus securing the distribution of Universal's films in Britain for GFD. By 1945 Rank was the biggest shareholder and he used his power to re-organize the company in such a way as to ensure the proper distribution of his films in America. A new production/distribution organization was to be set up, United World Pictures, with a capital of $10 million financed equally by Rank and Universal. It was to be supplied annually with eight films from Rank and eight films from International Pictures Inc., an independent American production company which had enjoyed considerable success with films like *The Dark Mirror, Casanova Brown*, and *The Woman in the Window*.

Exhibitors would be presented with the sixteen films as a package, and it was hoped that the popular International films would help sell the rather less commercially desirable British films. Such 'block-booking' practices were widespread in America, but in June 1946 the Justice Department won a court decision making them illegal. This was a considerable set-back for Rank, and United World Pictures had to be abandoned. But the links between Universal and International were tightened. From the beginning of October 1946, Universal was to concentrate entirely on distribution and to form a new subsidiary, Universal-International Productions, which would deliver twenty-five pictures annually for distribution by the parent company. Twelve Rank films would also be handled, though now they would have to rely on their own merits to attract bookings.[22]

Outside America, Rank was busy establishing a world-wide organization. In January 1945 he took over the hundred-and-ten-strong Odeon Cinema chain in Canada; in November he acquired a fifty per cent holding in the Australian Greater Union Theatre circuit; in March 1946 he bought the hundred-strong Kerridge circuit in New Zealand; in 1947 he extended his interests in South Africa and the West Indies and began building a large cinema in Cairo. By the beginning of 1947 Rank seemed set to prove that at last British films had arrived at the international market place.

5   Great Expectations

We've shown in this war that we British don't always muddle through: we've shown we can organise superbly – look at these invasions of the continent which have gone like clockwork; look at the harbours we've built on those beaches. No excuse any more for unemployment and slums and underfeeding. Using even half the vision and energy and invention and pulling together we've done in this war, what is there we cannot do? (J.L. Hodson, *The Sea and the Land*, 1945)[1]

War in Europe ended officially on 8 May 1945. Churchill had insisted, since taking power in 1940, that victory be the only aim and had devoted himself wholeheartedly to diplomacy and war strategy. But Britain's war effort was dependent on the morale and efficiency of workers in industry and it was here that the Labour ministers in the Coalition – particularly Ernest Bevin – played a crucial role. Despite Churchill's impatience and irritation with demands for social reform, he was persuaded that it was a necessary condition for winning the war. Paul Addison, in *The Road to 1945*, describes the Coalition government as

> the greatest reforming administration since the Liberal government of 1905–14. Here in the midst of war, was an astonishing example of the uses of adversity. Social security for all, family allowances, major reform in education, a National Health Service, Keynesian budgetary technique, full employment policies, town and country planning, closer relations between the state and industry – all these had been set on foot by the spring of 1943. By the spring of 1945 a new and wide-ranging prospectus of peacetime development was at an advanced stage of preparation within the civil service, while educational reform had already been embodied in the Butler Act of 1944 and had only to be administered. . . . When Labour swept to victory in 1945 the new consensus fell, like a branch of ripe plums into the lap of Mr Attlee.[2]

Though there were fears in some quarters that social revolution was on its way, the policies followed by the Labour party were hardly more radical than those favoured by moderate progressives in the Liberal and Conservative parties. Even nationalization was initially confined to ailing, undercapitalized industries and was carried out more as an exercise in managerial rationalization than as an attempt to deprive the rich of their ill-gotten gains.

The new Labour government faced daunting economic problems in 1945. According to Angus Calder, Britain ended the war:

> With external disinvestment amounting to four thousand million pounds; with her shipping, an important source of invisible exports, reduced by thirty per cent; with her civilian industries physically run down after six years of war and her visible exports running at no more than four-tenths of her pre-war level; with 355,000 of her citizens dead by enemy action at home or abroad.[3]

It is not altogether surprising, then, that reform should be slow and cautious. With hindsight it is possible to view the Labour government's policies as excessively timid, but it made sense to maintain the wartime consensus. Edgar Anstey, one of the pioneers of the documentary movement, made an unashamedly pro-nationalization film, *Coal Crisis*, for Rank's *This Modern Age* series and was summoned to explain himself. Rank's diffidence about interfering with his film-makers has already been remarked upon, but this was a political rather than an artistic matter and Rank was a staunch Tory. His response is revealing not only about his own methods and personality but of the climate of the time. After careful consideration he told Anstey:

> 'Well, if you assure me, as you have, that everything said in this film about the present condition and the economics of the coal industry is as you depict it, then we must put it out. A lot of my coal-owner friends will probably never speak to me again or not for a very long time, but if it's true we must show it.'[4]

Labour relations were unprecedentedly harmonious during the 1945–51 period. Trade union leaders were reluctant to encourage strikes which would make life difficult for the government, but equally important was the willingness of employers to make concessions. With the economies of Germany, Italy, and Japan disabled, the demand for British goods was high: the motor-car industry which before the war had depended entirely on the domestic market exported nearly two million cars between 1945 and 1952, and industries such as shipbuilding and cotton textiles which had suffered during the depression of the thirties enjoyed a revival. Full employment meant that skilled men were at a premium and those who were confined to unskilled jobs could pick and choose where they worked. With comprehensive national insurance, a National Health Service, and improved education opportunities there seemed the promise of a fairer and more equal society.

Plans and dreams

Huge numbers of documentaries, not all of them sponsored by the government, set out to explore the problems faced by post-war Britain and the proposed solutions. As early as 1941 Bernard Miles was insisting in *The Dawn Guard* that the old ways of living were 'gorn forever and the sooner we make up our minds about that the better'. By 1944 documentaries were asking what new ways were going to take their place now that the transitional period of the war was drawing to a close. The Scottish Co-Operative Wholesale Society put their view forward in *The Two Good Fairies*, written by Birkbeck professor and Brains Trust star Dr C. E. M. Joad. A working-class couple (with suspiciously plummy voices) look forward to the future with equanimity, despite the forebodings of the older generation, because they are able to live in a cheap, modern home and enjoy maternity benefits and hospital facilities thanks to the ministrations of the two good fairies – Sir William Beveridge and the Co-Operative Wholesale Society.

More searching and less optimistic is Humphrey Jennings' *A Diary for Timothy*. A film scrapbook of the last nine months of the war for a child born in September 1944, it has a dirge-like quality wholly appropriate for a nation emerging victorious but exhausted from a long and bitter struggle. Instead of euphoria, there is a grim stress on the problems of peace, on the need to combat the 'greed for money and power' that has dominated the past. E.M. Forster's commentary is occasionally pompous and overblown, but half-way through the film there is a magical fusion of poetry and imagery. Christmas jollity is interrupted by news of the German counter-attack and shots of city and countryside enshrouded in fog succeed one another until, following a train driver into the fog, we emerge into a bright, clear, frosty landscape and a choir singing 'O Come All Ye Faithful':

'In those days before Christmas, the news was bad, and the weather was foul. Death and darkness, death and fog. Death across those few miles of water for our own people and for others, for enslaved and broken people. The noise of battle getting louder. And death came by telegram to many of us on Christmas Eve. Until out of the fog dawned loveliness, whiteness, Christmas Day.'

Henceforward the film becomes more optimistic, but unlike most subsequent documentaries, there is no pretence that there are easy solutions.

'life is going to become more dangerous than before, oddly enough. More dangerous because now we have the power to choose and the right to criticize and even to grumble. We're free men, we have to decide for ourselves.'

When the Labour government came to power in 1945 the international situation was already de-stabilizing. The world was soon divided between the two super-powers despite the messy protests of the people who found themselves on the wrong side of the 'iron curtain'. 'Poor little Poland' over which Britain had gone to war was left to Stalin's tender mercies and the Greek guerrillas who had heroically resisted the Germans found themselves labelled Communists and thus ineligible heirs to the new Hellenic kingdom. So far from 'left speaking unto left', Labour found itself tied up in an increasingly cold war.

In 1943 Paul Rotha made *World of Plenty*, an ambitious documentary contrasting the potential wealth of the world with the poverty of so many of its peoples; there were two post-war sequels – *Land of Promise* (1946) and *The World is Rich* (1948). All three films are imbued with the sort of optimism about solving the world's problems which lay behind the foundation of organizations like UNESCO (where John Grierson established a mass media department) and inspired schemes like the Labour government's attempt to farm groundnuts and sunflowers in East Africa. The murky politics of the real world, however, tended to be left to the ·newsreels.

At home, the havoc wrought by enemy bombers on Britain's towns and cities seemed to present a heaven-sent opportunity to architects and planners who had decried the slum conditions of the thirties. Ambitious schemes were proposed for rebuilding badly blitzed towns like Portsmouth, Plymouth, Coventry, and London.[5] But it was in housing, more than any other area, where the discrepancy between ambition and achievement was most apparent. House building had been virtually at a standstill during the six years of war, a quarter of a million homes had been destroyed and four million damaged. The severe housing shortage was exacerbated once the war was over by the return of servicemen whose wives and girlfriends had been living in temporary accommodation and now wanted homes of their own. The government was wary of making grandiose promises about homes fit for heroes to live in and documentaries such as Jill Craigie's *The Way We Live* and the Rank Organization's *Homes for All* (an episode of their newsreel series *This Modern Age*) stress problems as much as achievements, though they share a faith in planning and the virtues of a progressive bureaucracy. This rather forced optimism precluded any mention of the twenty thousand squatters who took up residence in abandoned Army and RAF camps in the summer of 1946.[6]

Since the General Strike of 1926 the miners had been pressing for the nationalization of their industry. On 1 January 1947 it finally happened, but in the great majority of places the management remained the same and the atmosphere of suspicion and distrust was slow to dissolve. Films tended to play down the lingering bitterness that plagued labour relations and stress that a new era of co-operation and harmony was at hand.

Humphrey Jennings' last film for the Crown Film Unit – *Cumberland Story* – focuses on a pit, near Workington, exploring its troubled history, looking forward to its prosperous future. The spokesman of the new order is a mining engineer, James Adam Nimmo, who tells us that:

'The history of the Cumberland coalfield has been one of continuous struggle, first against the natural condition of the seams, secondly against the coal owners. But during the war we carried out experiments which changed the whole atmosphere here and gave us new methods of work to meet underground conditions. In the past the battles with the mine owners tended to divide the miner from the mining engineer. Our experiments have shown that both can work together and that both must work together. They've also shown that the miner himself can become a modern craftsman and he must become one. Now our battle with the coal owners is ended and the pits belong to us all.'

Cumberland Story lacks the resonance and conviction of Jennings' wartime films. For all the brave talk of reform and construction, peace was less cinematically exciting than the death and destruction wrought by war, and the blaze of glory around the British documentary gradually faded. This hardly affected the great mass of documentaries concerned with everyday instruction and exhortation. The Halas and Batchelor *Charley* cartoons, for example, where a comical 'ordinary man' is taught the benefits of the NHS and other aspects of the Welfare State, are by no means inferior to those wartime films telling people to dig for victory and eat potato pie. But post-war Britain lacked the sort of revolutionary fervour which might have inspired documentary makers to expand the boundaries of the cinema.

Not that there weren't attempts to arouse enthusiasm. In 1946 an impressive exhibition of British-designed goods, 'Britain Can Make It', attracted considerable attention, and in 1951 there was the Festival of Britain. 'Britain Can Make It' was supported only by a newsreel documentary of the same name, but the Festival of Britain commissioned a prestige documentary from Jennings, *Family Portrait*. In many ways it is an impressive film – there is the familiar stress on a common cultural heritage, on the beauty and magic of the English landscape – but there is something which doesn't ring true. Jennings' harmonious populist utopia is at odds with earnest, busy, and slightly vulgar Labour Party Britain, and light years away from the soon-to-be-realized affluent society.

The great expectations of the intelligentsia were not to be fulfilled, but the Labour government was remarkably successful in putting Britain's battered economy back into working order. By the end of 1948 when

Harold Wilson, the President of the Board of Trade, announced his 'bonfire of controls', most people were more prosperous than they had ever been. But there was a darker side to post-war Britain. As Harry Hopkins points out:

> There existed side by side, often overlapping in baffling fashion, an England of 'Plain living and high thinking', and an England of high living and distinctly low thinking, an England of 'Reality' and an England of 'Escape', the England of Sir Stafford Cripps, of equality of sacrifice and the export drive, and the England of the black market restaurant, the expense account, and Mr Sidney Stanley, 'the Pole of Park Lane'.[7]

In October 1948 a tribunal was set up under Mr Justice Lynskey to investigate possible charges of corruption at the Board of Trade. The Lynskey tribunal found that John Belcher, a railway clerk and union official who had been elected to Parliament in 1945 and appointed Parliamentary Secretary at the Board of Trade in 1946, had lucrative but improper links with, among others, Leonard Matcham, a Max Factor executive; Sir Maurice Bloch, a leading sherry importer; and Solomon Kohsyzcky (alias Sidney Stanley), a contact man and sometime dress manufacturer. The corruption revealed was reassuringly small-scale. Luxury, apparently, was a few days' holiday in Margate paid for by the eager-to-please Mr Stanley; export licences could be obtained after the discreet delivery of a bottle of luxury perfume or a hogshead of sherry. It was the sort of 'under the counter' black-market activity with which people were thoroughly familiar, and it was shown to have made only superficial inroads into the administrative machinery. Ministers like Cripps and Wilson were completely vindicated. If the Labour party's vision of a caring society lost out to get-rich-quick consumerism in the fifties, it did so honourably.

Ealing's social conscience

Documentary influence on feature film production was reckoned one of the main causes of the success of British films during the war. But in the post-war period the whole idea of a documentary-influenced realist British cinema became increasingly untenable. The independent producer/director teams – David Lean and Cineguild, Powell and Pressburger, Carol Reed, Launder and Gilliat – turned towards adventure stories, melodramas and literary adaptations which, with the exception of *Brief Encounter*, *Odd Man Out*, and *The Fallen Idol*, the critics found disturbingly irrelevant to the problems of post-war society. Del Giudice at Two Cities strayed into the political arena with the Boulting brothers' *Fame Is the Spur*, and Pilgrim Films, the company he set up after quarrelling with Rank, was responsible for *The Guinea Pig* and *Chance of a Lifetime*. Michael Balcon at Ealing and Sydney Box, who took over as head of production at Gainsborough in 1946, made attempts to explore social problems, but their methods, increasingly divorced from the documentary realism approved of by the critics, provoked only hostility.

Ealing is remembered for its war films and its comedies, but there is an interesting gap in the late forties when the studio had no formula to guide its production activities. Charles Barr in his authoritative book on *Ealing Studios* says that:

> From 1940 to *San Demetrio*, almost all the films dealt, directly or indirectly, with the fighting of the war; the emphasis then changes. War films do not stop entirely, but are isolated and fairly marginal. Likewise, comedies were made at Ealing before *Passport to Pimlico*, including one, *Hue and Cry* which is an Ealing comedy by any definition. But *Hue and Cry*, released at the start of 1947, has no successor for two years, being just one among a wide range of films which Ealing turns out in the years before and after the Armistice. Until *San Demetrio*, one can say that Ealing was broadly identified with the war film, and after *Passport to Pimlico* with a distinctive form of comedy. In the five years between, there was no such easy identity, and the twenty-one features of this period cover a greater range than before or since.[8]

One aspect of this diversity is the series of films made by Basil Dearden and Michael Relph. Dearden was taken from the theatre by Basil Dean and remained at Ealing when his mentor left. His first directorial assignments were in co-operation with Will Hay on *The Black Sheep of Whitehall*, *The Goose Steps Out*, and *My Learned Friend*. He then went on to direct *The Bells Go Down*, *The Halfway House*, and *They Came to a City*, on which Michael Relph acted as art director. They worked well together, and in line with Michael Balcon's policy of internal promotion, Relph became associate producer on Dearden's next film, *The Captive Heart*. Their partnership continued until Dearden's death in a car crash in 1971, by which time they had worked together on over thirty films.[9]

Charles Barr comments disparagingly that: 'it is well known that he [Dearden] was readier than anyone else to pick up and realise any project that was on offer rather than waiting for one that specially appealed to him'.[10] Dearden and Relph's prolific output does include a number of mediocre efforts but, over a period of twenty years, they made several impressive films dealing seriously, intelligently, and entertainingly with a range of social problems: race prejudice (*Frieda*, *Pool of London*, *Sapphire*, *All Night Long*); homosexuality, when it was still a criminal offence (*Victim*); adjustment to peace after the excitement of war (*The Captive Heart*, *Cage of Gold*, *The Ship that Died of Shame*, *The League of Gentlemen*); crime and juvenile delinquency (*The Blue Lamp*, *I Believe in*

You, Violent Playground, A Place To Go); and the conflict between principles and feelings *(Life for Ruth)*.

Raymond Durgnat jibes that their films are characterized by a benevolent paternalism according to which, 'all characters who drop their aitches need to have their lives sorted out for them, or their heads knocked together by the British bobby and his social superiors',[11] but he admires the skill with which they integrate serious subjects into popular entertainment formats. Other critics have been less kind, accusing Dearden and Relph of combining a flashily melodramatic technique with an irritatingly superficial approach to the serious issues they raise. Like John Baxter and Norman Walker, they have been ignored or derided because their films do not conform with what is considered tasteful, artistic cinema.

They Came to a City is one of the least well-regarded of Ealing's films. As film art it hardly bears comparison with better known allegories such as Renoir's *La Regle du Jeu* or Bunuel's *Exterminating Angel*, but for anyone interested in British culture in the forties it is fascinating. Priestley himself appears in the film's prologue, meeting a young couple on a hillside and discussing with them the sort of society they could hope for after the war. Looking into the future we are introduced to nine characters – a waitress, a stoker, a charlady, a bank manager and his wife, a businessman, and three members of the upper classes: Sir George Gedney, Lady Loxfield and her daughter Philippa. They have all been swept up from their everyday life and dumped before a utopian city, the gates of which are as yet locked.

They quickly reveal what sort of people they are, but the real test comes when they are invited into the city. All the working-class characters are attracted by a society which is 'entirely owned and run by the people who live in it. A place where men and women don't work for machines and money but machines and money work for men and women.' But the stoker and the waitress decide to go back, determined to build their own city of sweetness and light. Of the middle-class characters, the money-grubbing businessman hates it, but the bank manager (Raymond Huntley, who specialized in seedy middle-class types), a man used to listening to people's problems and finding himself unable to help, is warmed by the co-operative ethos of the city and wants to stay. He is dragged away by his wheedling, clinging wife, but he too goes back inspired with the idea of changing the world. Of the upper-class characters, Sir George (A. E. Matthews, who often played dotty but benevolent aristocrats) admits that his eccentric behaviour is a cover for the fact that he 'can't stand people' and thus finds the city's fraternal spirit distasteful. Lady Loxfield, spoilt, bigoted and crabby, is appalled by a society where she is not looked on as something special, but her daughter is inspired to break away from maternal domination and start a new life.

If one accepts the city as the Welfare State, Priestley gets it about right – working-class people are wholeheartedly for it, as are the more kindly or forward-looking members of the other classes, leaving only a rump of the selfish and the over-privileged. It is a difficult play to adapt – long message-filled speeches, a city which is impossible to visualize – and Ealing's decision to turn it into a film must have had as much to do with Michael Balcon's new-found social conscience as with a realistic assessment of its commercial prospects.

Dearden and Relph's next film, *The Captive Heart*, vies with Cavalcanti's *Went the Day Well?* as the best of the Ealing war films. The three men worked together on several films and they share a fondness for introducing exotic elements into their ostensibly realistic films. *The Captive Heart*, the progenitor of those Prisoner-of-War-camp films of the fifties in which Bryan Forbes, Richard Attenborough, John Mills, *et al.* organize concert parties and make daring escapes, was shot on location in a recently liberated Prisoner-of-War camp in Germany and is centred around a Czech partisan (Michael Redgrave) who has assumed the identity of a dead British officer before being captured. To maintain the pretence – and avoid being shot – he begins corresponding with the dead man's wife (Rachel Kempson, who was married to Redgrave in real life) and finds himself falling in love with her. It is a marvellously effective device – enabling the film to explore problems of loneliness and separation, of deep relationships between people who had had no time to get to know each other because of the war – and the film is richer and more resonant than Ealing's standard realist fare.

Unlike the fifties Prisoner-of-War films where it is almost exclusively an officer's war, in *The Captive Heart* the other ranks are vigorously represented by Ealing regulars Jack Warner, Mervyn Johns, and Jimmy Hanley. Redgrave's integration into the community of officers, who at first suspect him of being a spy, is paralleled by Hanley's growing friendship with Mervyn Johns and Jack Warner, steady working men whom he initially despises as mugs. There is an easy camaraderie between officers and men. 'Were you really? How awfully interesting!', exclaims the raffish Captain Grayson (Guy Middleton) on discovering that Hanley used to be a burglar, and they team up to break into the Camp Commandant's office.

Redgrave's long-distance romance is set against an assortment of other romantic relationships: between a young pianist (Derek Bond) and the newly-married wife he suspects of being unfaithful to him; between a Scotsman (Gordon Jackson) and the woman he loves but tries to push away from him once he discovers he has permanently lost his sight; and between Warner and Johns and their cosy, loving, working-class wives (Gladys Henson and Rachel Thomas). The letters Redgrave receives from his supposed wife summon up a traditional England of children, gardens, home-made toffee, and cricket on the village green. But his letters to her, with their stress on communal life, on co-operation and making the best of things, come much closer to the new society which it was hoped would emerge from the war.

Redgrave's description of life in the camp, accompanied by shots of men putting up pictures, singing, playing games, involving themselves in useful activities, invites comparisons with Butlins. But the less pleasant aspects of this enforced holiday are also made apparent. Redgrave writes home, as men wander listlessly about or lie on their bunks, sunk in despondency,

> Our third winter is approaching, bringing with it a new enemy. It's not the duration, it's the indefiniteness of duration. If a man knew the length of his sentence he could plan accordingly. Afterwards in our memories we shall re-live only the sunny days, the pleasant scenes, the freedom of mind and the comradeship. We shall forget the wet days, the wet weeks, those days when it seemed an effort to do nothing and our bunks were the only peace. Deep down in the hearts of all of us there dwells a lonely ache, a desperate yearning for those we love, and a fear of becoming forgotten men.

In fact all ends happily, but the film shares with *A Diary for Timothy* a moodily sombre attitude to the war and the problems of peace. *Frieda*, which Dearden and Relph made a year later, is more melodramatic, but it deals seriously with post-war problems.

Like *They Came to a City*, *Frieda* was a successful stage play (by Ronald Millar) and has a didactic message to convey. Bob, an RAF officer (David Farrar), escapes from a POW camp in the dying days of the war and is helped by a German girl whom he marries. When he takes his bride home, he meets unexpected hostility from his own family, particularly his aunt, a prospective Labour MP played by Flora Robson, and from the community at large. After a number of crises, Frieda begins to win acceptance, but her Nazi brother (Albert Lieven) arrives on the scene and re-activates the latent hostility. Only when Frieda is driven to attempt suicide do the family recognize her essential innocence. By 1947, when the film was released, Michael Balcon had signed a distribution agreement with Rank, and it was skilfully and aggressively marketed.

COULD YOU LOVE FRIEDA?
WOULD YOU TAKE FRIEDA INTO YOUR HOME?

the public was asked. As Frieda was played by the beautiful young Swedish actress Mai Zetterling the question was heavily loaded, but *Frieda* did indeed, as the posters claimed, COURAGEOUSLY PRESENT A GREAT CONTROVERSY OF OUR TIME.

Attitudes towards the Germans had been relatively tolerant throughout the war. Churchill bluntly declared 'the only good German is a dead

German', and Roosevelt thought that the German people 'should have soup for breakfast, soup for lunch and soup for dinner' until they had learnt their lesson. But this wasn't a war which generated the sort of hysterical nationalism that was apparent in the 1914–18 War. Tom Harrisson, in his book *Living Through the Blitz*, observes:

> Hatred there was – some. Surprisingly little of it was engendered by personal bombing experience, however. Mixed with this came, persistently, a form of affectionate respect for the Luftwaffe crews, 'only doing their job' etc. For every one reference to a Hun or Boche – Churchill's standard epithets – there must have been getting on for ten thousand to Jerry. 'Jerry' as Eric Partridge's *Dictionary of Slang* aptly remarks, 'is often half-affectionate'.[12]

With the end of the war the situation changed. There had been some knowledge of concentration camp atrocities but the First World War had inured people against horror stories and they were only half believed. Thus the scale and savagery of the Nazi 'final solution' was difficult to comprehend until the newsreels of Belsen and the other camps appeared.

10 Sisterly rivals Mai Zetterling (left) and Glynnis Johns. *Frieda* (1947).

There followed a wave of revulsion against the Germans which made it impossible to regard them merely as the defeated enemy.

On the other hand there were strong political reasons for helping Germany back onto its feet and tying it into a Western alliance against Communism. Cold War attitudes hardened rapidly and Labour's Foreign Secretary Ernest Bevin was unsentimental about the need to make up with the old enemy. By the time *Frieda* was released Britain was supplying eighty million pounds a year in aid to Germany. It would be wrong to suppose that *Frieda* ia a 'Cold War film' though. Its deeply humanist message is summed up in Flora Robson's admission that 'you can't treat people as less than human without becoming less than human yourself'.

In *The Captive Heart* Dearden and Relph match and interweave a broad spread of characters and stories. Though *Frieda* ostensibly deals with broad universal problems – how to deal with a defeated enemy, whether a nation can be held collectively guilty for the crimes carried out in their name – there is a rapid narrowing down to the problems of a particular foreigner trying to penetrate the woolly insularity of a close-knit English community, and yet further to the triangular relationship between Frieda, Bob, and Judy (Glynnis Johns), the young widow who was Bob's childhood sweetheart. In their different ways, though, both films manage to combine communal with personal concerns, deep emotional issues with social problems.

1947 was a good year for Ealing. Each of the five films released that year was impressive in one way or another: *Frieda*; Cavalcanti's *Nicholas Nickleby*; Charles Frend's *The Loves of Joanna Godden*; Charles Crichton's *Hue and Cry*, the first of a new type of Ealing comedy; and Robert Hamer's *It Always Rains On Sunday*, subsequently hailed as a landmark in realist cinema, though at the time it was viewed as a sordid descent into the low life of the East End. Though *Frieda* and *It Always Rains On Sunday* were popular enough at the box-office, they had no successors at Ealing. Dearden and Relph went on to the glossy heavyweight splendour of *Saraband for Dead Lovers* and then to a cosy and conventional saga of police life, *The Blue Lamp*. The jaundiced view of working-class communal life seen in *It Always Rains On Sunday* gave way to cheery, whimsical fantasies like *Another Shore*, *Passport to Pimlico*, and *A Run for Your Money*, where eccentric millionaires, ancient documents, and lottery winnings allow a temporary escape from the realities of austerity-bound Britain.

The Boxes at Gainsborough

Sydney Box, who took over at Gainsborough in 1946, was more willing to take on society and its problems. Box worked as a journalist in the thirties, and after marrying a continuity girl and aspiring scriptwriter, Muriel Baker, worked with her on one-act plays for the burgeoning amateur dramatics market. During the war the Boxes established a documentary company and became prolific producers of government information films. In 1944 Sydney produced two feature films for Two Cities – *English Without Tears* and *Don't Take it To Heart* – and leased the Riverside studio at Hammersmith to begin independent feature production. The following year he released *29 Acacia Avenue*, a risqué comedy about suburban infidelities which only just scraped past the censor; and *The Seventh Veil* which became the top box-office picture of 1945. · Box was now established as a successful producer and was considered by J. Arthur Rank a suitable successor to Maurice Ostrer at Gainsborough.

Bad feeling between Ostrer and Rank had meant that Gainsborough's operations had been gradually run down. Only three films – *Caravan*, *The Magic Bow*, and *The Root of All Evil* – had been made since the end of the war and only *Jassy* was in development. The Boxes turned things round with a vengeance. Muriel took charge of the script department and with her assistant Peter Rogers began energetically commissioning scripts and setting writers to work on adaptations. By the time she left in 1949 there were forty scripts in various stages of development. Despite the opposition of Michael Balcon, who with a seat on the Rank board of directors was able to overlook Gainsborough's affairs while brooking no interference with his own studio, Betty Box, Sydney's twenty-six-year-old sister, was given charge of the old Islington studio and produced twelve films in two years – a rate of production equalled only by Ted Black in the mid-thirties. With the films they produced independently at Riverside studios, the Boxes could claim responsibility for thirty-seven films in their short reign at Gainsborough.

Sydney Box was not a very inspiring figurehead for the brave new British film industry. Overweight and balding, he exuded an unctuous geniality which automatically made people suspicious. None the less he was one of the very few commercial film producers to unashamedly declare himself a socialist. In an address to the National Film Association, a body set up to co-ordinate the film interests of the Labour party, the TUC, and the Co-operative movement, he reminded his audience that the forces of reaction and capitalism 'are able to instil a great deal of propaganda into films from their point of view' and that: 'No film has been made of the Tolpuddle Martyrs, the Suffragette Movement, the National Health Service as it is today or the scandals of patent medicines, oil control in the world or armament manufacture for profit.'[13] There is no doubt that, as far as it was possible while toiling in the satanic mills of J. Arthur Rank, Box did try to make films which were socially critical but as Muriel pointed out:

'We were not under contract to Rank to make films with overt statements on social problems or those with strong propaganda themes. We were expected to produce a programme of films that would interest the general public and encourage people to go to the cinema more frequently and enjoy well-made dramas and amusing comedies. We were not engaged to indulge our own political or socialist views, however much we should have found satisfaction in doing so. *The Years Between* [the film version of Daphne du Maurier's play] gave a hint of the things we wanted to say politically, but it was an exception.'[14]

The Boxes had already begun production on *The Years Between* when they were summoned to Gainsborough, but they did succeed in producing a handful of 'problem films' – *When the Bough Breaks, Good Time Girl, The Lost People, Portrait From Life*, and *The Boys in Brown* – under the Rank aegis. *When the Bough Breaks*, produced by Betty Box at Islington, is a

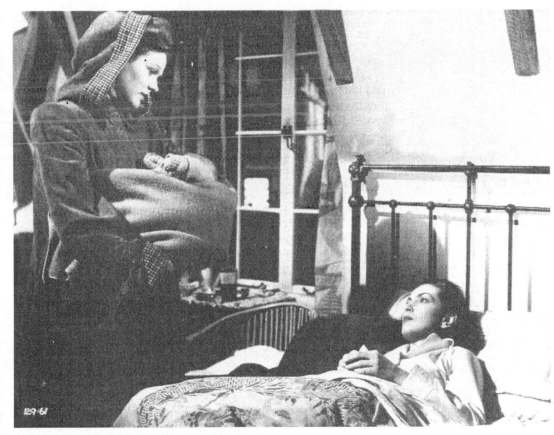

11 Working-class mother Pat Roc surrenders her son to middle-class Rosamund John. *When the Bough Breaks* (1947).

sober story about a young woman, Lily Bates (Pat Roc), who after giving birth to a son discovers that her husband is married to someone else. As she has to fend for herself, she allows her child to be adopted; but later she meets and marries a respectable Streatham tobacconist (Bill Owen) and wants to retrieve her child. The middle-class foster parents (Rosamund John and Leo Genn) reluctantly part with the boy, who is now eight or nine years old and thoroughly used to the comfortable lifestyle of his foster parents. Not surprisingly he finds it hard to adjust to life above the shop in Streatham, and his mother, anxious to make up for the lost years, succeeds only in alienating him with her shrill demands.

The film aroused conflicting opinions among the critics – Nina Hibbin in the *Daily Worker* considered it 'a fine piece of filmcraft and a richly human story' while at the other end of the spectrum C.A. Lejeune in the *Observer*, dismissed it as a 'supreme example of imbecility'.[15] As a low-budget picture it suffers from undistinguished photography and skimpy sets, but Pat Roc is at her best as the insecure working-class mum who can't relate to her child and the film is bitterly incisive about the divisions brought about by inequality of wealth.[16]

Good Time Girl is more sensational. It aroused considerable controversy and emerged, after protracted battles with the censors, under Box's own label, Triton, rather than as a Gainsborough picture. Good-time girls were supposedly a leftover from the sexual licence which flourished during the war. Ethel Mannin, whose novel *Julie: The Story of a Dance Hostess* had been set among the good-time girls of the thirties, disapproved of this new, brasher generation with their 'bleached or brassy hair, greasy scarlet mouths done up from corner to corner, no eyebrows to speak of, painted nails, blue shadows on their eyelids', and they were viewed as a serious threat to the moral fibre of the nation.[17]

The problem of juvenile delinquency had been explored by Jack Lee and Ian Dalrymple in a feature documentary, *Children On Trial*, in 1946, and the film is an interesting indication of how tame and conventional the documentary ethos had become. The young spivs and good-time girls are shown as misguided youngsters who have slipped off the rails because of their unhappy home lives. Sympathetic Juvenile Courts and caring Approved Schools get the girls interested in other things besides pictures, jazz, and men, and exhaust the boys in a busy round of swimming, farming, and cricket. The Boxes' *Good Time Girl*, which they jointly scripted with the young Ted Willis, was rather more adventurous in exploring the exciting life led by its heroine and in criticizing the attitude of the State towards juvenile offenders.

Gwen Rawlings (Jean Kent), a poor but very pretty girl, is sacked from her dull job in a pawnbroker's shop and runs away to the bright lights of London. Through the offices of Jimmy Rosso, a lecherous waiter (Peter Glenville), she becomes a hat-check girl in a Soho club and rapidly attracts admirers. Unfortunately she also attracts trouble, and despite the well-meaning attention of Red, a middle-aged musician (Dennis Price), a probation officer, and a magistrate (Flora Robson), she is framed by the jealous waiter and packed off to Approved School. Smarting under the injustice of her sentence and the drab uniformity of her new home, Gwen teams up with the dormitory toughie Roberta (Balcon's daughter Jill in an uncharacteristically unladylike role) and begins a reign of terror. When they are eventually exposed a riot ensues during which Gwen makes her escape.

The Principal of the Approved School (Nora Swinburne), talks of 'the salvaging of those youngsters whose natural growth has been marred by bad upbringing, bad companions, or plain bad luck'. But Gwen arrives at the school rebellious but essentially good-hearted and leaves it cruel, selfish, and deceitful. The lecherous motorsit (Garry Marsh) who offers her a lift is no match for her and her seduction by a smooth, flashy spiv (Griffith Jones) is something she willingly acquiesces to in return for a taste of the good life. A period of sybaritic luxury and drunken revelry ensues, but it ends abruptly when she runs over a Bobby on his bicycle, and she finds herself back in London with two American deserters who propel her rapidly towards a tragic denouement.

Much of this is adapted from Arthur La Bern's novel *Night Darkens the Street*, which in turn was inspired by the Cleft Chin murder of 1944. George Orwell, in his essay on the 'Decline of the English Murder', wrote unsympathetically but perceptively of the 'anonymous life of the dance halls and the false values of the American film', of the world of 'movie palaces, cheap perfume, false names and stolen cars' which the Cleft Chin murderers inhabited.[18] La Bern chose to remould the story in more traditional form, making his heroine an innocent victim of her environment, 'an ignoramus with starry eyes, a well-developed body and an underdeveloped mind' who escapes from a childhood of Dickensian squalor to the glittering world of London night-life.

With boisterous, sharp, bouncily sexy Jean Kent, *Good Time Girl* moves even further from the sad life of the real murderess Elizabeth Jones. But Muriel Box stresses that she spent long hours reading through Royal Commission reports on the Approved School system, and the film is extraordinarily outspoken about middle-class hypocrisy. To appease the censors, the film is told in flashback by magistrate Flora Robson to deter potentially delinquent Diana Dors from herself becoming a good-time girl; and by the end of the film she is suitably contrite and chastened. But it is Robson and her cronies with their posh, patronising voices and ridiculous hats who push Gwen off on the road to ruin. Though it makes nonsense of the film's logic – if Robson knew the truth of Gwen's circumstances why did she give her a three-year custodial sentence? – the moralistic framework clamped on to the film increases our exasperation with these middle-class busy-bodies and our sympathy goes out to the girl who just wanted to have a good time.

Good Time Girl was directed by David Macdonald, who after *This England*, had joined the British Army film unit and produced two celebrated war documentaries, *Desert Victory* (1943) and *Burma Victory* (1945). He obviously benefited from his wartime experiences, and with the aid of Gainsborough stalwarts Maurice Carter as art director and Stephen Dade as lighting cameraman, made a film which is full of atmosphere and telling detail – the brief glimpse of Red's wife, the nightmare presence of 'Smiling Billy', the embarrassing love scene presided over by a disapproving probation officer – and he handles the long and complex story with an assurance signally lacking in *This England*.

Critical reaction to the film was largely hostile. C.A. Lejeune condemned it as

a squalid British film about a young woman from a bad home who gets

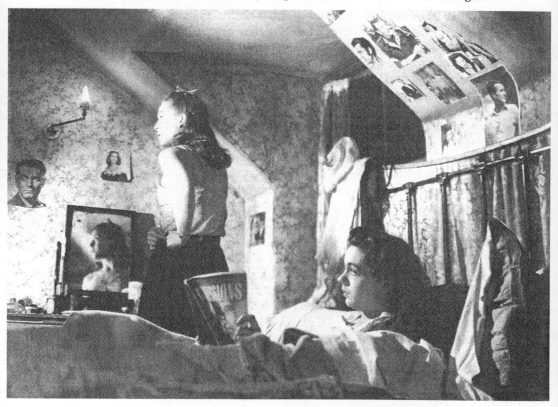

12 Gwen Rawlings (Jean Kent, standing) considers what the world outside her slum-land home has to offer. Her sister (Vera Francis) settles for fictional means of escape. *Good Time Girl* (1948).

into the company of thieves, seducers, drunkards, black marketeers, army deserters, razor slashers and vitriol throwers, and ends up with fifteen years for murder. It is not the sort of film I like and I like it none the better because it is presented, with a smug complacency that seems to me the last resort of hypocritical cant, as a cautionary tale within a tale.[19]

Box tried to distance himself from the Gainsborough tradition of salacious escapism and stoutly defended the integrity of his films. In a side-swipe at his predecessor Maurice Ostrer who had just released *Idol of Paris*, which featured a much publicized whip fight between two women, Box declared:

> When . . . a producer attempts to cash in on sadism and to exploit the lower emotions of his audience, his action is, to my mind, inexcusable and only encourages hooliganism and crime. Films based on sadism may prove a nine-day wonder, but in the long run can only bring their makers into disrepute and, more than that, prejudice the good name of the industry.[20]

His attempts to deal with serious subjects in terms of popular melodrama fell on stony ground, and the Boxes found themselves more and more constrained by the increasingly centralized Rank administrative machine. *The Boys in Brown*, made at Pinewood in 1949, during Gainsborough's brief half-life between losing its studios and losing its identity entirely, is as dull and conventional as *Children on Trial*, redeemed only by the spectacle of Richard Attenborough, Michael Medwin, Alfie Bass, Jimmy Hanley, and Dirk Bogarde in short trousers.

Del Giudice strikes out

Sydney Box was a shrewd, adaptable producer who had been brought in to run Gainsborough on business-like lines. Giudice's position at Two Cities was rather different. He had founded the company and he had been the architect of a string of successful pictures – *In Which We Serve, The Gentle Sex, The Demi-Paradise, This Happy Breed, Henry V, The Way Ahead, Blithe Spirit, The Way to the Stars* – which had done much to establish the critical reputation of the British film industry. Unfortunately, with the exception of *Odd Man Out*, none of Two Cities' post-war films had been a notable success and two – Thorold Dickinson's *Men of Two Worlds* and Maurice Elvey's *Beware of Pity* – had been costly failures. This led to friction between Giudice and John Davis, the accountant who had become Rank's right-hand man. According to Alan Wood:

> Between him and Davis there had grown up a violent antagonism which split the Rank Organisation in two. To Davis, Del Giudice was

extravagant and wasteful; to Del Giudice, Davis was an accountant with no soul for anything but figures, and no knowledge or appreciation of films. The struggle for power between the two was bitter and intense.[21]

Early in 1947 Giudice was forced to resign from Two Cities. He formed an independent production company, Pilgrim Films, but in an industry now dominated by the Rank empire he found it impossible to repeat the success he had enjoyed with Two Cities. In the three years of its existence Pilgrim managed to produce only three modestly budgeted films – *The Guinea Pig* (1948, d. Roy Boulting), *Private Angelo* (1949, d. Peter Ustinov), and *Chance of a Lifetime* (1950, d. Bernard Miles and Alan Osbiston).

The Guinea Pig, based on a popular play by Warren Chetham Strode, was by far the most successful. Collaboration between Giudice and the Boultings – all of them supporters of the Labour government – had begun with *Fame is the Spur*, one of the last films to be made under Giudice's regime at Two Cities. A prestigious adaptation of Howard Spring's novel about a Labour politician, Hamer Radshaw (loosely modelled on Ramsay Macdonald), who abandons his principles in the pursuit of power, it had proved disappointingly unpopular. Raymond Durgnat considers the film hostile to the Labour government, but Labour politicians like Cripps and Attlee were happy to distance themselves from Ramsay Macdonald and the 'greatest betrayal in the political history of the country'.[22] Exhibitors sought to blame the film's lack of success on its political subject, but a more likely explanation of its unpopularity lies in the film's unpleasant, exasperating central character with whom it is dificult for an audience to feel any sympathy or interest. As a critic was to complain of *Christopher Columbus*, Macdonald's life was the wrong shape for a satisfactory film. Howard Spring had to some extent solved the problem by shifting attention on to a second generation – Hamer's son and the daughter of Arnold Ryerson, his best friend – but this made for a very long novel and was jettisoned by the Boultings and their scriptwriter Nigel Balchin. Hamer's rise from fervently idealistic shop assistant to ambitious, pragmatic politician is well told, but after a very moving middle section in which the middle-class girl he has married, Ann Artingstall (Rosamund John), becomes a Suffragette, is imprisoned, forcibly fed and dies of tuberculosis, the film, like Hamer, begins a slow and inexorable decline.

Undeterred by *Fame is the Spur*'s failure at the box-office, Giudice and the Boultings proceeded to investigate the politically sensitive issue of public-school education in *The Guinea Pig*. Jack Read (Richard Attenborough), the son of a Walthamstow tobacconist (Bernard Miles), wins a scholarship to a public school where he encounters snobbery and hostility but is eventually accepted as an equal. *The Guinea Pig* is more optimistic than *When the Bough Breaks* about the ability of schoolboys to transcend class barriers and it now looks smug and condescending in its advocacy of mild reform. But if the film is compared with another celebration of the public-school ethos, *Goodbye Mr Chips*, made immediately before the war, then it is possible to see a great advance towards attitudes favouring a more equal and democratic society.[23]

The last of Pilgrim's efforts, *Chance of a Lifetime*, was the most controversial, though now it looks a model of sanity and moderation. A small factory owner (Basil Radford) tires of the troubles caused by his strike-prone workers and offers them the opportunity of running the business themselves. They accept but then find they need their ex-employer's expertise and ask him to come back and work with them. It was very much Bernard Miles' pet project – he co-produced, co-directed, and collaborated on the script with Walter Greenwood – and embodied that caring, idealistic, sentimental populism which had been an integral part of Britain's war culture. In 1950, though, there was a different social climate. The three major circuits refused to handle the film, and when a Board of Trade committee set up to prevent the circuits from abusing their monopoly power ordered that it be shown in Rank's Odeon cinemas it was a box-office failure.

The critical establishment

In an inflammatory contribution to Tom Maschler's *Declaration* in 1959, Lindsay Anderson complained that:

> In 1945, it is often said, we had our revolution. It is true we had something: though for a revolution it was a little incomplete. According to the British cinema, however, nothing happened at all. The nationalisation of the coalfields, the Health Service, nationalised railways, compulsory education – events like these which cry out to be interpreted in human terms – have produced no films.[24]

But there was little critical demand for such films at the time – least of all from Anderson and his fellow writers on the film journal *Sequence*.[25]

It is difficult now to share the attitudes and approach of British film critics of the forties. Though they claimed an allegiance to 'realism' they seem to have had no very clear idea of what they meant by it. In France André Bazin and in America Siegfried Kracauer attempted to work out coherent theories about realism. In Britain the most influential film theorists, Paul Rotha and Roger Manvell, had espoused the montage theories of Eisenstein and Pudovkin in the thirties and were never quite able to square them with the new fashion for realism. In an editorial in *The Penguin Film Review* for September 1947 a puzzled Manvell admitted that:

The film critic, as things are now, has too often to invent his own bread-and-butter principles and muddle along with a few outworn critical platitudes about composition, movement, editing and synchronisation.[26]

Critics tended to plump for anything which could be linked to the documentary tradition, or, as a second best, well-made plays with cleverly worked out plots and psychologically rounded characters. Thus a film like *The Way to the Stars* was praised to the hilt, while Powell and Pressburger's *A Matter of Life and Death*, a much more adventurous and innovative work, was criticized for its 'technical trickery'. Ealing's comedies, and even Herbert Wilcox's Mayfair cycle were accepted as light relief, while Gainsborough's achievements in art direction and photography, which made their films more atmospheric, more intense, more complex, were ignored because they were not directed towards making the films more realistic.

With the exception of Carol Reed's *Odd Man Out*, which was recognized as 'expressionist', and *Mine Own Executioner*, redeemed by the presence of Burgess Meredith, films that were moody and atmospheric were considered unhealthily gloomy, even morbid. Costume pictures as different as *The Wicked Lady, Blanche Fury*, and *The Bad Lord Byron* were lumped together and dismissed as 'tosh' – though Olivier's Shakespeare pictures were considered masterpieces. Anything that was violent, particularly the abhorred spiv films, provoked hostility; *No Orchids For Miss Blandish*, which had seemed inoffensive to the BBFC – not noted for its liberal attitude during this period – aroused such an hysterical outcry from the critics that in many areas of the country local authorities banned it.

In 1945 Sidney Bernstein, cinema owner, wartime MOI films advisor, and later television mogul, brought out a little pamphlet on *Film and International Relations*. He was concerned that British films should reflect the positive, attractive side of British society and praised the realist films of the war years. But shrewd showman that he was, he didn't hesitate to point out that audiences were more attracted to the exceptional than the everyday and that the realist path might be difficult to follow once the war was over:

Story films . . . are bound to concentrate for their subjects to a large extent on violence and passion, because such is the raw material of drama. Except for isolated attempts to break the rule, as with *Millions Like Us*, films deal with the exceptional in life rather than the usual. It is the unusual which exercises a strong appeal to the sense of curiosity which is innate in us.[27]

Ironically Bernstein's television company Granada was responsible later for *Coronation Street*, a successful saga of the everyday which itself grew out of post-war comedies like *Passport to Pimlico* and the Huggett films.

Documentaries, comedies, even some of the post-war problem films did try to deal with the mundane world of austerity-bound Britain in a cheery and optimistic way, but despite the strictures of the critics, film-makers and audiences found it difficult to wean themselves away from the melodramatic, the exotic, and the macabre.

It is easy to be sneeringly condescending (as they tended to be themselves) towards the critics who have bequeathed us such a meagre heritage of approved films. But their espousal of realism and abhorrence of sensationalism was inextricably bound up with the decency and generosity which made people want a new and fairer society. As Geoff Brown says of *The Penguin Film Review* which enshrined so many critical prejudices:

the Review was dominated by the earnest enthusiasms of the evangelists and educationalists – the kind of people who had worked in

13 Irene (Jean Kent) and Jenny (Sally Gray). Choosing between passion and respectability. *Carnival* (1946).

the war with Civil Defence groups, the Army Bureau of Current Affairs or similar organisations, helping to stimulate discussion about every aspect of 'modern society' which would emerge at the end of the fighting.[28]

But in this concern to improve public taste, much of what was most interesting and exciting in British cinema was pushed out into the cold.

In hindsight one of the lesser-known films of 1946, *Carnival* (directed by Stanley Haynes for Two Cities), appears as an instructive parable. Sally Gray, most tinsellish of English actresses, plays a chorus girl in love with a selfish, unreliable young artist (Michael Wilding). She decides to be sensible and gives him up, along with the glitter and excitement of the stage, to marry that archdeacon of realism and social responsibility, Bernard Miles. They return to his farm in Cornwall where he transforms himself into a possessive religious bigot, dominated by his old mother, and ends up shooting Ms Gray, who dies stoically regretting she made the wrong decision. The outcome of the love affair between British films and the critics was only slightly less drastic.

6 Passionate Friends?

'The human mind is rather like Salome at the beginning of her dance – concealed from the outer world by veil after veil of reserve. With friends and intimates the average person will drop two or three of the veils – with a lover, five or six. But in all normal human contacts, the mind still retains one veil, the ultimate protection against the nakedness of its innermost thoughts. This veil – the seventh veil – only a psychiatrist can tear down. (*The Seventh Veil*)[1]

So far, at all events, the real story of modern womanhood has not begun to be told. And it cannot be told except as part of the story of modern times. (Catherine de la Roche, *Penguin Film Review*, January 1949)[2]

Britain mobilized its women more efficiently and effectively than any of the other war combatants. Half a million women volunteered or were conscripted into the armed forces and a million more were mobilized as war-workers. By 1944 seven-and-a-half million women were working outside the home. 'A people's war meant to a large extent a women's war.'[3] The number of women on the battlefront was tiny, but the blitz ensured that those on the home front saw plenty of action. In the first three years of the war more civilians than soldiers were killed. During the First World War women had taken a great step forward towards equality only to be pushed back once the men returned from the trenches. They had the vote but high unemployment ensured that for all but a small minority their place in society was confined to the home. The Second World War produced a less ephemeral transformation.

Most women were demobilized from their war jobs just as they were from the armed services. But there was no concerted effort to drive women back into the home, no repetition of the scurrilous press campaign which had labelled women war workers limpets and parasites at the end of the First World War. Those women who were escaping domestic drudgery or who had broken through into skilled work were reluctant to give up their jobs 'just to be a wife and mother in a small house'.[4] But for the great majority, combining boring repetitive jobs with long hours of travelling and the difficulties of keeping a family, the end of the war and the end of war work came as a relief.

Concern was expressed, as it had been throughout the twenties and thirties, at the falling birth rate, but the concept of motherhood as woman's sole and sacred function was discredited by association with Hitler's Germany and there was a recognition of the need to make child-bearing materially more attractive. Anne Scott-James in an article titled 'Why Women Don't Have Babies', bluntly argued that: 'The country can't expect women to have larger families until we can offer them a much higher standard of social services. After the war there must be a real drive to relieve the drudgery of women.' She advocated better planned family houses – 'Houses of good size with plenty of room for children, with labour-saving equipment to save housework and washing up, and with space for the laundry and the pram' – and more nurseries.[5]

In its bid to recruit married women with children for the war effort, the government had had to provide extensive nursery facilities (72,000 nursery places for children under two by 1944), but this was regarded very much as a temporary measure.[6] In 1945 a Ministry of Health circular on correct child care had advised that 'the proper place for a child under two is at home with the mother', and argued that 'under normal peacetime conditions the right policy to pursue would be positively to discourage mothers of children under two from going out to work'.[7] None the less, over half the government-run nurseries were taken over by local authorities, and private companies, particularly those in industries such as textiles which had difficulty attracting back their female work-force, established work-place nurseries.

In 1943 Anne Scott-James had argued for facilities which would make it possible for women to combine a career with a family:

> There ought to be more and more opportunities for women to combine a home and outside life. Better social services will help them at home. More provision for part-time jobs, more encouragement for married women in the professions, in social work, and in industry, will help them outside. When you have this sort of attitude, then many women who have a real talent for professional work, and do not now marry, will be able to use that talent and marry as well – and so be in the running for having children.[8]

The sort of help which women got left much to be desired, but improvements in welfare services, the spread of labour-saving devices and the removal of restrictions on women resuming their careers after marriage did make things a little easier. (Before the 1944 Education Act married women were barred from teaching and until 1945 women civil servants had to choose between continuing their career or getting married.) The real advance was in women's expectations. Just as life in the services, despite its hazards, opened up new opportunities for men, war-work allowed women to discover a new independence and self-respect. Though many of the women who joined the ATS, the WRNS, the WAAFS, worked as cooks and cleaners, others drove trucks, crewed anti-aircraft guns or barrage balloons, became bomb-plotters, photographers, radio-operators, mechanics. The same applied to women working in the munitions factories, the railways, the Post Office and the land: though most were doing unskilled, repetitive work, it could, in some cases at least, open up new horizons. Mona Marshall, moving from domestic service in rural Lincolnshire to work in a Sheffield steel factory, found that despite the hard and dangerous work:

'To be quite honest, the war was the best thing that ever happened to us. I was as green as grass and terrified if anyone spoke to me. I had been brought up not to argue. My generation had been taught to do as we were told. At work you did exactly as your boss told you and you went home to do exactly what your husband told you. The war changed all that. The war made me stand on my own two feet.'[9]

Women in films

One of the livelier contributors to the *Penguin Film Review*, Catherine de la Roche, complained of the failure of the cinema to recognize the changed status of women after the war:

Our epoch has produced probably the most fundamental changes in the relationship between men and women ever known, changes which have not yet attained stability and which are still conflicting with the more long-standing traditions of the past. The emancipation of women, the advance of science, economic and international stresses have presented men and women with a set of choices and responsibilities, freedoms and restrictions, which affect their attitudes to each other, to marriage and to parenthood.[10]

Debates about the role of women in post-war society inspired Jill Craigie's off-beat documentary *To Be a Woman*, which argued strongly for equal pay, and *Women in Our Time*, an episode of Rank's news magazine, *This Modern Age*, which is also surprisingly outspoken in its demand for equal pay and insistence that women play a more active role in the running of society. After a lecture from Lady Rhondda, the formidable editor of *Time and Tide*, the film concludes with the message:

'Women are still excluded from the ministries of most religions and from the Stock Exchange; no woman has yet been a High Court judge or even a King's Counsel and Britain has not so far appointed a woman to any of the United Nations' councils. Hasn't the time come then for women to be recognised once and for all as equal partners with men? That is the answer to most problems of women in our time: a real partnership between men and women in this modern age.'

Such political issues were pointedly ignored in feature films. Sue Aspinall, in her survey of 'Women, Realism and Reality in British Films 1943–53', points out that:

> Although the realist films of the early 1940s were topical in relation to the war itself, very few films were made that attempted to deal with other aspects of contemporary reality. In particular, the most painful experiences of women during these years were not represented: the struggle to eat reasonably on rations, the long hours of work, the terror of air raids, prolonged separation from small children, the death of friends, acquaintances and loved ones, the shame of venereal disease and the emotional trauma involved in unwanted pregnancy were not shown on the screens.[11]

Women who discover hidden resources within themselves had featured in wartime films like *Millions Like Us, They Flew Alone*, and *The Gentle Sex*, but with the exception of Anna Neagle's Amy Johnson, they tended to be passive recipients of their good or bad fortune. In post-war films such as *The Years Between, I Know Where I'm Going, Black Narcissus, Root of All Evil, The Courtneys of Curzon Street*, and *The Loves of Joanna Godden*, women struggle more actively with their destiny. In *The Courtneys of Curzon Street*, for example, Anna Neagle plays a lady's maid who marries a baronet (Michael Wilding). After a brief period of idyllic happiness, she leaves him because she fears she has blighted his military career. It is a great sacrifice, but in her period away from her husband she is able to establish herself as a talented, self-sufficient woman, capable of making a life and a position in society by her own efforts.

Women had got used to a greater degree of independence during the war years and often resented the return of their menfolk. Mickey Lewis, an 'ordinary housewife' who had spent the war cutting gear wheels for guns, found:

> 'It was really difficult – suddenly he turned up and I didn't feel "how marvellous", I felt a bit resentful at first. I thought, oh he's come home to spoil it all. I hadn't made any relationships with other men. I was just living a broader kind of life and it was very difficult to change.'[12]

The problems of a woman who learns to cope without her husband and then has to cope with his return are explored in *The Years Between*, scripted by Sydney and Muriel Box from a play by Daphne du Maurier. Diana (Valerie Hobson) grieves heavily when she is informed that her husband is missing, believed killed. But she pulls herself together, wins his old parliamentary seat, and is about to marry a neighbouring farmer, when her husband (Michael Redgrave) returns. His experiences in a prison camp hardly equip him to deal with the situation. 'I don't want a wife forever sitting on committees and making speeches, I want the wife I left behind', he complains. But he is only able to regain his wife's affection by recognizing her new-found power and dignity.

Alexander Korda's comedy, *Perfect Strangers*, takes as its theme the transforming potential of wartime experience. A dull, prematurely middle-aged couple, Cathy and Robert Wilson (Deborah Kerr and Robert Donat), are drafted into the services and become bold, attractive, self-confident people. It is three years before they manage to get leave at the same time and by then they have both met someone they genuinely care for and want a divorce. When they meet they have difficulty recognizing each other. Surprise and admiration rapidly give way to anger and resentment as they each let slip the frustration and contempt which underscored their apparently happy pre-war marriage. Having become mature and sensible people, however, they manage to overcome their difficulties and begin a new and better phase of their marriage.

With its cardboard sets and caricatured characters, Korda's film drew down a barrage of critical disapproval. The *Monthly Film Bulletin*, for example, complained that it was 'a superficial film which assumes that all that is needed for marital happiness and success in life is physical well-being and glamour'. Audiences accepted it as an amusing fantasy and it was a big commercial success, but there is something unsatisfactory about the film. It is easy to enjoy the transformation of seedy, stoop-shouldered Robert Wilson into dashing Robert Donat and bespectacled, dowdy Cathy Wilson into beautiful Deborah Kerr. But the transformation is so complete that they do indeed appear perfect strangers and their shared experience of a failed marriage seems a flimsy and unconvincing basis for a happy new relationship.

Sydney and Muriel Box's *A Girl in a Million* (1946 d. Francis Searle), appears to justify female disgust at the way relations between the sexes were dealt with in British films. A scientist (Hugh Williams) is provoked by his nagging wife into a row which leads to divorce. Disillusioned with women, he gets a job in a remote research station but falls in love with a young girl (Joan Greenwood) who has lost her voice because of a traumatic accident. They marry and live happily together until another accident restores her voice. Her incessant chatter ruins their relationship and she leaves him. They are finally reunited after she gives birth to a son, but to retain the affection of her husband she pretends that her voice has disappeared again.

'So much for the new partnership of equals', sniffs Sue Aspinall. But the film is less concerned about keeping women in their place than in making fun of men who are unable to cope with anything but the most docile women. The other men in the film – played by Wylie Watson, Basil Radford and Naunton Wayne – are confirmed bachelors, Wayne and Radford because they are obviously frightened of women, Watson because his mother taught him that marriage was 'a modern form of slavery' which he refuses to participate in. He warns the heroine on the eve of her wedding that she is in danger of being exploited by men:

> 'By investing the small sum of 7/6d they become possessed of a housekeeper, cook, bottle-washer, char-woman, nurse, mistress, companion, wife and mother. All without further payment except for a small weekly pittance that would be refused by any one of those people in the open market.'

Greenwood marries anyway, relying on her female wiles to right the balance.

The impatience of film critics with films which refused to deal in a sensible, progressive, and realistic way with the world was an echo of a wider conflict between 'escapism' and 'realism' which agitated Britain in the forties. Significantly, the issue around which the position of women debate crystallized was not nursery care or equal pay but fashion, and in particular the length of skirts. In February 1947 a new designer, Christian Dior, shook the fashion world with what subsequently became known as the New Look. As one manufacturer commented:

> The Dior collection marked the re-birth of women as they had always existed in the minds of men – provocative, ostensibly helpless and made for love. He immobilised them in exquisite dresses which contained between fifteen and twenty-five yards of material; dresses with tiny waists in black broadcloth, tussore and silk taffeta, each with a built-in corset which was itself a deeply disturbing work of art. By day, superb beneath huge hats that resembled elegant mushrooms, they were unable to run; by night they needed help when entering a taxi. As these divine visions moved their underskirts gave out a rustling sound that was indescribably sweet to the ear.[13]

Not surprisingly this was anathema to those women who accepted the practical, simple, asexual styles of the war years as a token of women's emancipation. Mabel Ridealgh, a Labour MP, contemptuously lambasted the foolishness of male fashion designers:

> 'Can anyone imagine the average housewife and businesswoman dressed in bustles and long skirts carrying on their varied jobs, running for buses and crowding into tubes and trains? The idea is ludicrous. Women today are taking a larger part in the happenings of the world and the New Look is too reminiscent of a caged bird's attitude. I hope our fashion dictators will realise the new *outlook* of women and will give the death blow to any attempt at curtailing women's freedom.'[14]

Common sense and practicality was on the side of the anti-New Look campaigners: with cloth rationed and in short supply it seemed madness to bring down the length of skirts at the whim of a Parisian designer who was aiming primarily at the rich American market. But rather like the thirties unemployed whom Orwell found living on tea and jam and visits to the cinema rather than investing sensibly in wholemeal bread and fresh vegetables, Britain's glamour-starved women were prepared to sacrifice a lot to feel exciting and seductive. Heavy use of make-up, painted legs, the obsession with nylons, should have warned Mabel Ridealgh that more powerful forces than common sense were at work. By the summer of 1948 the New Look had transformed the appearance of British women, though popular appropriation transformed Dior's elitist, nostalgic vision of women into something less passive and restrictive than he had intended.

Catherine de la Roche and another bulwark of the *Penguin Film Review*, E. Arnot Robertson, adopted a Mabel Ridealgh approach to British films. In an article entitled 'That "Feminine Angle"', de la Roche castigated the men of Wardour Street for attempting to woo the female film fan by appealing to her baser instincts:

> Study advertising and trade press matter, and you will find that sentimentality, lavish and facile effects, the melodramatic, extravagant, naively romantic and highly coloured, the flattering, trivial and phoney – these are the elements in pictures, whatever their overall qualities, that are supposed to draw women. Above all (and not surprisingly, since it's the opinion of men), woman's chief and all-consuming interest in Men.[15]

She argues that women, having proved themselves competent and self-sufficient during the war, deserved more respect than this and warned that the cinema was falling behind the times, particularly in its depiction of relationships between men and women. E. Arnot Robertson agreed:

> Identifying myself for the moment with the heroine on the screen, as the female part of a good audience is supposed to do, I feel it is high time I was allowed to do something besides looking cute in order to inspire true love, of the undying variety, in the hero. Still, in ninety-nine films out of a hundred I don't have to do anything, say anything or be anything endearing; I just look cute.[16]

Both Robertson and de la Roche saw the scarcity of women on the screen with whom they could identify as a symptom of the cinema's general failure to come to terms with the modern world. It is easy to sympathize with their enthusiasm for a progressive, realist cinema which would serve as an agent of radical social change, but it is unlikely that the great mass of picture-goers shared their hostility to lurid sensationalism and a number of interesting films slip through their high-brow net.

British critics had a peculiar blindness towards the talents of British actresses. They enthused over stage actresses like Celia Johnson when they made occasional appearances in films but were sneeringly dismissive of women who had made their career in British films. Milton Schulman, for example, complained:

> Jean Kent is almost indistinguishable on the screen from Patricia Roc, Greta Gynt and Margaret Lockwood. Now I know some of them are blonde and others brunette, but they all have the same stereotyped, glassy, manufactured features which have somehow become the hallmark of British female stardom.[17]

Margaret Lockwood (in *The Man in Grey* and *The Wicked Lady*), Jean Kent (in *Caravan, Good Time Girl*, and *Trottie True*), Greta Gynt (in *Dear Murderer* and *Take My Life*), and Pat Roc (in *Millions Like Us* and *When the Bough Breaks*), show themselves capable of charismatic performances despite their limitations, and had Schulman looked more closely he would have noticed an impressive array of female talent in the British cinema: Rosamund John, Phyllis Calvert, Kathleen Ryan, Deborah Kerr, Lilli Palmer, Glynnis Johns, Valerie Hobson, Margaret Johnston, Joan

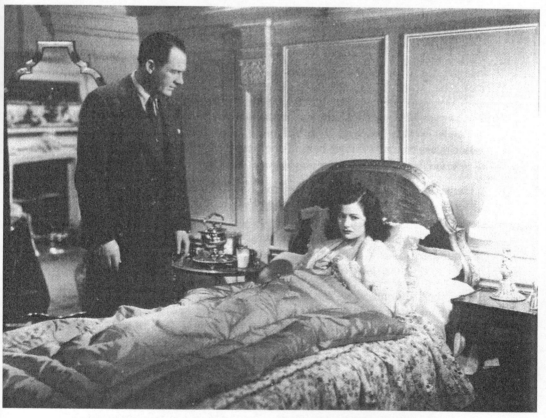

14 Charles (Ian Hunter) confronts his murderous wife Bedelia (Margaret Lockwood) – 'a spoilt child rather than a psychopath'. *Bedelia* (1946).

Greenwood, Sally Gray, Dulcie Gray, Anna Neagle, Ann Todd, Kathleen Byron, Googie Withers, Jean Simmons, and occasionally Vivien Leigh. Not surprisingly, those who chose to concentrate on their careers as film actresses went to Hollywood.

That said, there was no equivalent to the glittering femmes fatales who haunted the Hollywood cinema. A psychological comparison of British, French, and American films of the immediate post-war period came to the conclusion that 'British films do not, on the whole, take the destructive potentialities of women seriously'.[18] Margaret Lockwood's scheming vixens in *The Man in Grey* and *The Wicked Lady* might be considered exceptions, but they are essentially boisterous, good-natured villainesses, bold but unthreatening, and their 'evil' is always shared with the audience. Thus when Lockwood played a real femme fatale, the husband-murdering heroine of *Bedelia*, the results were not entirely convincing.

Made at Ealing by ex-British National producer John Corfield, and starring Gainsborough's most prestigious actress, *Bedelia* (1946 d. Lance Comfort) is one of those films which look fascinating on paper but make dull viewing. Adapted from a novel by Vera Caspary, whose *Laura* had been made into a successful film by Otto Preminger, it founders on the conventions of the British crime thriller. The detective (Barry K. Barnes) who tracks Bedelia from Monte Carlo to the Yorkshire Dales is always one step ahead despite his seeming inanity; Bedelia's fourth husband and potential fourth victim (Ian Hunter) is a gullible but worthy fool, and he commands the affection of a loyal secretary (Anne Crawford) who teams up with the detective to unmask the evil woman. Bedelia herself – a compulsive thief with a murderous fear of men beneath her sweet, loving exterior – is much more interesting. 'I hate men! They're beasts!' she shouts when cornered. But Lockwood is unable to convey any sense of ambiguity and danger, and Bedelia comes across as a spoilt child rather than a psychopath. The film might have worked better if Lockwood had been cast as the ingenue secretary and Anne Crawford, with her opaque, china doll prettiness, cast as the villainess.

Hollywood excelled in making sentimental melodramas which were thought to appeal particularly to women. Directors like John Stahl, Clarence Brown, John Cromwell, and Frank Borzage exercised great skill in bringing novelettish stories to life and were able to call on the services of formidable actresses such as Barbara Stanwyck, Bette Davis, and Joan Crawford. It is not surprising, then, that films like *Imitation of Life*, *Stella Dallas, Now Voyager*, and *Since You Went Away* were highly successful.

In Britain there was no real equivalent until Gainsborough decided to exploit the popularity of Phyllis Calvert, Margaret Lockwood, James Mason, and Stewart Granger after *The Man in Grey* in contemporary as well as costume subjects and made *Love Story* (Lockwood and Granger),

Madonna of the Seven Moons (Granger and Calvert), and *They Were Sisters*, (Calvert and Mason). They were all big box-office successes, but a mixture of studio politics and vociferous critical disparagement brought the cycle to a premature end. The Rank Organization decided to tighten its control over Gainsborough and replaced Maurice Ostrer, who had run the studio as an autonomous unit, with Sydney Box who had made his reputation by producing and co-writing (with his wife Muriel) *The Seventh Veil*, a commercially very successful re-working of the dominant motifs of *Madonna* and *Love Story*. But once he settled in at Gainsborough, Box concentrated on comedies and action pictures with only a few forays into costume pictures and social problem films as a concession to the Gainsborough tradition of melodrama. Only one Gainsborough 'escapist' melodrama appeared after the war ended, Brock Williams' *Root of All Evil*, produced in the dying days of the Ostrer regime.

The story concerns two young women, Jeckie and Rushie Farnish (Phyllis Calvert and Hazel Court), who have to fend for themselves when their father loses his farm. Jeckie's fiancé jilts her in favour of a better match, and the arrogant contempt with which she is treated by his family provokes her into suing for breach of promise. Anxious to avoid a scandal, the family pay up, and with the money she obtains Jeckie opens a grocery shop which undermines their family business. She becomes wealthy and teams up with a slick businessman, Charles Mortimer (Michael Rennie). They discover oil under the land of a poor farmer, Scholes (Moore Marriott). He sells to them not realizing the value of his land, but when he discovers he has been cheated he burns down their oilwell. Jeckie, who has failed to find happiness with Mortimer, loses all her wealth, but is consoled by Joe Bartle (John McCallum) who has loved her for years.

Predictably, the 'quality' critics had nothing to say in the film's favour and the review in the *Kine Weekly* illustrates Catherine de la Roche's argument about the insulting condescension of 'that feminine angle':

> It is not, however, so much the film's dizzy accountancy as its unblushing transactions with the obvious that weaken its drama and entertainment. The audience is required merely to sit back and see how a fresh cast deals with a time-honoured cycle. Fortunately, the average woman fan has no head for figures, and it is mainly because of this and its spectacular staging and artful title that we are prepared to give it the benefit of many box-office doubts.[19]

The 'average woman fan' proved more discerning than was expected. *Root of All Evil* failed to emulate the success of *Love Story*, *Madonna of the Seven Moons*, and *They Were Sisters*. Pam Cook courageously defends the film in her article on 'Melodrama and the Women's Picture', arguing that in *Root of All Evil*: 'romantic illusions about love and marriage are set up, questioned and relocated in order to mount a criticism of materialism, speculation and consumerism'.[20] But this seems an excessively generous assessment of such a poorly scripted, drably photographed, weakly directed film. Fortunately, powerful and resonant contemporary melodramas continued to be made outside Gainsborough.

Passion and restraint

The Seventh Veil had been released in October 1945. According to Muriel Box: 'with almost monotonous yet very comforting regularity it broke every known record, and was awarded the Oscar for the best original screenplay of 1946'.[21] It was the commercially most successful British film of the decade. Three months later David Lean's *Brief Encounter* was released, the most critically lauded British film of the forties and probably of British cinema generally. Surprisingly the two films have much in

15 Francesca (Ann Todd) defies her oppressive guardian (James Mason). *The Seventh Veil* (1945).

common, and they share a thematic concern with a woman having to choose between lovers with two other films released around the same time, Herbert Wilcox's *I Live in Grosvenor Square* and Powell and Pressburger's *I Know Where I'm Going.*

In *The Seventh Veil* Francesca (Ann Todd), a gawky schoolgirl, is orphaned and sent to live with her guardian Nicholas (James Mason), a cultivated but misanthropic man who ignores her until he realizes she has real ability as a pianist. He sends her to a music academy where she flowers into an attractive young woman and falls in love with a happy-go-lucky American jazz enthusiast (Hugh McDermott). When Nicholas discovers what is happening he whisks her away to Europe where she becomes a successful concert pianist. They lead a busy but reclusive life together until Francesca falls in love with an artist (Albert Lieven) commissioned to paint her portrait. She elopes with him but their car crashes. Francesca is only mildly injured but the shock unbalances her.

16 'Threateningly expressive shadows'. Celia Johnson and Trevor Howard at Milford Junction. *Brief Encounter* (1945).

She is convinced that her hands are damaged and that she will never play again. After attempting suicide she loses her memory but she is brought back to sanity by a psychiatrist, Dr Larsen (Herbert Lom), who gets her to tell her story under hypnosis. She is then able to decide which of her three suitors she really loves, and chooses Nicholas.

The film received muted critical approval for its use of classical music and its clever construction, but as a romantic melodrama it was not taken very seriously. *Brief Encounter*, by contrast, aroused real critical enthusiasm. For C.A. Lejeune:

> it seems to me to catch, in words and pictures, so many things that are penetratingly true. The whole colour, the spring, the almost magical feeling of the discovery that someone's in love with you, that someone feels it's exciting to be with you; that is something so tenuous that it's hardly ever been put on the screen. And yet it's done here.[22]

As Sue Aspinall points out:

> *Brief Encounter* is a rarity in combining women's picture material with 'quality' in its writer (Noel Coward), director (David Lean) and actors (Celia Johnson and Trevor Howard). . . . It was unusual for a realist and a 'quality' film to base its narrative on a woman character at all – and, even more so, to make that narrative the story of her sexual feelings.[23]

With its dimly-lit interiors, its hysterical heroine, its threateningly expressive shadows, its theme of doomed love, its creation of a hostile and repressive world, it is difficult to understand how the film fits into an aesthetic of realism at all, but at the time it was greeted as a sign that British cinema was capable of the same sort of truth to life seen in Italian Neo-Realism and the films of Orson Welles and William Wyler. The French critic André Bazin enthused:

> Nothing could be more tightly structured, more carefully prepared, than *Brief Encounter* – nothing less conceivable without the most up-to-date studio resources, without clever and established actors; yet can we imagine a more realistic portrait of English manners and psychology?[24]

As such, it would seem to be at the opposite pole to *The Seventh Veil*. Yet there are many similarities between the two films. Both stories unfold in flashback, Laura's as a reverie as she listens to Rachmaninov's Piano Concerto in her over-comfortable home, Francesca's under hypnosis on the psychiatrist's couch. Both heroines have to make a choice between different sorts of love – Francesca between the dominating, possessive love of Nicholas and the less exacting demands of an American jazz-band leader and a successful portrait painter; Laura between the passionate, idealistic Doctor Harvey (Trevor Howard) and her steady, predictable, crossword-puzzle-playing husband (Cyril Raymond). Laura is subject to irrational decisions and fainting fits but she loses control only momentarily; Francesca cracks under the strain and collapses into amnesia.

Though *Brief Encounter* is anchored to the suburban reality of Milford Junction it is none the less a world of portents and threatening shadows. Laura doesn't have a sadistic guardian to contend with but, like Francesca, she is wracked by guilt and indecision and almost driven to suicide. She renounces her lover and returns to the domestic fold, whereas Francesca pursues the passionate, dangerous option. But this difference in resolution seems less important than the fact that both women undergo traumatic but thrilling experiences.

Celia Johnson's Laura Jesson is a very idiosyncratic, unusual heroine with few of the attributes of conventional stardom. The enhanced realism of her portrayal was highly praised by the middle-aged, middle-class critics, but audiences outside 'the better class halls' were alienated by her prim mannerisms and unsympathetic to her moral dilemma. One is tempted to believe that *Brief Encounter* was popular with the critics not so much because of its reflection of contemporary reality but because it satisfied their own fantasies about the excitement and passion of forbidden love affairs. *The Seventh Veil* offered different rewards. Ann Todd's Francesca, though as distant from most picture-goers as Laura, is something of a Cinderella to be loved and pitied. Laura's suffering is of her own making, Francesca suffers because of the sadistic, possessive love of her guardian. The sequence where Nicholas, driven by jealous fury, raps his young ward's hands with his cane to stop her playing the piano, seems to have had a shocking effect out of all proportion to the actual level of violence used.

Women had played unusually strong roles in Powell and Pressburger's wartime films – Valerie Hobson in *The Spy in Black* and *Contraband*, Googie Withers, Pamela Brown, and Joyce Redman in *One of Our Aircraft is Missing*, Sheila Sim in *A Canterbury Tale* – and as war subjects gave way to romance this emphasis became more marked. *I Know Where I'm Going* takes up *A Canterbury Tale*'s conflict between materialism and the mystical values associated with the countryside, but the story is more straightforward. Joan Webster (Wendy Hiller), a successful woman who throughout her life has known exactly what she wants, decides to marry a rich businessman who is much older than she is. She journeys up to Scotland for the wedding, but on the very last stage of her journey she is frustrated by wind and fog from reaching her destination, a small island off the West coast of Scotland. By the time the weather has cleared she realizes that she loves the impoverished Scottish laird of the island (Roger Livesey).

As with most of Powell and Pressburger's films, passion is dealt with wryly and obliquely. Roger Livesey's laird is charismatic less in his personal appearance than in the traditions he represents. (It might have been a different story if the film had been made with James Mason and Deborah Kerr, Powell's first choice for the parts.) Despite the wild, romantic setting, the film displays none of the angst of *The Seventh Veil* and *Brief Encounter*. Joan is frustrated and puzzled by the people she finds herself stranded amongst, but she is not humiliated or humbled, and the process by which she awakens to the beauty and terror of the world is untraumatic in comparison with that which Francesca and Laura have to undergo. Guilt-ridden, they attempt suicide. Joan by contrast, comes close to death through her own pig-headedness.

She bribes a young boatman to defy the storms and ferry her across to the island, and the laird has to rescue them from the consequences of her folly. Suitably chastened, she surrenders her materialist ambitions, her self-satisfaction, and her right to live a comfortable and easy life. But it is her reckless energy which make her able to appreciate the values of this rough, egalitarian community where dogs and eagles share the draughty houses, and it is she, the bold outsider, who breaks the old curse which holds the laird in thrall. It is a very moving film, like the three Technicolor films which follow it – *A Matter of Life and Death*, *Black Narcissus*, and *The Red Shoes* – a modern fairy story where complex ideas are expressed in powerful dramatic form.

If Lean and Powell represented the best of the talented young directors who had made their mark in the forties, Herbert Wilcox was one of the very few survivors from the silent era. In the thirties he had been responsible for essays in patriotic nostalgia like *Victoria the Great* and *Sixty Glorious Years*, starring his wife Anna Neagle. After a brief sojourn in Hollywood, they had returned to England to make *They Flew Alone* and *The Yellow Canary*, and then embarked on the highly successful 'Mayfair' cycle. The five films – *I Live in Grosvenor Square* (1945), *Piccadilly Incident* (1946), *The Courtneys of Curzon Street* (1947), *Spring in Park Lane* (1948), and *Maytime in Mayfair* (1949) – have much in common, but the first two are wartime melodramas, *The Courtneys of Curzon Street*, a family saga, and the last two light musical romances.

In *I Live in Grosvenor Square* Neagle is an upper-class young woman whose engagement to her childhood sweetheart, an upper-class young army officer, is disrupted when she falls in love with an American bomber pilot. In its concern to foster Anglo-American relations and to pay homage to the bravery of American flyers, there are obvious similarities with *The Way to the Stars* which was released a few months later. The Wilcox film, with its tough-talking but soft-hearted Americans and its kindly aristocrats doing their bit, is more clichéd, but in contrast to the passive, suffering women who wait for their men in *The Way to the Stars*, Neagle's Lady Pat Fairfax is a strong, positive woman who struggles to control her own destiny. She is grief-stricken when her American lover (Dean Jagger) is killed but has no qualms about turning to the young major (Rex

Harrison) she jilted for support. He is on the verge of embarking for the invasion of France, but because of a delay he manages to get away for a few hours and they meet in their old village pub, now packed with service personnel, and with the sort of restrained passion which Lean and Coward were to use so effectively in *Brief Encounter*, he tries to comfort her. After gossiping and joking, he confesses, 'Oh Pat darling, I don't know what to say', and she replies stoically, 'That's all right David, don't say anything and I won't either.' It is left open whether or not they will marry, but they now have a relationship based on trust and respect rather than the complacent chumminess with which they treated each other at the start of the film.

Box and Wilcox were both unabashedly commercial producers and did their best to cash in on the success of *The Seventh Veil* and *I Live in Grosvenor Square*. Before moving to Gainsborough, Box made *A Girl in a Million* which, though a comedy, has a climactic sequence during a piano recital; *The Years Between*, which involves its heroine in deciding whether to leave or stay with the husband she thought was dead; *Daybreak*, with Ann Todd torn between a hulking Swedish seaman and a possessive husband; and *The Upturned Glass* with James Mason as a brilliant surgeon who attracts and then murders a woman he thinks is a murderess. Wilcox followed up *I Live in Grosvenor Square* with *Piccadilly Incident*, the most luridly melodramatic of the Mayfair cycle, in which the heroine, Diana 'Sunshine' Fraser (Anna Neagle) has a lightning romance with the aristocratic Captain Pearson (Michael Wilding) and then has to spend several years on a desert island resisting the advances of a passionate Canadian sailor; and *The Courtneys of Curzon Street*, in which Neagle's below-stairs heroine marries a baronet and then defies convention further by bringing up their son by herself and earning a good living as a popular entertainer.

Lean and Powell also returned to re-explore the issues they had raised in *Brief Encounter* and *I Know Where I'm Going*. *The Red Shoes*, Powell and Pressburger's last film for Rank, was their most extravagant but also their commercially most successful film. In England, though it was handled with noticeable lack of enthusiasm by the Rank Organization, it attracted more business than most films in 1948. But it was in America that it became a box-office smash. Despite the poor relations between Hollywood and the British film industry at this time, it became the first British film to gross over five million dollars.

Like *I Know Where I'm Going* it is a fairy story, but this time with a bloody and frightening ending. Vicky Page (Moira Shearer), a young dancer, is accepted into a prestigious ballet company and given the chance to become a famous prima ballerina. After initial success she has to decide between dedication to her career and life as an ordinary married woman. She is unable to and leaps to her death onto a railway track. It is a dazzlingly confident film, clichés are transcended, rules are broken, prejudices trampled on. In contrast to the fragility of Ann Todd, the brittleness of Celia Johnson, Shearer, with her flaming red hair and her muscular dancer's body, seems a symbol of life and vitality. There is no hint of neurotic self-doubt, of frustration or repression: Vicky Page is a beautiful, talented, and well-adjusted young woman. But Powell and Pressburger skilfully entwine her life with that of the doomed heroine of the ballet performed within the film, so that her death, though superficially the result of her internal conflicts, is a sacrifice – the price society exacts for her short reign as a fairy princess.

The Red Shoes, with its larger-than-life characters and rich Technicolor photography, is flamboyantly extrovert. Lean's *The Passionate Friends* returns to the gloomily introspective world of *The Seventh Veil* and *Brief Encounter*. Its similarity with *Brief Encounter* was noted and disapproved

17 Our first glimpse of Vicky (Moira Shearer), already looking like a fairy princess, in the box with her aunt (Irene Browne). *The Red Shoes* (1948).

of by the critics. It is a much less warm and romantic film and its
sophistication was mistaken for glossy detachment.

Mary Justin (Ann Todd), the wife of a rich banker, arrives at a French
mountain resort a day or two ahead of her husband. Although she doesn't
realize until the morning, the man who takes the room adjoining hers is
Steven Stratton (Trevor Howard), with whom she had an affair nine years
earlier. She recalls their meeting at a New Year's Eve party in 1939, some
time after she had chosen a cold but comfortable marriage with Howard

18 Mary's dejected return to her embittered husband. Ann Todd and Claude Rains.
The Passionate Friends (1949).

Justin (Claude Rains) in preference to the passionate interdependence she had shared with Stratton. Continuing the flashback, which makes up the main body of the film, we see how their love affair is rekindled but finally ends when Mary refuses to jettison her marriage. Their encounter in the mountains is purely platonic, but when Howard sees them together he understandably misconstrues the situation and insists upon a divorce. When he expresses his feelings of bitterness and betrayal Mary attempts suicide, but this brings them both to a realization that their marriage is, after all, worthwhile.

It is an extraordinarily powerful film but much more cerebral than *Brief Encounter* and *The Seventh Veil*. 'I see your point of view, but it's a cold, bloodless, banker's point of view and I don't believe a word of it,' Stratton tells Howard when he says his marriage to Mary is based on 'freedom and understanding, and a very deep affection'. With their separate beds and brittle politeness to each other, one is inclined to agree. But Howard, despite his wealth and power and status, is extraordinarily vulnerable, and the relationship between him and Mary commands interest and respect by the end of the film. At his lowest ebb he confesses to her: 'I didn't expect love from you, or even great affection. I'd have been well satisfied with kindness and loyalty. You gave me love and kindness and loyalty. But it was the love you'd give a dog, and the kindness you'd give a beggar, and the loyalty of a bad servant.' But passion seethes beneath the iron restraint they impose on their emotions and Mary's refusal to give herself completely to a man is shown not to be the awful mistake Stephen Stratton tells her it is.

Between *I Know Where I'm Going* and *The Red Shoes*, Powell and Pressburger made two films – *A Matter of Life and Death* and *Black Narcissus* – both of which are love stories but of such a unique nature that they defy classification. In *A Matter of Life and Death*, an RAF bomber pilot, Peter Carter (David Niven), establishes contact with an American radio controller, June (Kim Hunter), before crashing his plane into the sea. Washed up on a sandy shore, he assumes he has passed into the other world but is confused when a woman cycles by whom he guesses rightly to be June. They fall in love at first sight.

Peter is convinced that he is only alive because of some celestial oversight which is constantly in danger of being put right. June enlists the help of her friend Dr Reeves (Roger Livesey) who discovers that Peter's concussion has brought about a rare brain disorder and that a risky operation is necessary if his life is to be saved. On the night of the operation, Dr Reeves is killed, which in Peter's fantasy world makes him eligible to plead his cause in the Celestial Court where the issue of whether or not Peter should be reclaimed has become entangled with that of Anglo-American relations. Dr Reeves convinces the Court that if June truly loves Peter it would be wrong to deprive her of her chance of happiness. Her tears of anguish during the operation prove that she does. Peter is allowed to remain on Earth. The operation is a success. The critics sneered condescendingly at this 'audacious, sometimes beautiful, but basically sensational film about nothing' (Dilys Powell). But it was chosen as the first film to be presented for a Royal Command Performance and was a popular international success.[25]

Powell, now established as a major director, thought he deserved a holiday and went to South America where the Inca city of Machu Picchu inspired in him the idea of a grandiose location epic. However, when he returned to England he found his partner Emeric Pressburger equally inspired with the more concrete idea of making a film from Rumer Godden's novel *Black Narcissus*. Powell reluctantly acquiesced but he insisted with perverse but, as it turned out, irreproachable logic that the film, which is set in a convent in the Himalayas, be shot in the studio with

19 Clodagh's flashback to happier times in Ireland. Deborah Kerr. *Black Narcissus* (1947).

only occasional excursions to a tropical garden in Horsham, Sussex, for local colour.

The story concerns a group of five nuns who are sent out from the mother convent in Delhi to a remote area of the Himalayas where the local ruler has offered the use of a palace – which used to be his 'House of Women' – as a base from which they can offer medical and educational services, as well as religion, to the local population. The five nuns are very clearly delineated – Sister Briony (Judith Furse) understands medicine; Sister Philippa (Flora Robson) is a natural gardener; Sister Honey (Jenny Laird) has a way with children; Sister Ruth (Kathleen Byron) is well-educated, if neurotic, and is expected to be a good teacher; Sister Clodagh (Deborah Kerr), the Mother Superior, is a capable organizer. These are not the usual stereotypes of women (even of nuns) on the screen and the film continually confounds expectations in its combination of conventional and mysterious elements.

All the women are affected by the atmosphere of the place and find it difficult to deal with the superstitious, unruly locals. They are given considerable help by Mr Dean (David Farrar), the agent responsible for managing the ruler's estates, but he is rude, dissolute, and hostile to their presence. Moreover he has a down-to-earth sexuality which disturbs and arouses both Ruth and Clodagh. In a dramatic climax Ruth breaks her vows, puts on make-up and a red dress and declares her love for Mr Dean. He rejects her and sends her back to the pleasure palace where, mad with jealousy, she stalks her rival Clodagh and tries to push her over a precipice.

Had the film chosen to concentrate on Ruth and Clodagh's choice between God and Mr Dean, *Black Narcissus* would have fitted neatly into the pattern established by *The Seventh Veil*, *Brief Encounter*, and *I Know Where I'm Going*. As it is, neither their religious nor their romantic feelings are given much weight. Mr Dean's vehement denial that he loves Clodagh is not entirely convincing, but it embodies a rejection of romantic illusion. There is an effective contrast between Ruth's attempted seduction of Mr Dean, shot in a disturbing expressionist style, and Clodagh's soft-focus lyrical daydreams about the fiancé who jilted her. Ruth's delusions become part of her world and lead to madness and death, Clodagh shakes herself free from illusion and leads her remaining nuns back to Delhi. She has learnt enough to know when to give up but her honesty forces her to acknowledge a wary but passionate attachment to Mr Dean.

7   Exotic Dreams

Essentially, melodrama is a dream world inhabited by dream people and dream justice, offering audiences the fulfilment and satisfaction found only in dreams. An idealization and simplification of the world of reality, it is in fact the world the audiences want but cannot get. (M.R. Booth, *English Melodrama*, 1965)[1]

Costume drama has played a major role in British film culture. Will Barker, most ambitious of early showmen/film-makers, made films about Henry VIII and Jane Shore (the mistress of Edward IV), and after a long period of eclipse, the fortunes and reputation of the British film industry were revived by the international success of Korda's *The Private Life of Henry VIII* in 1933.[2] British film producers embarked on a spate of unwieldy epics, many of which flopped disastrously and helped create the slump which hit the industry in 1937. But Korda and another crafty entrepreneur, Herbert Wilcox, continued to exploit costume pictures to advantage. Wilcox cast his wife Anna Neagle as *Nell Gwyn*, as *Peg of Old Drury*, and then as Queen Victoria in *Victoria the Great* and *Sixty Glorious Years*. Korda's *Rembrandt*, one of his most charming films, was a commercial failure, but his Technicolor celebrations of the great days of the British Empire, *The Four Feathers* and *The Drum*, were big box-office successes.

The war intensified patriotic feelings but made manifestations of heroism and imperial might seem slightly ludicrous. The typical costume films of the early years of the war – *Lady Hamilton*, *The Young Mr Pitt*, *The Prime Minister* – incorporate a different sort of propaganda. Nelson, Pitt and Disraeli are cast as popular heroes and Britain is shown as the upholder of liberty and democracy against Continental tyranny.

Popular melodrama

At the opposite end of the market to the lavish historical epic was a different sort of costume film, derived from Victorian stage melodrama. Theatrical melodrama had been very popular before the advent of the cinema. Melodrama halls like the Grand at Islington, the Standard in Shoreditch, and the Britannia in Hoxton, the Surrey Theatre at Blackfriars, and the Pavilion, Mile End, catered for audiences of two thousand people and upwards. This sort of entertainment gradually died out between the wars, but the last of the great melodrama stars, Tod Slaughter, appeared in a series of film adaptations of some of the old favourites: *Maria Marten or the Murder in the Red Barn, The Ticket of Leave Man, It's Never Too Late To Mend, Sweeney Todd, the Demon Barber of Fleet Street*, and *The Face at the Window*. During the war the only addition to the cycle was an adaptation of Wilkie Collins' *The Woman in White* (retitled *Crimes at the Dark House*), but the tradition of grand guignol villains and frail but intrepid heroines lived on.

Shambling, sinister Laird Cregar appeared in two Hollywood films set in the foggy London town of the imagination – *The Lodger* and *Hangover Square* – both of them directed with expressionist fervour by German expatriate John Brahm. Thorold Dickinson cast Anton Walbrook, best known to the public as Prince Albert of *Victoria the Great* and *Sixty Glorious Years*, as a suave, sadistic murderer relentlessly pushing his wife into madness in *Gaslight*, made for British National shortly after the outbreak of war, and the film was sufficiently popular to tempt MGM to remake it four years later.[3] Paramount-British made *Hatter's Castle* with Robert Newton, one of the few actors who could equal Slaughter in eye-rolling histrionics, as a Victorian patriarch who ruins the lives of his womenfolk; and Gainsborough initiated a new cycle of costume melodramas with *The Man in Grey*.

The Slaughter films and their successors concentrated their attention on the villain, but there was a tradition of melodrama which followed the trials and tribulations of women. Theatrical impresarios were not slow to discover the allure of the colourful adventuress who pursued a career of lurid sinfulness before love or death made her see the error of her ways. In the 1890s plays such as *The Female Swindler, A Disgrace to her Sex, The Girl Who Wrecked his Home*, and *That Wretch of a Woman* were normal fare at theatres like the Mile End Pavilion.[4]

Censorship ruled out the possibility of this sort of subject being explored in contemporary guise in British films (though there was a cycle of 'bad girl' films – *Jennie Gerhardt, Ladies They Talk About, Blonde Venus, Susan Lenox, Her Fall and Rise*, etc. – made in Hollywood in the thirties). The Gainsborough melodramas combined the British practice of using the past to explore contemporary issues with the concerns of popular melodrama with sex, violence, and the possibility of happiness. But they were also much more attuned to a modern female audience. Their main female stars, Margaret Lockwood and Phyllis Calvert, were not really sex symbols (though Jean Kent certainly was) and most of their fan mail came from women.

Despite the success of *The Man in Grey, Fanny By Gaslight*, and *The Wicked Lady*, it was a formula which was difficult to maintain. Their stars grew restive and wanted to move on to more critically respected roles; Arthur Rank was unhappy about their salacious sex appeal and was unable to maintain a good working relationship with Maurice Ostrer. The resources of talent which Ted Black had attracted to the studio were gradually run down. In the year before Sydney Box took over only three films had been made – *Root of All Evil*, a contemporary melodrama set among the oil fields of East Anglia, and two costume pictures, *Caravan* and *The Magic Bow*.

Caravan, like *The Man in Grey*, was based on a novel by Lady Eleanor Smith and it has similarly star-crossed lovers and a similarly convoluted plot. Richard Darrell (Stewart Granger) and Oriana Camperdene (Anne Crawford) are childhood sweethearts and despite the difference in their class status plan to marry. Richard is sent on a mission to Granada, where his rival for Oriana's affections, Sir Francis Castleton (Dennis Price), arranges for

20 Two kinds of love. Rosal (Jean Kent) and Oriana (Anne Crawford). *Caravan* (1946).

him to be ambushed by a band of gypsies. Richard is left for dead, but a fiery gypsy girl, Rosal (Jean Kent), who has tried to warn him of the danger, takes him to her mountain retreat and nurses him back to health.

Richard recovers physically but he has lost his memory and is content to believe Rosal's story that he has always been in love with her until she inadvertently mentions Oriana's name and the past comes flooding back. Meanwhile, back in England, Oriana, believing Richard dead, has married Francis. When Richard learns of the marriage he feels angry and betrayed. He writes to Oriana, bitterly congratulating her on the good match she has made and proceeds to marry Rosal. Undismayed by Richard's bitterness ('that sort of hatred *is* love' she tells Francis) and thrilled that he is alive, Oriana hotfoots it for Spain with her husband in pursuit.

Dennis Price's Sir Francis Castleton is as odious a villain as any played by Tod Slaughter. He is no match for Richard man to man and has to achieve his ends, with the help of his slimy assistant Wycroft (Robert Helpmann), by unfair play. Having tricked Oriana into marriage he makes her suffer the grossest indignities when she refuses to submit to his desires. Even the London prostitutes, with whom he tries to humiliate his wife, despise him; and he dies, trying to escape his rival's wrath, swallowed up by a treacherous quagmire.

The film is directed by Arthur Crabtree with more dash than he had shown with *Madonna of the Seven Moons*. As in *The Man in Grey*, there are four almost equally balanced characters, but the atmosphere is much lighter. In place of the treacherous friendship between Hesther and Clarissa, there is open conflict between Rosal and Oriana. But they are both good women, and when Rosal discovers that Oriana commands Richard's heart despite her 'cold English ways', she works with her to save the man they both love.

There is no tragedy: Richard suffers but is rewarded by an idyllic convalescence in the arms of the loving gypsy girl. Oriana suffers but it is an ordeal she must undergo in order to deserve future happiness. Rosal dies, but she happily sacrifices her life for the man she loves. Francis disappears into the quagmire, but that is a fate he richly deserves.

Caravan is the Gainsborough picture which comes closest to stage melodrama:

In this world life is uncomplicated, easy to understand, and immeasurably exciting. People are true to their surface appearances and always think and behave in the way these appearances dictate. One of the great appeals of this world is clarity: character, conduct, ethics, and situations are perfectly simple, and one always knows what the end will be, although the means may be temporarily obscure. The world of melodrama is thus a world of certainties where confusion, doubt, and perplexity are absent; a world of absolutes where virtue and vice coexist in pure whiteness and pure blackness; and a world of justice where after immense struggle and torment good triumphs over and punishes evil, and virtue receives tangible material rewards.[5]

From his first appearance as a bullying little boy, we are never left in any doubt that Francis will grow up to be the Demon King. And it is no accident that Oriana, the woman who has always loved Richard, is blonde and wears white, while Rosal, the interloper, is dark and dresses in black. As with all good popular theatre, though, contemporary issues intrude. The new sort of egalitarian society forged by the war is endorsed by the relationship between Francis – who is an insufferable snob and think his landed status makes him a superior being – and Richard, who insists he is equal to any man despite his poverty. The dilemmas for women facing the return of their husbands and boyfriends is explored in the two kinds of love represented by Oriana – certain that even Richard's marriage to another woman and her own marriage to another man cannot destroy their lifelong love – and Rosal, whose reckless passion has won her a man who is, in reality, another's.

After this *The Magic Bow* is something of an anti-climax. Jean Kent and Dennis Price have much less interesting roles and the story is disappointingly thin. The original idea was to cast James Mason as the violinist Paganini, Margaret Lockwood as his childhood sweetheart Bianchi, and Phyllis Calvert as Jeanne, an aristocratic lady he falls in love with. Mason read the script and resolutely refused the part. Margaret Lockwood and Phyllis Calvert were equally disgruntled and together decided to appeal to Rank:

> 'We thought no, this is the end, we cannot do this. So we held hands and went to see Mr Rank. . . . Margaret was very timid about it, I wasn't at all. I thought, I'm not going to do this film. We went to Park Lane, and there was this huge room with an onyx table stretching right across the room, with a huge figure – he was an enormous man – sitting at the end. And one of us went one way round the table and the other went the other way, and as we got to him, he rose up from his seat and said, "I hear you want more brass". So where were you? Anyway, Margaret got out of it and I didn't. I was given a lot more brass and I did it. I would have been breaking my contract if I hadn't done, but I thought that perhaps a little persuasion might have got me out of it.'[6]

In fact Calvert copes very well with Jeanne, Paganini's well-born lover, and Stewart Granger gives a performance of extraordinary magnetism as the romantic violinist.

Despite their personal indifference to one another, Calvert and Granger had managed to sustain a convincing love affair over three films – *The Man in Grey, Fanny by Gaslight,* and *Madonna of the Seven Moons.* It is the continuation of this screen affair which provides the main excitement in *The Magic Bow.* Despite the impossibility of a match between a penniless fiddler and a member of the aristocracy, Jeanne and Paganini fall in love at first sight. After a series of frustrations, she takes the initiative, kisses him and encourages him to declare his love. They plan to marry but Jeanne is whisked away to Paris to wed a Napoleonic General, Paul de la Rochelle (Dennis Price). Paganini wins fame and fortune but when he thinks he has lost Jeanne for ever he can go on playing no longer. At the prompting of Bianchi (Jean Kent), Jeanne defies convention, her fiancé, Napoleon, and her mother and marries Paganini after all.

21 Duel at dawn. A wounded Paganini (Stewart Granger) is comforted by Germi (Cecil Parker) and Bianchi (Jean Kent). Jeanne (Phyllis Calvert) stands by her fiancé (Dennis Price) but her heart is with Paganini. *The Magic Bow* (1946).

The critics were predictably dismissive. Dialogue such as 'You've learnt so much about music but so little about life' and 'With this violin I could talk to the world', was hardly calculated to impress highbrows like C.A. Lejeune. As history the film is nonsense, but as melodrama it is very satisfying. Clichéd though it is, Calvert's handling of the scene where she asks Paganini to play for her while she steadies herself to leave him for ever, for example, is superb.

As with the other Granger/Calvert romances, the path of true love does not run smoothly. Despite Napoleon's disruption of the old order, class barriers appear almost insuperable in *The Magic Bow*. At one point the thwarted Paganini accuses Jeanne of choosing the easy way out:

'Isn't it rather that you won't sacrifice all the trumpery and vanities of a life you've been accustomed to? Don't try to spare my feelings by denying it. There's no room for people like me in your world. Go on, marry your Paul. Fill a nursery full of pale-faced aristocratic parasites.'

But as she points out, her spirit is willing enough, it is the massive obstacles put up by society which stand between them and a happy union. For a time it looks as if the odds are against them. But then in an extraordinary sequence played out before the Pope, their love is made manifest and everything holding them apart drops away. A fitting happy end to this unique cycle of films.

The Boxes' costume pictures

When the Boxes took over at Gainsborough they switched the emphasis away from costume melodrama. But, perhaps to reassure the studio staff that there would be some continuity, they decided to make, as their first production at Shepherd's Bush, Graham Greene's *The Man Within*, a story of smuggling and treachery set in eighteenth-century Sussex. Though it was directed by Bernard Knowles, who had been responsible for *The Magic Bow*, and Jean Kent appeared again as a lascivious schemer, the film has little in common with the earlier Gainsborough melodramas. Geoffrey Unsworth's Technicolor photography gives a completely different atmosphere to the film and its mood of gloomy foreboding is accentuated by the Boxes' convoluted narrative structure.

Francis (Richard Attenborough), a cowardly and unsympathetic young man, is adopted by his uncle, Carlyon (Michael Redgrave), the skipper of a smuggling ship. The crew despise Francis and trick Carlyon into flogging him for a theft of which he is innocent. He gets his own back by betraying them to the Excise men and is pursued by a vengeful Carlyon into the Sussex countryside. He is influenced by two very different women – Elizabeth, a downtrodden country girl (Joan Greenwood) and Lucy, the mistress of the Public Prosecutor (Jean Kent) – to testify against his former comrades, but he draws the line at betraying Carlyon.

The narrative unfolds in several flashbacks as Francis faces up to the threat of torture by the authorities. *Sight and Sound* was suspicious:

This is a curious film – a sort of introverted freak, with no apparent purpose and aimed at no clearly-defined audience. If it were a nightmare, brought to a psychiatrist by one of his patients for analysis, it could be fitted into the Freudian framework without serious difficulty.

22 Passion between men. Francis (Richard Attenborough) and Carlyon (Michael Redgrave) in the torture cells. *The Man Within* (1947).

The central figure is a boy who hates his father but madly hero-worships his father's friend after the father's death; suffers from persecution-mania and finds a haven only in the arms of two women, each suspected of having loose morals; betrays his hero, behaves in a cowardly way, and suffers frightful remorse, but ends by redeeming himself and earning his hero's pardon. The fact that this all takes place in period-costume, against a Technicolor background of ships and smugglers ('the gentle-men') and the sea, also no doubt has a bearing on something or other – a practised psychiatrist could presumably say what.[7]

More sophisticated critics like Basil Wright found the stylized settings, the complex psychology, the unresolved relationships, fascinating. But even Wright failed to point out that despite the presence of the two women, the real love affair is between Francis and Carlyon.

The new Gainsborough's second costume picture, *The Brothers*, seemed to confirm the critics in their opinion that the Boxes were up to no good. Set in Skye at the turn of the century and shot in black and white, it is a much more austere film than *The Man Within* but it is equally disturbing. Elspeth Grant, reviewing it under the heading CRUELTY PAYS DIVIDENDS – BUT IT DOESN'T ENTERTAIN ME, complained:

Sadism, it seems, can be considered a selling point: brutality is booming, flogging is fascinating, fist fights are fun – particularly when staged in such surroundings that the fighters are liable to break every bone in their bodies – and morbidity makes money. So, at least, one would gather since that astute gentleman, Mr Sydney Box, shrewd judge of public taste, has chosen to make such a gloomful and violent film as *The Brothers*.[8]

Mary Lawson, a pretty orphan (Pat Roc), is sent to live with distant relations on the Isle of Skye. Her unfamiliar charms soon ensnare the sons of two feuding families, the McFarishes, and Mary's relations the Macraes. Feuding inevitably intensifies and ends in a number of deaths, including that of Mary herself.

Pat Roc had played a similar role in Ealing's *Johnny Frenchman* where she had inspired rivalry between a Breton and a Cornish fisherman. But the essence of her appeal was as a modern, town-bred girl and she appears artificial and incongruous in this primitive Celtic world. The Boxes had originally intended to cast Ann Todd whose fragile, witch-like beauty would have been perfect for the part. Unfortunately Maxwell Reed was to play Fergus Macrae, and Todd, who had been knocked about by him in *Daybreak*, had no intention of allowing herself to be whipped, wooed, and finally murdered by the big, clumsy Irishman. Though the film is irrevocably flawed there are some splendid sequences and to his credit Maxwell Reed acquits himself honourably among a cast of Scottish character actors – Will Fyffe, Duncan Macrae, Andrew Crawford, Finlay Currie, Morland Graham, and John Laurie – who obviously relished the chance of appearing in a raw, barbarous film which made no concessions to English sensibilities.

Jassy, released two months later in July 1947, consolidated the Boxes' bad reputation with the critics. Paul Dehn, lamenting the presence of 'TOO MUCH SADISM IN OUR FILMS', accused Sydney of being the worst culprit. 'Producers and directors have their recognisable weaknesses. Hitchcock likes appearing in his own pictures, De Mille likes crowds, Lubitsch likes staircases. Sydney Box likes torture, flogging and bloodshed.' And he looked forward with trepidation to *Son of Jassy* in which a mad baby will be flogged to death in a hot bath.[9]

In fact *Jassy* was a project inherited from the Ostrers and made with little enthusiasm by the Boxes, at Denham, away from their mainstream of thrillers, comedies, and contemporary social problem films. Its faults lie less in its violence – conventional footage of brutal blacksmiths and drunken squires – than in its passionless relationships.

Jassy Woodruff, a gypsy girl with second sight, whose father is shot by the brutal squire Nick Helmar (Basil Sydney), appears initially to be an ideal Lockwood heroine. Like Hesther in *The Man in Grey*, she is sent to work in a school and is befriended by a rich girl – Dilys (Pat Roc), Squire Helmar's daughter. Jassy, like Hesther, insinuates her way into her friend's household and wins the favour of the Squire. Dilys, meanwhile, dallies with the affections of Barney Hatton (Dermot Walsh), whose family once owned the house and land her father now occupies. Barney is now merely a poor farmer though, and Dilys passes him over to marry a titled landowner. However, Jassy loves Barney and sympathizes with his desire to repossess his ancestral home. She marries old Nick, who is besotted by her charms, on condition he makes her a gift of the house. Nick, enraged at being tricked, gets very drunk and falls off his horse. The conscience-stricken Jassy assiduously nurses him back to health. But while she is out visiting, Lindy, a deaf-mute she has taken under her wing (Esma Cannon), puts rat-bane in Nick's brandy and kills him. Jassy and Lindy are tried for murder and found guilty, but after sentence has been passed the mute manages to cry out and assert Jassy's innocence before collapsing and dying. Jassy is able to make Barney a present of the house, and in gratitude he marries her.

Norah Lofts' novel, told from four overlapping points of view, is one of the most interesting and complex of the 'costume' novels. But as far as the Gainsborough formula is concerned it has a basic flaw – Jassy is a good character and she is unjustly executed. The film solves part of the problem by getting Lindy to save the heroine from the gallows, but this only makes the film more unsatisfactory. Director Bernard Knowles makes Jassy oscillate between being an unscrupulous schemer – like Hesther or the wicked Barbara Skelton – and a brave, resourceful, virtuous woman like Fanny and Oriana.

Commercially the film was successful enough and the Boxes were encouraged by Rank to make two more expensive costume pictures – *The Bad Lord Byron* and *Christopher Columbus*. Both were directed by David Macdonald, who had been responsible for two of the best Box/Gainsborough films, *Good Time Girl* and *The Brothers*. He looked set fair to become a major British director, but the box-office failure of these two expensive costume pictures fatally blighted his career.

The origins of *Christopher Columbus* are obscure, but someone within the Rank hierarchy had commissioned, at considerable cost, a script from the novelist Rafael Sabatini. Gainsborough, with its tradition of costume drama, was the obvious home for such a production. The Rank organization was trying to make films which would be popular with American audiences and, no doubt, a film about the man who discovered America looked seductively marketable. However, there were good reasons why Hollywood had passed over the subject itself. From an entertainment point of view, there was very little action in the Columbus story. As the film critic of the *Daily Telegraph* pointed out:

> Columbus was a great man who changed the history of the world; but that doesn't necessarily make him a good subject for a film. Without agreeing with the wag who said that Columbus 'when he started out' he didn't know where he was going, when he got there he didn't know where he was, and when he got back he didn't know where he'd been', we may still think that dramatically, his life was the wrong shape.[10]

On the basis of Sabatini's previous work – novels like *Scaramouche, The Black Swan*, and *Captain Blood* – one might have expected a swashbuckling Columbus beset by pirates and savage Indians. The Boxes were unhappy with what they had inherited. According to Muriel, 'After a good deal of research I found this long script both inaccurate and inferior in quality. I passed on my opinion to Sydney and we asked to be excused from producing it, but to no avail.'[11] They were able to insist, however, on writing their own script which boldly, but perhaps unwisely, encompassed a painstakingly researched historical account of Columbus's involvement in the power politics of the Spanish Court.

The film is long and slow with few action sequences – resembling the history films made by Roberto Rossellini in the 1960s – but it is by no means a bad film. The sets, designed by Maurice Carter, look impressively authentic and Stephen Dade's delicate Technicolor photography is superb. Fredric March gives a thoughtful, sensitive portrayal of Columbus as a blindly obsessed man who against all the odds turns out to be right in his obsession. Florence Eldridge, Linden Travers, and Kathleen Ryan give good performances as the three women in his life, and Francis L. Sullivan is given more to do than usual as the bombastic villain.

The production was dogged by trouble. On location in the West Indies, one of Columbus' ships sank and another caught fire. Court parrots plagued the sound men with outbursts of bad language and Florence Eldridge, who was playing the Queen of Spain, burnt her face and held up production. By the time the film was released it had few champions and its slow pace and lack of adventure and excitement alienated audiences.

The Bad Lord Byron was equally ill-fated. In 1983 Muriel Box (by this time Lady Gardiner) was still puzzled by its lack of success:

'It was most beautifully photographed and everything was totally authentic. Nothing was artificially concocted, everything that was in the film was exactly as Byron described it. It also had a beautiful cast. Joan Greenwood was wonderful as Lady Caroline Lamb – exactly right – and I thought Dennis Price gave a most creditable rendering of Byron in every way. But it received terrible notices. They quite shocked us.'[12]

Indeed the film does have many fine qualities, but the Boxes, who had astutely gauged what the public wanted with *The Seventh Veil*, were sadly offbeam with Byron. Their attempts at accuracy only provoked the ire of perfectionists such as Harold Nicolson, who insisted publicly that

Byron did not limp in the way that is here represented, he slithered; he did not talk with the voice of a BBC announcer, he talked with the Devonshire House drawl with an undertone of Scotch; in no circumstances would he ever have dreamt of bringing a walking stick into a drawing room or calling Hobhouse 'John'.[13]

It is unlikely that many members of the cinema-going public would have welcomed a drawling, slithering Byron; but Dennis Price's foppish gentleman was also some way away from the popular image of Byron as a Romantic hero. The Ostrers would have gone unerringly for the misanthropic libertine of *Childe Harolde*; the Boxes chose the world-weary sophisticate of *Don Juan*. In *The Seventh Veil* they had used an elaborate narrative structure and a semi-open ending to intensify the melodramatic power of the film. *The Bad Lord Byron* whisks us away from Byron's death-bed at Missolonghi to a heavenly court where his past life – or at least his past loves – unravel before us, and we are invited to judge for ourselves whether he was a hero and great poet or a scoundrel and a seducer. But the bitty, episodic structure as Byron's friends, lovers, and enemies each give their evidence makes identification with the hero difficult, and romance and drama seep away in the urbane atmosphere of the heavenly courtroom.

Ealing's costume pictures

The box-office success of the Gainsborough melodramas did not go unnoticed by the rest of the industry. Ealing tried its own brand of costume picture in 1944 with *Champagne Charlie* and followed it up with *Pink String and Sealing Wax*, the first film of promising young editor-turned-director, Robert Hamer.

Despite subtle direction and a charismatic performance from Googie Withers, *Pink String and Sealing Wax* doesn't quite manage to take off from its theatrical origins. The story is centred upon two contrasting worlds: a suffocatingly middle-class household dominated by a bullying patriarch, and a glittering, sordid tavern queened over by a magnificently bosomed landlady. Edward Sutton (Mervyn Johns) is a well-established pharmacist in Brighton, and rules his wife and three children with a rod of iron. His son David (Gordon Jackson) begins frequenting a local hostelry and falls for the landlady, Pearl Bond (Googie Withers). He thinks she reciprocates his feelings but in fact she is using him as an unwitting accomplice in the murder of her drunken husband (Garry Marsh).

Poor David, caught between the repressive sadism of his father and the callous amorality of the woman he loves, is potentially a tragic figure. But in a distinctly hurried denouement, things are taken out of his hands. Sutton senior grasps the seriousness of the situation and confronts Pearl. Disappointingly, this arrogant, unscrupulous woman is reduced to a crumpled mass of guilt and tears. Rather than face arrest and trial for murder she jumps off the promenade into a raging sea; leaving the bourgeois family chastened, but intact.

This sad and gloomy film found some supporters among the critics but was not a commercial success, and it was not until 1947 that Ealing attempted period pieces again with Cavalcanti's *Nicholas Nickleby* and Charles Frend's *The Loves of Joanna Godden*. Sheila Kaye-Smith's novel about a turn-of-the-century gentlewoman farmer was an unusual subject for Ealing, a studio with a strong male bias. But in a policy statement made in 1945 Balcon had promised 'films with an outdoor background of the British scene' and *Joanna Godden* offered the opportunity of location filming on Romney Marsh.[14]

On the death of their father, Joanna and Ellen Godden (Googie Withers and Jean Kent) inherit a substantial sheep farm. Though Joanna is engaged to a neighbouring farmer, Arthur Alce (John McCallum), she resents his assumption that he will become master of the farm and she sacrifices her romance in order to prove she is capable of running it herself.

Britain had something of a tradition of sheep farming films, though the heroine (Margaret Lockwood in *'Owd Bob*; Helen Perry in *Sheepdog of the*

Hills) generally had to vie for attention with a canine co-star. Googie Withers' Joanna Godden puts sheep, dogs, and men firmly in their place. The Australian 'looker' (Chips Rafferty) she brings in to introduce new methods is soon sent packing when they prove inappropriate to Romney Marsh; and though, like Jeckie Farnish in *The Root of All Evil*, she ends up in the arms of John McCallum, it is very much as an equal partner.

Despite its title, the film is by no means exclusively concerned with Joanna's loves. Her relationship with Arthur Alce is a low-key affair and her happy marriage to Martin Trevor (Derek Bond) ends abruptly when he drowns. Joanna's sheep-breeding experiments are afforded rather more realism than Jeckie Farnish's entrepreneurial ventures. Attempts to adopt a modern approach to farming had considerable contemporary relevance at a time when, under the pressure of food shortages, Britain's agriculture was undergoing a revolution and the Labour government was attempting to plant five thousand square miles of Tanganyika jungle with groundnuts. Joanna, like the groundnut farmers, comes up against unexpected obstacles, but she perseveres and wins the respect of her conservative neighbours. Joanna's determination to defy convention and be a farmer rather than a lady works surprisingly well as a device, bringing together a set of concerns about progress and the need for innovation with the more familiar romantic problem of a woman's difficulty in combining success in the 'man's world' with a happy domestic life. Refreshingly, Googie Withers is for once allowed to portray a strong, intelligent woman who deals with her problems with vigorous common sense and ends up prosperous, wise, and as happy as one has a right to be.

Both *The Loves of Joanna Godden* and *Nicholas Nickleby* were modestly successful and the studio, now under the Rank aegis, was encouraged to embark on a more lavish costume drama, *Saraband for Dead Lovers*. It was made in Technicolor and directed by Basil Dearden, most showy and melodramatic of the Ealing directors. But despite this, and the presence of Stewart Granger, it fitted more into the doom-laden tradition of *The Man Within* than the mainstream of Gainsborough melodramas.

As befitted Ealing's adherence to realism, the film was based on real historical events, albeit filtered through a novel by Helen Simpson and a screenplay by John Dighton and Alexander Mackendrick. In 1694 George Louis, Prince of Hanover (and subsequently King of England), discovered a love affair between his estranged Queen, Sophie Dorothea, and a Swedish soldier of fortune, Count Philip Konigsmark. With the aid of an ageing courtesan, the Countess von Platen, George had Konigsmark killed and Sophie Dorothea was imprisoned for life in the Castle of Ahlden.

Michael Relph's production design with its subtle use of browns and reds to create a warm but dangerous atmosphere is very impressive. But the story unfolds unevenly. As *The Times* pointed out:

the emphasis is more on situation and scenery than on character drawing. Indeed the splendour of some of the scenes and the magnificent scale on which they have been reconstructed frequently turn the characters into romantic ciphers.[15]

The critics had little time for costume pictures, even from Ealing, and the accusation of flashy technique and trite characterization is one that has often been levelled at British directors like Basil Dearden and Michael Powell who have an eye for the startling effect. But in *Saraband* there is some justification. Dearden never quite manages to impose order and coherence over this ambitious, sprawling melodrama.

Literary adaptations

Saraband for Dead Lovers was part of a general boom in costume pictures. Between 1946 and 1950 at least seventy were made in Britain, ranging from creaking epics like *Bonny Prince Charlie* to Tod Slaughter's *The Curse of the Wraydons*; from respectful adaptations of Dickens and Shakespeare to bodice-ripping exploitation films like *Idol of Paris*.

Adaptations of literary classics were better received than other costume pictures, though there were critical rumblings that money and talent would be better spent on contemporary subjects. When David Lean followed up *Brief Encounter* with *Great Expectations* there was a general reluctance to backtrack on the hopes held out for him as a great British director. Richard Winnington argued that *Great Expectations* emulated what its predecessor had achieved but on a larger scale, signalling to the world the superiority of British films:

> As proof of this, I ask you to note a definite break from discreet miniature and delicate water-colour into full canvas. I ask you to pay attention to the first *big* British film to have been made, a film that confidently sweeps our cloistered virtues into the open. The film is *Great Expectations*. . . . It is a landmark in the history of British films: not only because it is taken from the most shapely, mature and filmable of all Dickens' novels, not because it has the best photography I've seen for years or because the casting is nearly perfect or because of its knife-edge cutting or its furious pace, but because it casts a complete spell derived from some inner power.[16]

When Lean went on to *Oliver Twist*, however, there was a definite feeling that things were not going according to plan. Arthur Vesselo in *Sight and Sound* warned,

> It is clear from the first moment of *Oliver Twist* that Messrs. Lean and Neame have concocted it with the success of *Great Expectations* in the

forefront of their minds. Such a success can be a danger as well as an inspiration; and to let the atmosphere of the earlier film extend and obtrude itself into the later, as it does emphatically in the *Oliver Twist* opening sequence, is a cardinal error.[17]

Great Expectations is a relatively cheerful novel about growing up and coming to terms with the world. *Oliver Twist* is a different sort of novel entirely. Dickens' Fagin, Sikes, and Bumble are acidly drawn portraits of the sort of degraded characters who presided over the seething, poverty-stricken netherworld which existed beneath the thin crust of Victorian prosperity and respectability. But by 1948 Lean had moved a long way from the realism of *In Which We Serve* and *This Happy Breed* and was determinedly not a director of social comment films. John Bryan's elaborate sets – the cavern-like workhouse, the bizarre London landscapes, Fagin's labyrinthine den – would not have been out of place in a German Expressionist film of the twenties and Guy Green's shadowy lighting gives a nightmare feel to much of the film. In this larger-than-life world the characters inevitably emerge as caricatures, and something of Dickens' indictment of Victorian society is lost. But it is still an extraordinarily rich and satisfying film.

The other Dickens adaptation, Cavalcanti's *Nicholas Nickleby*, with more justification and fewer pretensions, turns a sprawling, untidy novel into a fairy story. Nicholas (Derek Bond), a fine, upright young man, stands up to the grotesque Squeers, rescues Smike from Dotheboys Hall, saves his sister's honour, defeats his uncle's wicked machinations and wins the woman he loves. In Lean's films it is the macabre sequences which are most memorable: Magwitch in the windswept churchyard, Miss Havisham and Estella in their eerie, cobweb-strewn house, the grim, tomblike workhouse into which Oliver Twist is born, Fagin in his den counting his money. *Nicholas Nickleby* is much more sunny, the benevolent glow from the Crummleses, the Cheerybles, the cottage at Bow, sending a reassuring warmth through the film.

Two Cities, even more than Ealing, had been associated with realistic, contemporary subjects during the war years. Their only venture into the past was Olivier's *Henry V*, a lavish celebration of English military valour, worlds apart from Gainsborough's costume melodramas. However, in 1946 Two Cities released three costume films – *Carnival*, *Beware of Pity*, and *Hungry Hill* – though it is not clear how much these were Giudice's own projects and how far they were foisted on the company by the Rank hierarchy. None of them made much of a mark with critics or audiences, but all three have their good points. Maurice Elvey and his biographer Linda Wood both consider *Beware of Pity* his best film, and it certainly provides Lilli Palmer with her most substantial and satisfactory role.[18] *Carnival*, with Guy Green's photography and Sally Gray's hesitant, delicate performance, has an enchanting quality which more than makes up for the film's ramshackle construction and deserves rather more recognition than it has received. Brian Desmond Hurst's attempt on Daphne du Maurier's *Hungry Hill* founders on the problem of fitting a three-generational family saga into a ninety-two minute feature film, but Margaret Lockwood's performance as Fanny Rosa, an Irish femme fatale who develops into a bitter, drug-dependent matriarch, is startlingly ambitious if, in the long run, unconvincing.

Henry V had proved unexpectedly popular in America, and in 1947 Two Cities allowed Olivier to embark on his long-cherished project to film *Hamlet*. Although the decision was made to film in black and white, costs soared alarmingly (the final budget was £580,000), and before the film was completed Giudice left to work as an independent producer.

None the less, *Hamlet* is a fitting monument to his efforts to make

23 'The wary, polite but irreligious men of the racing fraternity'. William (Dirk Bogarde) takes Esther (Kathleen Ryan) to see the Derby. *Esther Waters* (1948).

expensive, artistic films for a discerning mass market. Desmond Dickinson's moody deep-focus photography and the gloomy interiors of Roger Furse's Elsinore are typical of the post-war fashion for expressionism and angst, but Olivier's Hamlet is as vigorous and unneurotic as the swashbuckling hero of *Caravan*. With a degree of taste and subtlety Hollywood would have found it difficult to emulate, Olivier and his team turn a philosophical play, where very little seems to happen, into an action-packed psychological thriller. Hollywood responded generously by awarding *Hamlet* the Academy Award for Best Picture of the Year.

In 1949 John Mills, who had played Pip in *Great Expectations*, teamed up with director Anthony Pelissier in order to produce two films which allowed him more flamboyant roles: *The Rocking Horse Winner* where he plays a groom and uses his Suffolk accent for the first time, and an adaptation of H.G. Wells' novel *The History of Mr Polly*.

Mr Polly is a simple, dreamy chap who loses his job, inherits a small portion of wealth, marries, and lives in domestic purgatory, until just when middle-aged despair seems about to overtake him, he escapes to the English countryside, and becomes a happy man. Mills' Polly, perpetually talking to himself in overblown schoolboy slang, is an irritating hero and Anthony Pelissier directs with the subtlety of a sledgehammer, but the film's optimism, like that of *Nicholas Nickleby* is infectious. 'If you don't like your life you can change it', Polly tells himself after fifteen years of married misery. His escape from his dull existence might seem improbable, but his needs are so simple, his mistakes so out of proportion to the price he has had to pay for them, that it is extremely satisfying to see him act on his inspiration and save himself.

There are two other interesting, offbeat films in this cycle of literary adaptations. *Esther Waters* is the one major film directed by Ian Dalrymple, who headed the Crown Film Unit during most of the war. It is a forthright and intelligent version of George Moore's novel about a mid-nineteenth-century housemaid who insists on bringing up her illegitimate child herself, before eventually marrying the bookmaker/publican who has been her lover.

Given Dalrymple's links with the documentary movement, it is not surprising that *Esther Waters* has more in common with the low-key realism of *Nicholas Nickleby* and *The Loves of Joanna Godden* than the baroque splendour of the Lean films or the whimsical extravagance of *The History of Mr Polly*. But although Cavalcanti eschews the caricature and stylization employed by David Lean, *Nicholas Nickleby* is still largely a studio-made film and, with its black and white characters and clear sense of right and wrong, very much a melodrama. *Esther Waters*, shot largely on location and with characters who are unconventional and morally ambivalent, attempts a much more thorough-going realism.

Esther (Kathleen Ryan), is wilful, ignorant, and bad tempered; her lover

William Latch (Dirk Bogarde) is shallow, glib, and of doubtful honesty. Esther's scorn of the popular romances read by the other servant girls is exposed as hypocritical when they discover she can't read. Her attitude to gambling gradually becomes more liberal, but she retains a 'good woman's' suspicion of pub life and the racing scene. But her experience of the world's injustice does teach her to detect humbug. After six years of bitter struggle on her own, she is offered the chance of marriage by the now prosperous William, and by Fred Parsons, a kindly lay preacher who has befriended her. Fred (brilliantly played by Cyril Cusack) tries to be nobly impartial about her decision: 'I don't want you to give yourself to someone – to Latch, or even to me. I want you to be happy', he tells her. But then he can't resist adding, 'And I know you can't be happy without God.' In a Norman Walker film, this no doubt would have clinched things. But Esther, with her illegitimate child, requires a more muscular Christianity. She bursts out in exasperation: 'Oh Fred, I'm not just another soul to save. I'm a woman too.' And goes off to the King's Head, Soho, to join the wary, polite, but irreligious men of the racing fraternity.

Dalrymple undertakes a deliberate de-melodramatization of both character and situation. The workhouse infirmary where Esther has her baby looks more like an NHS hospital than the hell-hole where Oliver Twist is born – though the matron soon tells her to get on her 'peggy weggies' and make room for someone else. In contrast to the Dickens films and *Mr Polly* which are populated with instantly recognizable character actors – Stanley Holloway as Vincent Crummles, Bernard Miles as Newman Noggs and Joe Gargery, Moore Marriott as Uncle Penstemon, Edie Martin as Annie and the Old Lady on the Roof, Francis L. Sullivan as Jaggers and Mr Bumble, Finlay Currie as Magwitch and Uncle Jim – *Esther Waters* employs less familiar faces and their peculiarities are more subdued. The baby-minder murders babies for a fiver, but she does so in a kindly, no-nonsense way; the racing men win some and lose some without making a fuss; the servants gossip bitchily but rally round in a crisis.

Bogarde's William Latch, a sort of nineteenth-century racing spiv, with his check suit and his oily ways, is an impressive creation, even if his accent does slip occasionally. Like many of the heroes of historical romances, he comes from a noble family which has gone down in the world. But unlike Barney Hatton in *Jassy* or Philip Thorn in *Blanche Fury*, he has no burning desire to repossess his heritage. He aims to get rich, but is quite happy to sacrifice respectability for the glitter and excitement of the racing world. His contrived and untimely death is the main flaw of a film which is quirkily independent of other British costume pictures.

Esther Waters aroused little interest among critics or the public, and as it was an expensive film it blighted relations between Dalrymple's company, Wessex, and the Rank organisation. Thorold Dickinson's *The Queen of Spades*, though not a spectacular commercial success, was very highly praised by the critics, and despite its polished look was made on a shoe-string budget. Dickinson had shown his talent and versatility during the war by directing a Victorian melodrama, *Gaslight*, and a grimly realistic war film, *The Next of Kin*. After two years working on *Men of Two Worlds*, an over-ambitious epic set in Africa, he was brought in to replace Rodney Acland as director of *The Queen of Spades*, which had begun shooting at the decrepit old Welwyn studios. Dickinson, more of an intellectual than most directors working in the commercial industry, tended to become indulgent when given his head, but his impressively fertile visual imagination worked well under pressure, and with the help of cameraman Otto Heller he achieved a triumph of improvisation and ingenuity:

'After the first day I cast convention overboard and aimed in every scene at colourful, conscious contrast. . . . When the story went out of doors (the film was shot entirely indoors), there was always a wind blowing. Mist was dense, snow abundant, tobacco smoke almost impenetrable, artificial lighting by candles was always apparently from below unless chandeliers were visible. The tempest evoked by the ghost of the countess nearly blew the camera and its crew off their rostrum. Dust was thick as after a sandstorm. Gems and silks glittered, rags and sores looked stinking. And Otto Heller's camera captured it all while his camera operator Gus Drisse traced camera movements of outlandish and intricate composition.'[19]

With Dickinson as director, Edith Evans and Anton Walbrook as stars, and a story by Alexander Pushkin, *The Queen of Spades* had high art credentials which warded off accusations of unhealthy morbidity. But there is a certain irony in the critics preferring this gruesomely disturbing venture into the supernatural to the impeccable realism of *Esther Waters*.

The decline and fall of the British costume film

Attempts to continue the Gainsborough tradition outside Gainsborough started promisingly but ended in ignominious failure. Leslie Arliss and Ted Black teamed up again to make *A Man About the House* (1946) – a patchy but effective melodrama about the involvement of two fading English spinsters (Margaret Johnston and Dulcie Gray) with a handsome and unscrupulous Italian (Kieron Moore). Then Black was set the Herculean task of producing *Bonnie Prince Charlie* for Korda and died before completing it. Arliss joined Maurice Ostrer who had set up his own production company to continue the tradition of *The Man in Grey* and *The Wicked Lady*. But without the backing of the Gainsborough actors and technicians or the common sense of Ted Black, their first venture, *Idol of Paris*, turned into an embarrassing fiasco. Beryl Baxter, plucked from obscurity to be made into a second Margaret Lockwood, proved pathetically

24   Ambitious outsiders: Philip (Stewart Granger) and Blanche (Valerie Hobson).
     Blanche Fury (1948).

inadequate, and Michael Rennie was hardly better in the James Mason
role. The professionals of the Gainsborough scenario department ensured
that *The Man in Grey* and its successors went out with logical, well-
worked-out plots. *Idol of Paris*, which charts the rise of Theresa – a late-
nineteenth-century ragman's daughter – to become Queen of the Parisian
demi-monde, is slow, clumsy, and incoherent. Even the presence of Miles
Malleson as Offenbach and Christine Norden as Cora Pearl, the honest
whore who threatens to expose Theresa for the virtuous woman she is,
fails to bring the film to life.

The relative failure of *Idol of Paris* can be seen as further evidence that
the appeal of costume pictures was primarily to women – for whom
titillating near-rapes and sadistic whip fights were unlikely to be
satisfactory substitutes for sympathetic female protagonists and a well-
constructed fantasy world. Its lack of success virtually ended the film
careers of Maurice Ostrer, Leslie Arliss, and Beryl Baxter.

Idol of Paris was an uninspired re-working of an old formula but in three films made in the late forties – *Blanche Fury* (1947), *So Evil My Love* (1948), and *Madeleine* – a serious attempt was made to combine the quality of production lavished on big-budget literary adaptations with the passion and intensity of the wartime Gainsborough melodramas.

So Evil My Love and *Blanche Fury* (and two other films made at the same time, *The Mark of Cain* and *Moss Rose*) were based on novels by Joseph Shearing, a pseudonym for the prolific Gabrielle Margaret Vere Long (who also wrote books as Marjorie Bowen). Jeffrey Richards points out that all the Shearing novels: 'centred on female protagonists, all featured the classic "sensation" ingredients (secrets, double lives, accidents, intricate plotting), and all highlighted the disastrous consequences of repression and marital tyranny.'[20] In *Blanche Fury* (directed by Marc Allegret for David Lean's Cineguild), Blanche (Valerie Hobson) is rescued from domestic servitude by her rich relations and employed by them as a governess. She is treated with respect and has little difficulty enticing

25 Ambitious outsiders: Mark (Ray Milland) and Olivia (Ann Todd). Muriel Aked looks on in disdain. *So Evil My Love* (1948).

Laurence, her cousin (Michael Gough in his first screen role), into marriage. On her wedding night she realizes that she loves the estate steward, Philip Thorn (Stewart Granger), the illegitimate heir of the Furys. Blanche connives at Philip's murder of her husband and his father, but exposes him when he attempts to do away with Lavinia, the solemn little girl who is now the legitimate heir to the family fortunes. Lavinia is killed in a riding accident, Thorn is hanged, and Blanche dies giving birth to his son, who inherits the Fury estates.

The film invites comparison with *Jassy*: Thorn, like Barney Hatton, is a dispossessed son, more in love with his family estates than with the heroine; Blanche, like Jassy, is a poor woman who uses her beauty to ensnare a rich man she does not love. But the love affair between Blanche and Philip is turbulent and intense, in marked contrast to the insipid romance between Jassy and Barney; and there are no sub-plots to distract from the main conflict. Superficially Blanche and Philip are similar – ambitious outsiders denied the position in society to which their talents entitle them. Blanche has no scruples about manipulating her cousin – she allows him to marry her but puts him firmly in his place when he tries to exert his authority. ('I have no intention Laurence, contrary to the fashion of our time, of being ordered about by my husband,' she tells him contemptuously.) Philip has no scruples about killing Laurence and his father when they try to drive him from the estate. But the deed done, their differences are revealed.

'Nothing and no one ever shall remain between me and the absolute possession of Clare [the Fury estates]. I thought you should have realized that by now,' a surprised Philip tells Blanche when she objects to the removal of Lavinia. Philip has described himself earlier as 'an unwanted tree that nothing can destroy'. His love for the land is something strong and solidly rooted. But it is not something Blanche shares. When it becomes clear to her that his love for her, or the death of an inoffensive child, mean little to him in comparison with his possession of the Fury estates, she becomes implacably hostile and sacrifices everything to thwart him.

In *So Evil My Love*, made for Paramount-British by Hal Wallis and Lewis Allen, Ann Todd plays a missionary's widow, Olivia Harwood, who, on a boat returning from Jamaica to England, nurses a typhoid victim, Mark Bellis (Ray Milland), back to health. Though he considers himself 'the best painter in London' his talent is unrecognized by the public and he makes a living as an art thief.

He takes a room in the respectable widow's house as a safe base from which to work. But Olivia too is not quite what she seems. Underneath her demure exterior lurks a passionate and ambitious nature. 'My life was to be rich and full and complete,' she tells Mark bitterly, and she recaptures her lost hopes by falling in love with him. He encourages her to resume an old friendship with Susan Courtney (Geraldine Fitzgerald), the wife of a leading barrister. Soon she has established complete dominance over her friend ('Poor Susan, so pampered, such a fool'), and at Mark's bidding attempts to blackmail her husband (Raymond Huntley). The scheme backfires, but Henry Courtney has a heart-attack, and by a judicious juggling of medicine bottles, Olivia gets his wife to finish him off. Before Susan can be executed for murder, however, Olivia discovers that Mark has been unfaithful to her. She kills him and gives herself up for both murders.

So Evil My Love doesn't have the visceral impact of *Blanche Fury* with its rich Technicolor photography, but what it loses in intensity it makes up for in sophistication as a psychological thriller. The performances of the four principals are remarkably good. Geraldine Fitzgerald, who had appeared in Norman Walker's *The Turn of the Tide* in 1935 before making her name in Hollywood, returned to play the silly inadequate woman who inadvertently murders the husband she hates and fears, with great aplomb. Raymond Huntley (the bank manager in *They Came to a City* and *Passport to Pimlico*) gives the best performance of his forty-year career as her stiff, sneering, impotent husband. The weakness and viciousness of these unhappy representatives of upper-middle-class respectability seem almost to excuse Mark and Olivia's bungled attempt at villainy.

'A missionary's widow, a painter before his time. We belong among the rejected,' Mark tells Olivia. But as with Blanche and Philip, similarities in social position conceal differences in temperament. Ray Milland, a British actor who had found success in Hollywood, had played a similar sort of gentleman of uncertain virtue in the American costume film *Kitty*. But though his treatment of pickpocket-turned-duchess Paulette Goddard had been caddish in the extreme, she had forgiven him when he showed he loved her and all had ended happily. In *So Evil My Love* he again realizes he loves the woman he has exploited and disregarded, but Olivia doesn't accept his change of heart and murders him.

Ann Todd's Olivia is a sympathetic and complex character. Unlike Blanche, she has resigned herself to failure in life, to becoming an obscure, repressed, unhappy woman. When Mark reawakens her suppressed hopes and ambitions she quickly learns to enjoy having power over others and she becomes bolder, more glamorous and more self-assertive. Her driving force, though, is her obsession with Mark, and when (mistakenly) she comes to see his love as false, she kills him and surrenders herself to the police.

Ann Todd had had an undistinguished film career in the thirties, acting the part of silly, upper-crust heroines in films like *The Return of Bulldog Drummond* and *The Squeaker*. Victor Saville gave her the opportunity to display her luminous intensity as the mad wife of Ralph Richardson in *South Riding*, seen in flashback riding her horse up the staircase of a country house; and as the long-suffering spouse of disgraced officer Clive Brook in *Action for Slander*. But her stage work was more interesting and it was her impressive performance in the lead role of *Lottie Dundass* in 1943 which persuaded the Boxes to cast her as the heroine of *The Seventh Veil*. For a brief period she managed to exploit her talents to the full – singing and dancing in *Gaiety George*, playing a fragile femme fatale in *Daybreak*, and developing her persona of a complex, vulnerable, enigmatic woman in *So Evil My Love* and three films by David Lean (whom she married), *The Passionate Friends* (1948), *Madeleine* (1950), and *The Sound Barrier* (1952).

In 1944, before she found fame in *The Seventh Veil*, she had appeared as Madeleine Smith in *The Rest is Silence*, a play based on a nineteenth-century murder case. Madeleine Smith was accused of poisoning her French lover, Emile L'Angelier. He had been blackmailing her and endangering her prospective marriage to a respectable Glasgow burgher. Scottish juries do not have to bring in a verdict of 'guilty' or 'not guilty' and with Madeleine Smith they decided the case against her was 'not proven'. In the play Madeleine is obviously a murderess. In David Lean's

26   Madeleine (Ann Todd) hiding her sensuality behind the prim reticence expected of a Victorian lady. *Madeleine* (1950).

film we are never quite sure of Madeleine's guilt. Discreetly objective, Lean builds up a picture of Madeleine's life which shows her capable of murder and justified in carrying it out, but we are shown no concrete evidence that she did poison her lover.

The men who surround her are universally unsympathetic – her father (Leslie Banks) is a fire-eating patriarch, her potential husband (Norman Wooland) a bore, her lover (Ivan Desny) a preening bully; after her arrest she has to endure the furious rantings of a male mob on her journey to the courtroom. But Ann Todd's Madeleine is no helpless victim of male oppression. She dares to expose and enjoy her sensuality, making love to the pretty but socially unacceptable L'Angelier and then exploiting the prim reticence expected of a Victorian lady to put off submission to marriage. Unlike Blanche Fury or Olivia Harwood, Madeleine's self-assertion goes unpunished. Though the evidence is against her, the jury find it impossible to believe that a woman who in appearance conforms to the norms of Victorian respectability could be capable of the flagrant violations of which she is accused. With an enigmatic smile she walks from the courtroom a free woman.

As a piece of film-making, *Madeleine* equals *Brief Encounter* and *The Passionate Friends* in sophistication, but its ambiguity and objectivity alienated both critics and audiences. Guy Green's attempt to light Ann Todd in as lush and elaborate a way as Sternberg presented Marlene Dietrich in the thirties was dismissed as a vulgar manifestation of Lean's affection for his new wife. As so much rests upon Madeleine's character though, it is entirely justified, and Ann Todd, with her sad, fragile face, responds with a performance full of nuance and subtlety.

There was obviously still a demand for costume pictures. Henry Hathaway's *The Black Rose*, Byron Haskin's *Treasure Island*, Hitchcock's *Under Capricorn*, made for American companies in Britain, were all commercial successes in 1950, and as the fifties progressed American historical spectacles like *Ivanhoe* and *Quentin Durward* were joined by cheap, popular Italian peplum epics. But British producers seemed to have lost the knack. However in the brief hiatus between losing its studios and being finally extinguished, Gainsborough managed one more costume picture, *So Long at the Fair*. Set in Paris at the time of the 1889 Exhibition and pairing Jean Simmons and Dirk Bogarde, the film inventively re-tells the old story of someone disappearing and their existence being denied by everyone they came into contact with. It was moderately successful but Terence Fisher, who co-directed it with Anthony Darnborough, could only find subsequent work directing 'B' films until 1957. Then, with *The Curse of Frankenstein*, he began a new cycle of sensational British costume pictures. With its theme of corruption and decay eating away at the heart of polite society, *So Long at the Fair* provides a fascinating link between the Gainsborough melodrama and Hammer horror cycles.

8   The Spiv Cycle

Not only my own mob, but all thieves were so prosperous that they adopted a sort of competitive spirit to display their wealth by dressing up their wives and girl-friends in as expensive jewellery and clothes as they could buy – from the black market of course. By common consent, Monday was regarded as truce day. It was the day after weekend working, when most screwing goes on anyway. It was the start of the week. Usually we all had bombs to spend, and we congregated in a club in Archer Street. What with all the villains in their genuine Savile Row suits and their wives and girl-friends wearing straight furs and clothes by the best West End dress-makers, that club looked like the Ascot of the underworld. (Billy Hill, *Boss of Britain's Underworld*, 1955)[1]

Wartime crime

Though the twenties and thirties were far from the crime-free golden age they sometimes appear in retrospect, the police remained firmly in control and were treated with a certain amount of deference. But the war shifted the balance of power in favour of the criminals. One might have expected that with the country in danger of invasion, differences would be forgotten in the common struggle and crime would diminish. The altruistic intentions of individual criminals, however, were more than counter-balanced by the new opportunities for crime which the war opened up. The war made even the most mundane commodities – from bacon to gardening tools, from stockings to safety pins – valuable, and thus significantly expanded the market for stolen goods. Rationing, which meant that those who had money were unable to buy as much as they wished, meant there was a steady supply of eager customers for black-market goods. The black-out and the shortage of policemen – the youngest and fittest of whom had been drafted into the army – meant that goods stored in warehouses, railway depots, docks, and factories were vulnerable to determined bands of thieves.

Officially the black market operated on a minor and unimportant level during the war. According to Lord Woolton, the Minister of Food:

The penalties for infringement of the food regulations were literally

ruinous . . . and the consequence was that [black marketeering] became
so perilous an occupation that few indeed dared embark on it . . . in spite
of all scarcity of supplies and the rigidity of rationing, there was little or
no black market in Britain.[2]

This is patently untrue. Though the rationing system never actually broke
down, it suffered severe haemorrhages. In 1944 14,000 ration books were
stolen from a government office in Hertfordshire, 600,000 supplementary
clothing coupons from a London employment exchange, and 100,000 ration
books from the Romford Food Office. The Romford ration books were
reckoned to be worth half a million pounds on the black market, making it
the most lucrative haul until the Great Train Robbery of 1963; the thieves
were never caught and none of the ration books were recovered.[3] By the
middle years of the war the underworld had become sufficiently aware of
the profits to be made from the black market to organize large-scale
depredations in the form of lorry hi-jacks and warehouse robberies. In one
theft alone 1,366,000 cigarettes were stolen.[4]

Very little of this sort of activity found its way into the films of the war
period. A Crown Film Unit short, *War and Order*, sought to reassure the
public that though the ranks of the police were depleted, gaps were being
filled by keen amateurs whose odd appearance (initially they had no
uniform and their status was insecure) did not necessarily mean that they
were ineffective. In 1942 the MOI commissioned from Gainsborough a
rather more forthright effort, *Partners in Crime*, written and directed by
Launder and Gilliat. The film astutely juxtaposes traditional crime – a
burglar stealing jewellery – with black marketeering. Robert Morley as
the judge is particularly harsh on the receiver, whom he holds responsible
for instigating the robbery:

> 'In the world in which we live, you prey upon our society. If it were not
> for you and similarly unpleasant specimens, thieves could not make a
> living. You create the demand, you offer the market, you are the real
> criminal.'

There was nothing particularly novel here, but Launder and Gilliat rudely
push their comparison to its logical conclusion, equating the housewife
going away with her 'under the counter' meat with this traditional villain
of the underworld. In a postscript Morley's judge sternly addresses a
cinema audience among whom sits the offending housewife (Irene Handl):

> 'Let you and others like you, whether you buy or sell, who have seized
> the opportunities offered by a war – which is a war for life – to line your
> pockets or your cupboards or your stomachs on the miserable and
> illogical plea that if I don't someone else will; let those of you consider
> just exactly who and what you are and whether you are any better than
> common criminals, parasites preying on the body of a community at
> war.'

This was hard-hitting stuff and the film had to weather complaints from the Master Butchers, the Pawnbrokers Association, Parliament, and Scotland Yard.[5]

Strict censorship had ensured that British crime films of the thirties kept a respectable distance from the sordid realities of the underworld. No reference to drugs or prostitution was permitted, scenes inside prisons were forbidden, depiction of criminals carrying out a crime in a realistic way was discouraged. Scripts such as *At the Blue Café, Soho Racket*, and *Murder in Soho*, which featured prostitutes and drug addicts, were given short shrift by the British Board of Film Censors, and it was only occasionally in low-budget thrillers by Arthur Woods and Walter Summers, comedies like *Convict 99* and *A Fire has been Arranged*, or in the fevered imaginings of Edgar Wallace, that one caught glimpses of an uncosy underworld. In the early days of the war there was a spate of comedy thrillers – Gordon Harker and Alastair Sim's *Inspector Hornleigh* films, Formby's *Spare A Copper*, Elsie and Doris Waters' *Gert and Daisy Clean Up*, Askey's *Back Room Boy* and *The Ghost Train* – which exploited

27 British cinema's first spiv. Ted Purvis (Stewart Granger) shows Tillie Colter (Joy Shelton) that there's more on offer than bombers and mash in wartime Britain. *Waterloo Road* (1945).

topical fears about the underworld supporting a fifth column, but their black marketeers and saboteurs tended to be almost interchangeable cardboard villains. Not until *The Bells Go Down*, in 1943, did Mervyn Johns' unrepentant little fireman thief show that the 'common criminal' could be a more complex and interesting figure.

The rise of the spiv

The idea of using a working-class setting which included members of the underworld, introduced in *The Bells Go Down*, was more fully developed in *Waterloo Road*. It was originally intended as a portmanteau film with six stories set in the Waterloo area, but Gilliat decided to concentrate on the one which interested him most, that of a soldier, Jim Colter (John Mills), who goes AWOL to check on his wife's fidelity. It was a common enough problem, with barely consummated marriages having to withstand the strain of prolonged separation and the temptations of new relationships. The threat to the Colter marriage comes not from a glamorous GI or an amorous factory foreman but from a small-time gangster, Ted Purvis (Stewart Granger). He is undoubtedly a no-good wastrel but he is able to offer Tilly Colter (Joy Shelton) a good time. As a cynical ex-girlfriend tells the vengeful husband:

> 'Okay, now let's see. Ted might have taken her to the dogs, only there's no dogs today, he might be at the pictures picking up a few 'ints from Victor Mature, or he might be at the Alcazar, jitterbugging. I think that about covers his war effort.'

The reviewers call him 'the local pin table king, racketeer and bully', 'an amorous artful dodger', 'the local bad lot', but with his flash suit, his loud tie, his easy money, and his dangerous charm he is easily recognized as the screen's first spiv.

David Hughes does his best to provide a definition of this peculiar forties phenomenon:

> A spiv, it was agreed, was a relentless opportunist who earned his living by not working, preferably within the law. In fact they were not averse to a touch of crime, provided it looked (and perhaps felt) like something else, just as they didn't mind driving lorries as long as their clothing vividly proclaimed that they weren't lorry-drivers. They never planned their opportunities, as criminals did; they merely took them, snatched and improvised, inventing as they went along.[6]

In its original sense of a 'contact man', the spiv was as much a specialist as a peterman (safebreaker) or a buyer (receiver), but during the war the spiv became a sort of popular generic term for someone who dressed flashily and had underworld connections. Thus it was used to describe anyone from a barrow-boy to a gang-leader. The style of dress came from the more fashion-conscious of the racing gangsters of the thirties – a sizeable contingent of whom were Jewish or Italian with friends or relations in the rag trade.

The pre-war underworld was almost a separate caste: they spoke a language so riddled with argot and rhyming slang that it was virtually impossible for an outsider to comprehend. Spivs were generally tactful, unobtrusive characters who through judicious lounging, gossiping, and gambling acquired a comprehensive knowledge of who was who and what was what, and operated as intermediaries between various members of the underworld. The war caused something of a dilution of this criminal subculture as large numbers of amateurs – deserters and petty racketeers – swelled the ranks of the underworld. More important, the black market transformed the links between the public and the criminal world and required a different sort of contact man – a recognizable type who could be approached in the same way that a prostitute was approached – with a certain confidence that illicit requests would not be rejected.

The wartime black market was much bigger than was officially admitted, but it was a secretive, disreputable affair. When the war ended people expected conditions to improve, an end to shortages and restrictions, the beginning of the good life for which they had fought. Austerity meant more rather than less restrictions and shortages, and for many members of the respectable classes this was too much to take.[7] The spiv, as the representative of the black market, became something of a popular hero, celebrated in the music-hall sketches of Arthur English and Sid Field, in the cartoons of Osbert Lancaster, in the gossip column of Arthur Helliwell in the *People*, and in a cycle of feature films.

David Hughes sees the spiv as a manifestation of working-class spontaneity:

> They were, more than trade union leaders, more than the politicians, the voice of the working class – busy undermining (oh, the irony) the future of their own people. The spivs, flashily displaying all the suppressed energies of the back streets, were an unconscious, dramatic protest, a form of civil disobedience that millions of English people found endearing.[8]

The seeming moderation of the post-war Labour government and its defeat in the 1951 Election has tended to obscure its quite remarkable achievements in steering the country away from economic disaster and, despite vociferous media hostility, retaining a high level of popular support. Richard Acland, the founder of the Common Wealth party, standing as a Labour candidate in a marginal by-election in Gravesend in

1947, won decisively with a slogan 'Tough Times: So What?'; and the 1951 Elections were very closely fought.

It is easy to glamorize the black market – to see it as a healthy protest against bureaucratic strangulation – but there was a very seedy side to it. Arthur Helliwell, whose close contact with the underworld brought progressive disillusion, declared that Britain had become 'the land of the well-greased palm':

> We've developed into a nation of bribers. Everyone is on the game, from the big shot who buys the motor dealer's wife a fur coat and gets delivery of a new car in a week, to the housewife who slips the fishmonger a packet of cigarettes after the queue has gone. The butcher runs a car, but he can't get much petrol – slip him a couple of coupons and get an extra steak for yourself. The coal merchant can't get eggs – send him a couple of dozen and there's a ton of coal in your cellar. A page of clothing coupons to your tobacconist – and there'll always be a packet of twenty under the counter for you.[9]

The pre-war underworld had been concerned either with semi-legal activities such as gambling, drugs, and prostitution, or with the traditional criminal pursuit of robbing the rich. It was not until the war years, with the growth of commodity crime and the black market, that the underworld became parasitic on the community at large. Except for a small minority of working-class people who participated in its profits, the black market inevitably benefited the rich more than the poor by subverting a rationing system designed to ensure equal shares for all. It is in this context that one has to understand the hostility of film critics – who like most intellectuals of the period were vaguely left-of-centre – to the cycle of spiv movies which flourished between 1945 and 1950.

Waterloo Road had been almost universally praised by the critics. According to Richard Winnington in the *News Chronicle*:

> besides being a melodrama of the London blitz, the film is a fascinating portrait of a London locality. No soft music, but the harsh rattle of trains over the viaduct, the clamour of the street market, the wailing of sirens and the crash of bombs accompany this war-time love story.[10]

There were some complaints that the film was 'plot-bound', that 'the chasing of villain by hero and of hero by military police too much dominates the normal human traffic of the mean streets', but it was after all 'the people that count, not the plot', and they were solidly working class.[11] Granger's South London spiv, whose actions were rather more honourable than his intentions, was accepted as an indigenous member of the working-class community and, apart from the occasional sneer about his accent, did not come in for criticism.

The next three attempts to penetrate the underworld provoked mixed reactions. British National's *Appointment with Crime* concerned a smash-and-grab thief's attempt to avenge himself on the gang who had left him in the lurch. For William Whitebait it was:

> a genuine attempt at the popular level to create an English counterpart to the Hollywood gangster legend. Its merits are a certain neatness and speed in execution, bits of slang, glimpses into the oddly assorted criminal world.[12]

Though other critics maintained that it was merely an imitation of a Hollywood gangster film and Dilys Powell complained of 'the taste of blood which I am beginning to find all pervasive in the contemporary cinema', the film was praised for its intelligent use of its limited resources and hopes were expressed that William Hartnell, the thin-lipped criminal hero, might become 'a British James Cagney'.

Dancing with Crime was made by John Paddy Carstairs (with the help of his three brothers Tony, Basil, and Roderick Keys) for Alliance at the Riverside studios at Hammersmith which Sydney Box had used before transferring to Gainsborough. Alliance had been set up as an Anglo-American enterprise by Rank and RKO but it seems to have quickly distanced itself from its parents and pursued a vigorously independent existence of its own. Carstairs, the maverick son of comedian Nelson Keys, had shown a propensity for murder mysteries as far back as 1933 when he had submitted a script to the BBFC titled *Riverside Morgue*, though he had subsequently been side-tracked into directing comedies such as *Spare a Copper* and *He Found a Star*.[13]

With Richard Attenborough as a taxi-driver whose best friend is found murdered in his taxi, and Sheila Sim (his wife in real life) as his show-girl fiancée, *Dancing with Crime* was inoffensive enough to attract mild praise For William Whitebait

> *Dancing with Crime* has an appealing London background of pubs, the palais, smash-and-grab, dance hostesses, and lone taxi-driving. A genial thug (whose name I didn't catch) dies much too soon; Richard Attenborough and Sheila Sim make a pretty pair of babes in the Soho-cum-Camberwell wood.[14]

The 'genial thug', whose name was Bill Rowbotham, was touted by some enthusiasts as another 'British James Cagney'. Being a realist, he changed his name to Bill Owen and became a reliable British character actor.

Black Memory, made at the very old, very small Bushey studio by Gilbert Church, Oswald Mitchell, and John Gilling, the team responsible for the post-war revival of Tod Slaughter in *The Curse of the Wraydons* (1946) and *The Greed of William Hart* (1948), was an old-fashioned melodrama with a very modern spiv (Michael Medwin) cast in the villain's role. Medwin, with his bland, cheerful good looks, normally played upper-class twits (Edward Courtney in *The Courtneys of Curzon Street*, Yellow Bingham in *Another Shore*, the Duke in *An Ideal Husband*), and obviously relished the opportunity of dropping his RADA accent. Whereas Granger's Ted Purvis was something of a joker, a big pussy cat at heart, Medwin's Johnny, living in a grubby fantasy world of pseudo-toughness, was altogether more dangerous and unpleasant. But *Black Memory* was the sort of film considered beneath critical contempt and Johnny escaped detection.

Ironically, the first 'spiv film' to draw a full barrage of criticism, *They Made Me a Fugitive* (also from Alliance), was directed by the architect of Ealing realism, Alberto Cavalcanti. Based on a slim expressionist novel by Jackson Budd, *A Convict Has Escaped*, the film marks a return to the best tradition of thirties crime thrillers, though the atmosphere is notably blacker.

Clem Morgan (Trevor Howard), a disillusioned ex-RAF officer who misses the excitement of war, is recruited by Narcy (Griffith Jones), a black marketeer who (several years before Spats Colombo in *Some Like It Hot*) uses an undertaker's business – the Valhalla Funeral Parlour – as a cover for his illicit operations. Everything proceeds smoothly towards establishing Narcissus and Morgan as 'the poor man's Fortnum and Masons' until Clem discovers that, unlike F. and M., their business deals in drugs as well as whisky, bacon, and nylons. When he objects, Narcy, who covets Clem's girlfriend, frames him and gets him sent down for fifteen years in Dartmoor. The core of the film concerns Clem's escape and subsequent revenge on his perfidious partner.

Howard gives a fine performance as the ex-serviceman who drifts disastrously into crime and he is ably partnered by fragile, brave, glamorous Sally Gray as the chorus girl who penetrates his armour of jaundiced cynicism. But the film is stolen by Griffith Jones as Narcy, the spiv-like gang-leader. Narcy is one of the great villains of British cinema – along with Ernest Thesiger's sinister sex murderer in *They Drive By Night* and Robert Newton's suave acid-bath murderer in *Obsession*. He is a truly rotten working-class hero and almost succeeds in proving that the civilized rules of society have not survived the war. He beats up his middle-class girlfriend when she tries to assert her class privileges and he treats Clem, the war-hero, with contempt as a 'noorotic ammerchoor'. If Clem finally succeeds in bringing him to justice, it is as a pawn of the police, and Narcy, the sole surviving witness to his innocence, dies, in the best traditions of villainy, blindly swearing that he is guilty.

Cavalcanti's skill at bringing the story to life was fully acknowledged by the critics, but he was condemned for using his talents on such a socially undesirable subject. Arthur Vesselo in *Sight and Sound*, saw the film as a symptom of a general malaise:

Cavalcanti's *They Made Me A Fugitive*, a tale of sordidness, corruption and violence almost unrelieved. It is too easy to claim that this film is merely a copy of the American gangster-model, or that it is defectively put together. In fact, the atmosphere of London's underworld is all too plausibly conveyed (let us hope it is no more than imagination); and as for technique, the film is horrifyingly well-made.

It is the mood which is wrong, a mood bearing all the emblems of post-war depression and spiritual confusion. The returned RAF officer, out of place in civilian life and straying into racketeering for an adventurous livelihood, is an unconscious personification of decent humanity demoralised by war and unfitted for peace, and his wild but helpless twistings and turnings in the dark trap in which he finds himself are sinister reflections of our own state today. From the hero's first step off the path, moral issues become clouded and the end obscure.[15]

This sort of serious moral questioning was valid enough in a society where

28 Narcy (Griffith Jones) cracks open a coffin with the boys from the Valhalla Funeral Parlour. *They Made Me a Fugitive* (1947).

29 Jewish wide-boys: Lou Hyams (John Slater) and his brother Morry (Sydney
    Tafler). *It Always Rains on Sunday* (1947).

enlightenment seemed threatened by the forces of darkness. But it easily
degenerated into prissiness and prurience. Paul Dehn, in the *Sunday
Chronicle,* complained that: 'Cavalcanti, one of our best directors of
documentary [has] turned suddenly bacteriologist – hauling muck to the
surface and smearing it, for our minute inspection, under glass.' Ewart
Hodgson in the *News of the World,* a self-confessed 'squeamish old
sourpuss', moaned: 'Such brutalities certainly made me a fugitive from
this film. Before the end I sought escape into the sunshine, desperately
longing to encounter again the simple sentimentalities of *The Courtneys of
Curzon Street.*' Nevertheless, *They Made Me a Fugitive* was one of the top
box-office pictures of 1947, and it was closely followed by two more 'spiv
films' – *It Always Rains on Sunday* and *Brighton Rock* – which were
equally popular.
    Cavalcanti could be written off as a good director who having left the
safety of Ealing had lost himself in the commercial jungle. After all he was

a foreigner. But when Ealing produced its own spiv film, *It Always Rains on Sunday*, directed by promising young director Robert Hamer and solidly situated within the realist tradition, critics were pulled up short in their knee-jerk response to the sordid and violent. Or rather, some of them were. C.A. Lejeune, though grudgingly admitting that the film had its merits, launched into a tirade against 'the adulation of the spiv and all that goes with him', exclaiming

> But what a dreary round of squalor it all is! What a one-eyed way of looking at life, deliberately shutting out of sight anything that might seem tender or happy or noble! I dare swear there is as much merriment and kindliness and beauty in the East End even on a Sunday, as anywhere else in the world of men and women. No picture can really catch the mood of London without giving a hint of these things. But *It Always Rains on Sunday* fixes its microscope on the microbes, shuts the other eye, and squints resolutely. The actors in this sordid drama never smile, save cynically, and how right, how very right, they are![16]

This sort of attitude was responsible for the film being banished from the respected canon of British realist films until it was resurrected in the early seventies.[17] But several contemporary critics were amused rather than horrified at the array of East End spivs, and won over completely by the concentration of realistic detail. Paul Dehn, in an ecstatic review headed 'SEE IT TWICE', wrote:

> What is extraordinary about this ordinary story is that the life, which the three principal actors have breathed into the three principal characters, has also been breathed by director Robert Hamer into their background. This bedroom lives because of its eiderdown; that front door, because of its post-war scaffolding; this wall because it has a cat on it; that newspaper, because the house-number has been pencilled on its top right-hand corner.[18]

Arthur Vesselo, judiciously summing things up in *Sight and Sound*, decided that the film's mild, chummy realism redeemed its unsavoury subject matter.

> Sordidness and depressionism certainly need no encouragement; but do they really sum the film up? It is a film with vitality, humour, and more than a gleam of atmospheric magic, as well as back-street squalor; and only the hasty will deny the naturalism of much of its visual and spoken language. Are we to reject these qualities in the context? There appears to be no good reason for doing so. If the total effect were of gloom and subterranean violence it would be another matter, but to object to a picture of Bethnal Green because it includes aspects of low life and dwells on some of them seems to be pushing the argument too far.[19]

The debate continued with the first spiv film of 1948, the Boulting brothers' *Brighton Rock*. Graham Greene's novel is part of a thirties cycle of novels set in the underworld, several of which – *There 'Aint No Justice* and *They Drive by Night* (by James Curtis); *Wide Boys Never Work* (Robert Westerby); *The Creaking Chair* (Laurence Meynell); *Ten-A-Penny People* (Jim Phelan); *Night and the City* (Gerald Kersh) – were made into films. Greene's concern with the metaphysical conflicts wracking his juvenile

30 Pinkie (Richard Attenborough) threatens Spicer (Wylie Watson) with his chiv. *Brighton Rock* (1947).

gang-leader Pinkie Brown gave *Brighton Rock* a serious appeal absent in the rest of the cycle, but the underworld setting is vividly realized.

At the beginning of the film we are informed that:

'Brighton today is a large, jolly, friendly seaside town in Sussex, exactly one hour's journey from London. But in the years between the two wars, behind the Regency terraces and crowded beaches, there was another Brighton of dark alleyways and festering slums. From here, the poison of crime and violence and gang warfare began to spread, until the challenge was taken up by the Police. This is a story of that other Brighton – now happily no more.'

Greene wrote his novel in 1937, shortly after 'the Battle of Lewes' brought the racetrack gangs to public attention. Lewes, which had a small but prosperous racecourse a few miles from Brighton, had been the setting for a serious challenge to the Darby Sabini Mob, which though unsuccessful had paved the way for the rise to dominance of Alf White's King's Cross Mob. Once the new gang was installed, violence was kept to a minimum. But, ironically, by 1947 the Whites were tottering and violence flared as Jack Spot took control. Despite the images of happy, laughing holiday-makers from which the film flashes back into the murky past, Brighton was not the safest of places to be in 1947, and the film-makers had no difficulty finding unsavoury-looking extras for the racecourse scenes.

The film, co-scripted by Greene and Terence Rattigan, stayed fairly close to Greene's story of a seventeen-year-old boy who succeeds to the leadership of a small protection gang, commits murder, marries a naive waitress to keep her quiet, and is hounded to an untimely end by a loud, cheery concert-party pierrot with a strongly defined sense of right and wrong. Several critics complained that the religious aspects of the novel had been swamped by the violence and the stern moral message lost in a sentimental ending. For Richard Winnington, its serious pretensions were 'not enough to lift the film out of the sadistic norm of British gangster films', and he came to the conclusion that it was 'an empty, unsatisfactory and careless piece of film-making'.[20] But there were others (including Lejeune) who were prepared to defend the film. Joan Lester in *Reynold's News* took up an attitude exactly opposite to that of Winnington: 'this well-made, excellently acted film with the imprint of Boulting sincerity, is not just one more story of the underworld. It is a serious analysis of spivery.'[21] Greene himself stepped into the fray to protest at the unfairness of the *Daily Mirror* reviewer who had labelled the film 'false, cheap, nasty sensationalism' while continuing to uphold the virtues of the book on which it was based. However, *Brighton Rock* was popular with the public and Greene was encouraged to return to underworld themes – though this time on the larger stage of war-ravaged Europe – in *The Third Man*.

Wide boys and good-time girls

Meanwhile more mundane spiv films continued to appear. *Good Time Girl* had gone into production at the same time as *It Always Rains on Sunday*, early in 1947, though because of censorship difficulties it was not released until May 1948. Both films were based on novels by Arthur La Bern which offered a selection of spivish characters who gravitated around a central story. In *Night Darkens the Street/Good Time Girl* it was that of a girl's slide into dangerous company and murder; in *It Always Rains on Sunday*, that of an escaped convict's attempt to evade the law, and his relationship with his ex-lover, Rose Sandigate, who gives him shelter.

Good Time Girl's censorship problems were partly due to the controversial nature of the book – its criticism of the Approved School system, its vitriol-throwing racing gangsters – and partly due to the fact that Gainsborough treated its subject in a melodramatic style which was looked on less favourably than the meticulous realism aimed for in its Ealing counterpart. Surprisingly, no one compared *Good Time Girl* with *It Always Rains on Sunday*, though their similarities and differences are revealing. La Bern's characters would be able to stroll from one of his books into the other. Not so the characters in the films. Mr Sandigate (Edward Chapman) is a finely observed portrait of working-class respectability with his favourite chair, his regular hours in the local pub, and his basic requirement of pipe, slippers, and three meals a day; Mr Watkins (George Carney in his last role), who alternates between drunken brutality and shame-faced servility comes straight out of a Victorian melodrama. Syd and Lou Hyams – the Jewish wide boys who tempt the Sandigate girls with pretty things and illicit pleasures – would not be out of place in a television soap opera like *East Enders*; Peter Glenville's snivelling, vicious Jimmy Rosso and Griffith Jones' Danny 'I'm a rough boy' Martin, are the stuff of nightmares.

This does something to explain the current disparity in the critical standing of the two films – *It Always Rains* is now regarded as a landmark on the route to kitchen-sink realism, *Good Time Girl* is rarely seen and written about only disparagingly. Yet the harsh, cold, dangerous world of *Good Time Girl* where mistakes have to be paid for heavily, often in blood, and friendship suddenly turns to violence, is as evocative and as real as the tough, cheerful, and fundamentally cosy community of *It Always Rains on Sunday*.

Four more spiv movies were released in 1948: *Night Beat, The Flamingo Affair, A Gunman Has Escaped*, and *Noose*, though arguably one could also include Sidney Gilliat's *London Belongs To Me*. The hero/villain of Norman Collins' novel, Percy Boon, is undoubtedly a spiv in the David Hughes sense of a small-time dabbler in crime, but the novel and the film are set in the supposedly spiv-free time of 1938. Percy works in that hot-bed of spivery, the second-hand car trade and, in his purple suit and snap-brimmed trilby, certainly dresses like a spiv. In Sidney Gilliat's film he is played by Richard Attenborough who had already established his spivish credentials in *Brighton Rock*. In marked contrast to the demonic Pinkie, though, Percy is a weak and incompetent character and Atten-borough, reduced to ineffectual whining, is dwarfed by the gallery of eccentrics – particularly Alastair Sim's Mr Squales – who surround him in the seedy Kennington lodging-house where most of the action takes place. In its depiction of a low-life milieu, there are similarities with the novels of Robert Westerby and Arthur La Bern, but Collins' real mentor is Dickens and there is a sentimentality about the book – which Gilliat embraces wholeheartedly in the film – which puts it outside the spiv cycle.

The Flamingo Affair and *A Gunman Has Escaped* have disappeared from circulation, and *Night Beat* is a disappointingly shabby affair. The film is centred around two newly demobilized commandoes, Don (Hector Ross) and Andy (Ronald Howard), who, disillusioned by the lack of opportunities for returning heroes, decide to join the police force. Their initial impression of police life – cold feet and humiliation at the hands of petty criminals – is not encouraging; but Don perseveres and is transferred to the CID. Andy, the less steady of the two, falls under the influence of king spiv Felix Fenton (Maxwell Reed), who has designs on his sister Julie (Anne Crawford). Disgrace and dismissal follow, and Don is given the unpleasant task of arresting his wartime pal. When Andy is sent down for three months, Julie, who had planned to marry Don, marries Felix instead. The film ends rather messily with Felix murdered by a dance-hall singer whom he had cast aside and both Julie and Andy accused of the murder.

The script, by Guy Morgan, a *Daily Express* journalist who had written an interesting and useful book about the Granada cinema chain during the war (*Red Roses Every Night*), introduces new elements into the spiv cycle, but the plot is clichéd and the dialogue weak. A talented young cast struggle valiantly to bring their characters to life, but without much success. The film was directed by Harold Huth, a Gainsborough producer not noted for his handling of actors – though he himself had acted in the thirties. Christine Norden, as the dance-hall singer ('Miss Jacqueline Delaney – free, white and twenty-one'), assumes a tawdry, worldly-wise glamour which makes Diana Dors and Jean Kent look positively virginal; and ex-barrow-boy Maxwell Reed certainly looks the part of the working-class wide boy made good. But their performances never quite gell. Michael Medwin is more successful in a neat little cameo as a pick-pocket and Sid James is convincingly ugly as 'Nightlife' Nixon, but it is a disappointing film.

31 Bar Norman (Nigel Patrick) presses flowers and his unwelcome attentions on Linda Medbury (Carole Landis). *Noose* (1948).

Noose – based on a popular play by Richard Llewellyn – was more successful. Linda Medbury (Carole Landis), an American fashion journalist seconded to a British newspaper to write about Dior's New Look, launches on a crusade against the black market and vice racketeer 'Knucksie' Sugiani. She enlists the help of her English fiancé, sports writer and ex-commando Jumbo Hoyle (Derek Farr), who in turn recruits a tough bunch of taxi-drivers and market porters to take the law into their own hands and smash Sugiani's criminal empire.

This might seem an unlikely subject for the author of the best-selling mining saga *How Green Was My Valley*, but Llewellyn had submitted a very similar script, *Murder in Soho*, to the British Board of Film Censors in 1937. Sugiani is called Luciani and deals exclusively with vice; Medbury is called Dora and is a whore rather than a journalist; Jumbo is called Squeaks and is a bruiser instead of a sports writer, but the story is virtually the same. In 1937 it had provoked strong words and been decisively rejected but by 1948 the censors had grown slightly more tolerant and with certain changes they reluctantly approved it.

Noose is rather more humorous and stylized than most of the spiv films, though there were some critics who failed to see the joke. C.A. Lejeune was left 'with a strong feeling of nausea' but *The Times* reviewer who observed that 'In its own somewhat shop-soiled, black market comedy thriller convention *Noose* does well enough', was more typical.

Carole Landis was obviously not at her best – she committed suicide before the film was released – and her performance is disappointingly artificial. But her weakness doesn't seriously mar the film, she serves as something of a clothes-horse, displaying all the fashions of the New Look while inveighing against the triviality of fashion-writing at a time when women are being exploited by racketeers. And she is surrounded by an experienced and competent cast, directed with considerable verve by Edmond T. Greville.

The other Hollywood import, Joseph Calleia, is excellent as Sugiani 'the nastiest thug in Europe' and the presence of old stalwarts like Edward Rigby, John Salew, and Hay Petrie – who like Landis was dead by the time the film reached the screen – ensured that his underworld operation was no pale reflection of Hollywood/Chicago. The goodies are less impressive: Derek Farr makes Jumbo into something of a *Boy's Own* hero and Stanley Holloway is not a very convincing policeman. Certainly there is nobody on the right side of the law to measure up to Nigel Patrick's Bar Norman. As Sugiani's business manager he is the brains behind the operation. With his long camel-hair coat, pencil-thin moustache, non-stop patter, and quaintly phrased threats, he is the quintessential up-market spiv.

Noose was almost the last of this cycle of spiv films to feature a charismatic underworld figure. In 1949 only three films were released which could possibly be categorized as spiv films. *Man on the Run* (Derek Farr again) was a second feature, competently directed by Lawrence Huntington, about a deserter who gets involved with professional gunmen. *The Adventures of PC 49*, one of Hammer's early efforts, was equally low-budget. The hapless PC 49 (Hugh Latimer) disguises himself as a spiv in order to penetrate the Rossini gang, and spends a good deal of his time in Ma Brady's transport café, a hot-bed of vice and corruption. The dialogue – a peculiar mixture of Americanisms, underworld argot, and schoolboy slang – is racy, the action fast, and the spivs vicious and villainous.

The Third Man – a productive collaboration between Graham Greene and Carol Reed – was a more sophisticated operation. Harry Lime, the international racketeer who fakes his own death in order to continue his nefarious activities in anonymity, might seem worlds away from the tea and Chianti swigging spivs pursued by PC 49, but the nearest real-life equivalent to Lime, Max Intrator, was regarded as a sort of super spiv at the time.

Throughout 1947 he figured regularly in *The Times*, assisting unpatriotic persons such as Fred Cannell, gown manufacturer of Ealing, Sassoon Ezra of Hyde Park Mansions, and Commander Archibald Boyd Russell overcome the currency restrictions imposed by the Labour government which would have deprived them of their holidays in the South of France and other Continental playgrounds. Max was also concerned with shipping arms to Palestine in preparation for the conflagration which would soon break out there. Harry Lime was more straightforwardly evil, peddling drugs and precious medical supplies in an impoverished and battered Europe, but he shares Max's ability to fascinate as he repels.

The film was shot on location in Vienna, but in a very stylized, non-realist way by the Australian-born cameraman Robert Krasker who had been responsible for *Brief Encounter* and *Odd Man Out*. Starting from an idea rather than an existing novel, Greene was able to respond flexibly to the demands of director Carol Reed. Reed in turn was a powerful enough figure to withstand pressure from his two notoriously interfering producers, Alexander Korda and David Selznick. Greene's characters remain insistently enigmatic and Reed's idiosyncratic touches – the zither music, the audacious ending – succeed splendidly.

Reed, an actor's director, elicits superb performances from his international cast – Alida Valli as the mysterious, vulnerable Anna; Joseph Cotten as the fallible Holly Martins; Trevor Howard as the brittle, stiff-upper-lip British officer; Welles, larger than life, enticingly corrupt as Harry Lime – and there is none of the blandness which afflicts so many Anglo-American productions. In a bad year for British films, *The Third Man* was an overwhelming success. Reed was nominated for an Oscar, Krasker won one for Best Photography; and in Britain the film was the top box-office attraction of the year.

The success of *The Third Man* encouraged Twentieth Century-Fox to try their hand at an up-market spiv movie, generously employing Jules Dassin, who was on the run from McCarthyism, to direct *Night and the City* in London. Dassin was well-respected for his slice-of-life crime dramas *Brute Force*, *The Naked City*, *and Thieves Highway*, and might have expected sympathetic treatment from the English critics of his attempt to apply the same semi-documentary techniques to a story of the London underworld. Unfortunately this was not to be.

The Third Man, set in Vienna and shot in a pretentiously artistic way, could be seen as something more profound than a thriller. *Night and the City*, with Richard Widmark as a small-time promoter up against underworld boss Herbert Lom, was unmistakably a spiv movie, and it provoked a string of petulant, small-minded, unfair reviews. Dilys Powell came to the conclusion that:

Jules Dassin has given us a conglomeration of night-clubs, thieves kitchens, all-in wrestling and river-rats, the never-never city which does service in the cinema for any capital. . . . Except for its camerawork it is squalid and brutish: and one stretches with relief when Mr Widmark, having trotted non-stop from Waterloo to Hammersmith, runs into the Strangler and, with a pardonable gurgle, allows himself to be dropped in the Thames. *Night and the City* will presumably pass for a British film. It is about as British as Sing-Sing; and it will do the British cinema nothing but harm.[22]

In fact Dassin brings more of London to the screen than any film before the 'Swinging London' films of the sixties, and the liberties he takes with geography are insignificant compared to Reed's treatment of Belfast and Vienna.

Harry Fabian, the hero of Gerald Kersh's novel on which the film is based, is a tiresome little rat whose braggadocio reaps its well-deserved reward in an underworld where deeds count more than words. Widmark manages to transform him into something resembling a tragic hero: he has ideas, he has brains, but he over-reaches himself and is hounded to his doom.

Gene Tierney's role as Harry's long-suffering girlfriend is weak and Mike Mazurki, as The Strangler, is required to do little more than grunt and throw people about. But the British actors excel themselves. Maureen Delany as a waterfront black marketeer and Gibb McLaughlin as a forger do a neat, clean job in stealing scenes from the star. Francis L. Sullivan gives a sad and moving performance as the lugubrious Phil Nosseros – gross and flabby and repulsive in his huge shabby suit. Herbert Lom isn't quite frightening enough to be boss of the underworld, but with his Italianate chiv-man and bespectacled crooked solicitor at least he looks the part. Dassin's picture of the London underworld may be no more accurate than anyone else's but at least it is original and coherent and believable, and the film conveys a marvellously evocative impression of London at night.

The film fared badly at the box-office and, as hostile criticism had not harmed the commercial prospects of earlier spiv films, this indicates that public tastes were changing, an impression reinforced by the huge success afforded Dearden and Relph's *The Blue Lamp*.

Order is restored

In the British tradition of crime-writing policemen tended to play second fiddle to gifted amateur detectives. Edgar Wallace cast an aura of glamour and excitement around the Flying Squad and by the late forties real-life Scotland Yard detectives – Robert Fabian, Ted Greeno, John 'Charlie Artful' Capstick – had acquired a certain public prestige. But the uniformed policeman remained a figure of fun, if not contempt.

32   Helen (Googie Withers) prepares to walk out on Phil Nosseros (Francis L. Sullivan), the husband she finds so repulsive. *Night and the City* (1950).

In most thirties films policemen, when not being ridiculed, were solid but rather stupid. The spiv cycle introduced a new breed of cynical detectives, aware of their limited resources and the difficulties involved in bringing slippery, well-heeled spivs to justice. *Night Beat* attempted to go a step further and show the problems of the Bobby on the beat. It was not very successful but old Fred Groves, who persuades Don and Andy to join the force, offers an attractive picture of life as a village copper:

> 'I never had much money but there's not many as I'd change my lot with. I've three villages in my section. I've me marrows and me roses and four thousand folk big and small to count as friends. That may sound soft to you youngsters, but on that score I reckon myself a rich man.'

The subsequent presentation of police life as cold, wet, and boring seemed to show that city coppers didn't have it so idyllic. But at a time when most people were getting as sick of racketeering and the black market as they were of rationing and austerity, the climate was right for a favourable reassessment of the forces of law and order.

When the Gainsborough studios were closed down in 1949 and Muriel Box's scenario department disbanded, a script by Ted Willis about police life was passed on to Michael Balcon at Ealing. T. E. B. Clarke, Ealing's top scriptwriter, had worked as an auxiliary policeman during the war and welcomed the opportunity of drawing on his experiences, and Balcon was able to secure the full co-operation of the Metropolitan Police. A story was worked out which would cover some of the issues causing concern – the use of firearms in robberies, violence against policemen, and the problem of attracting suitable recruits to the police now that there were more attractive jobs on offer.

The film juxtaposes the lives of two young men: Andy Mitchell (Jimmy Hanley), who joins the police and is assigned to a beat in Paddington Green; and Tom Riley (Dirk Bogarde), an ambitious thief who robs a cinema in the Edgeware Road. In terms of box-office appeal Bogarde wins hands down over the ungainly Hanley. But the forces of law and order are shored up by Jack Warner, who, as the friendly old copper George Dixon, acts as Mitchell's mentor.

Warner was one of the most popular character actors of the period. He was flexible enough to play villains – the leader of a gang of crooks in *Hue and Cry*, a treacherous double agent in *Against the Wind*, an escaped convict in *My Brother's Keeper* – but it was the solid, sensible Cockney character he had created in Dearden's *The Captive Heart* that he was most closely identified with. He reappeared in Gainsborough's *Holiday Camp* and then in a series of spin-off films built around his fictional family the Huggetts (with Hanley as his son-in-law). Warner had played a detective in *It Always Rains on Sunday*, but PC George Dixon was essentially Joe Huggett in a policeman's uniform.

The murder of this familiar and well-loved figure half-way through the film must have had great dramatic impact on contemporary audiences – as it does for anyone to whom Dixon of Dock Green's 'Evenin' all' was a regular weekly event – and weights sympathy heavily in favour of the police. But if the policeman is the hero of *The Blue Lamp* it is not the 'spiv' who is the villain. From the very beginning of the film to its climax in that palace of popular spivvery, the White City Stadium, the film is at pains to distance the amateurish young thugs, who need to use guns to make up for their incompetence, from the real underworld professionals. Bogarde's Tom Riley is like Attenborough's Pinkie in terms of his age and appearance and ambivalence towards women. But Pinkie is a phenomenon – a boy so cold and ruthless that older men fall under his sway. He operates entirely within the ethos of the underworld. Riley is a 'juvenile delinquent' whom the professionals despise and betray.

In *Hue and Cry* the schoolboys of London converge from all corners of the city to attack the villains. In *Noose* the porters of Billingsgate, Smithfield, and Covent Garden smash up the crooked enterprises of racketeer Sugiani. In *The Blue Lamp* the underworld joins forces with the police to trap the young killer who has broken rules observed on both sides of the law. Charles Barr writes perceptively about T.E.B. Clarke's 'daydream of universal benevolence'. But the practice of killing policemen was frowned upon by professional criminals for the unsentimental reason that it jeopardized the 'live and let live' attitude it was in their interest to maintain.

From the late forties to the mid-fifties the crime rate actually fell. The police force was built up to its pre-war strength and the problems caused by deserters and foreign soldiers gradually disappeared. Full employment and the promise of affluence meant that a career in crime became less of a necessity for the poor. And conflict within the underworld was almost eliminated as Jack Spot and Billy Hill entered upon an uneasy alliance and kept order in an underworld where there was plenty to go round for everyone.

As the black market shrank, relations between criminals and the public were once again reduced to a minimum and the underworld became more deeply shrouded in obscurity. The spiv became a figure of fun – George Cole's Flash Harry in the *St Trinians* films – and British crime films sank back into the netherworld of the second feature.

9   Morbid Burrowings

Soft voices call from dark doorways as you pass, furtive figures loom out of the shadows, hands pluck at your sleeve. The return of the blackout seems to have boosted this nasty business. . . . Many of the nastier dives are gateways to all kinds of vice, from gambling to 'queer' erotic parties and private 'blue' kinemas where a seat costs you a fiver. (Arthur Helliwell, *People* March, 1947)[1]

In his review of *They Made Me a Fugitive*, Arthur Vesselo launched into a general attack on films which, instead of celebrating the new Jerusalem that was being built in Britain, indulged in 'morbid burrowings' similar to those of the German Expressionist films of the twenties which were thought to have presaged the coming of Fascism. Despite their English subject matter, Vesselo thought they

> have nevertheless an unpleasant undertone, a parade of frustrated violence, an inversion and disordering of moral values, a groping into the grimier recesses of the mind, which are unhealthy symptoms of the same kind of illness.[2]

This hostility was not confined to the critical establishment. Herbert Wilcox complained that the public 'do not want sadism, abnormality and psycho-analysis', and exhorted his fellow film-makers to make 'what one might call open pictures, happy unclouded pictures'.[3] Wilcox's films were not so happy and unclouded as he pretends, and the public showed no sign of losing its interest in the darker side of life. But film-makers did turn away from morbid themes and fifties British cinema is dominated by comedies and conventionalized war films until the eruption of horror and realism towards the end of the decade.

In America the morbid thrillers of the forties and early fifties have attracted a great deal of critical interest as 'film noir'. There have been attempts to excavate their roots, define their visual appeal, examine their thematic concerns, interrogate their treatment of women and sex, explain their relationship to American society. Despite the efforts of a handful of discerning scavengers, the British equivalent has been consigned to the dustbin of history.[4] American film noir is generally supposed to have been caused by a combination of post-war social malaise – in particular a disruption of the sexual status quo by women doing war-work and men being posted overseas – and the expressionist techniques favoured by expatriate mid-European directors and cameramen whose ranks had been swollen with refugees from the Nazis. It is a wide and amorphous field, but there are common characteristics. Most films noirs are set in a big American city, much of the action takes place at night, and interiors and daytime scenes are given a sense of foreboding and menace by the use of mirrors and shadows. The hero is generally beset by temptations: the prospect of easy money and the love of a beautiful but enigmatic woman, whose evil is often contrasted with that of a less glamorous but more wholesome woman. The resolution of the plot often involves the death of this femme fatale and sometimes that of the hero as well. Even those films with a happy ending, where the enigmatic woman turns out to be honest and steadfast – *Laura*, *The Big Sleep*, *The Blue Dahlia* – the general ambience of the film is one of world-weary cynicism.

The British 'morbid' films are much more diffuse and it is virtually impossible to contain them within a single genre. Here I have concentrated on murder mysteries and two smaller groups of films which feature a 'man on the run' or a man who has been physically or mentally damaged by the war. But they share an interest in psychological disturbance, in sex, violence, the exotic, and the unusual with many of the films dealt with in the previous three chapters.

Shadows are my friends

There was a strong tradition of the macabre in British cinema. As early as 1905 that morbid interest of the British public in murder, which was responsible for selling so many Sunday newspapers, manifested itself in two versions of the life and crimes of charismatic murderer Charles Peace.[5] The British Board of Film Censors, established two years later, ruled against the depiction of 'persons who have obtained notoriety in court proceedings', but allowed in older, fictionalized villains like Spring-Heeled Jack, Sweeney Todd, Jack the Ripper, and Burke and Hare the bodysnatchers. They were already the backbone of popular stage melodrama and were transferred without much refinement to the screen.

The hostility of the censors to anything which came close to real-life crime encouraged film-makers to introduce exotic or comic elements into their crime stories which led them away from censorial disapproval into the realm of the fantastic. Though British cinema had no distinct horror genre until Hammer re-invented Frankenstein in the fifties, bizarre and horrific strands appeared in British crime films and murder mysteries. Films based on Edgar Wallace novels, such as *The Frightened Lady*, *The Terror*, and *The Dark Eyes of London*, made the most of Wallace's penchant for mad criminal masterminds with sinister and often deformed helpmates.

Films aiming at greater realism, like *Sabotage, They Drive by Night*, and *A Window in London* displayed a murky, seedy world where violence is always unpredictably present.

During the war appetites for the macabre were no doubt satisfied to some extent by real events, but they were still fed by a regular diet of low-budget thrillers from Gainsborough (*Alibi, They Came by Night*, the *Inspector Hornleigh* films); British National, (*The Dummy Talks, Candles at Nine, The Trojan Brothers, Murder in Reverse*); and, above all, Welwyn (*Poison Pen, Traitor Spy, The Door with Seven Locks, East of Piccadilly, This Man Is Dangerous, The Night Has Eyes*). Initially there was little to distinguish the wartime films from their thirties predecessors, but gradually bridges were built between the nightmare world they inhabited and the drab reality of wartime Britain. The process can be clearly seen in a comparison between two films made at Welwyn – *The Door with Seven Locks*, directed by Norman Lee in 1940, and *The Night Has Eyes* directed by Leslie Arliss in 1942.

The Door with Seven Locks, based on an Edgar Wallace story, has a suitably bizarre villain, Dr Manetta (Leslie Banks), with an eye-patch, a pet monkey, and an obsession with instruments of torture (his ancestor was a Grand Inquisitor). He almost ensnares the plucky heroine (Lilli Palmer), but she is rescued by silly-ass detective Dick Martin (Romilly Lunge). The ingredients are similar in *The Night Has Eyes*. There is, again, a sinister man with a pet monkey (Wilfrid Lawson), an innocent but intrepid heroine (Joyce Howard), and an innocuous young man with protective feelings towards her (John Fernald). But the story is complicated by the presence of a misanthropic and darkly handsome man (James Mason) whose war wounds may or may not have turned him into a murderous psychopath.

Two women teachers, Marion and Doris (Joyce Howard and Tucker McGuire), spend their holiday hiking on the Yorkshire Moors, following in the footsteps of a colleague who mysteriously disappeared a year earlier. Lost in the mist and rain, they seek shelter in an isolated house and are then marooned there by flood-water. Their host, Stephen (James Mason), a pianist and composer who has been wounded while fighting with the Republicans in the Spanish Civil War, begrudges their presence, but Marion breaks through his barriers of bitterness and reserve and they fall in love.

It is difficult at this point to know whether Stephen is hero or villain. His attitude to Marion, though sincere, appears to be distinctly sadistic. He humiliates her, he humps her around like a sack of potatoes, he dresses her up in his grandmother's clothes, and he persistently insults her. When she declares her love for him and her willingness to help him, he angrily replies:

'You're getting no unctuous glow out of saving me. You fool! You think I'd turn my back on real women, lovely women, to change it all for a sentimental little school-marm. . . . What've you got? No beauty. No brains. Just a lot of half-digested ideas about life picked up in a teachers' common room.'

Pre-war heroines had not had to suffer such abuse, even in Hitchcock films, and Marion has already met a conventional chinless hero figure who admires her and disapproves of her 'morbid' insistence on going out on the moors. But, as she admits to Stephen, she wants rather more from a relationship than conventional chumminess: 'I've met men whose characters I've liked, whose brains I admired, but who meant nothing to me. I've met others, brainless and brutal you know . . .' and Stephen, nodding understandingly, says, 'Yes, I know, the queer fascination with cruelty.'

What Shelley calls 'the tempestuous loveliness of terror' had been drawn on heavily by English Gothic literature but had been kept at bay by the censors in British films. During the war the barriers began to break down as more meaningful relationships were established between murderers and victims. As it turns out, in *The Night Has Eyes*, Stephen is an innocent victim of his housekeeper (Mary Clare) and handyman (Wilfrid Lawson), and he is able to save the sorely put-upon Marion from being thrown into the quicksands. But his sadistic, ambivalent character was to reappear in two of the key films of the forties, *The Man in Grey* and *The Seventh Veil*.

Though art director Duncan Sutherland and cameraman Gunther Krampf work wonders with their limited resources and Arliss directs with considerable flair, *The Night Has Eyes* is still very much confined within its low-budget, 'B' movie limitations. Ealing's *Dead of Night*, by contrast, is something of a prestige production with contributions from all of Ealing's regular directors except for Harry Watt who was in Australia, and Charles Frend who had to drop out because of illness. *The Monthly Film Bulletin* calls it 'the smoothest film yet to come from an English studio'.

Death became an everyday experience for most people during the war and it is not surprising that there should have been an upsurge of interest in spiritualism and the supernatural. This movement found a limited expression in films like Gainsborough's *A Place of One's Own*, British National's *Latin Quarter*, Ealing's *The Halfway House*, and after the war in Lance Comfort's *Daughter of Darkness* (1947) and Anthony Pelissier's *The Rocking Horse Winner* (1949), but it is most satisfactorily explored in *Dead of Night*, one of the top box-office pictures of 1945 and one of the few 'non-realist' films to have found favour with the critics.

As with an earlier Ealing effort, *Halfway House*, *Dead of Night* consists of a series of discrete episodes held together by a loose linking story. An architect, Walter Craig (Mervyn Johns), arrives at a Kent country house and meets a group of people he is shocked to realize he has already met in a recurring dream. Though he cannot remember what happens in his nightmare, he knows it is something terrible and makes determined attempts to break the spell cast over him. All of the guests, with the exception of a pompous, pedantic psychiatrist, Dr Van Straaten (Frederick Valk), are sympathetic to Walter's plight and, though not unduly worried, accept that something supernatural is at play. Five of them, including Dr Van Straaten, tell a story of their own experience of an inexplicably uncanny event, and though Van Straaten attempts to provide rational explanations, the party's faith in the supernatural is confirmed rather than shaken. After the last tale is told, events move rapidly towards their macabre denouement. Lighting, perspective, reason, become increasingly distorted until it becomes apparent we are in Walter's nightmare. He is awoken by a telephone call from someone with a country house in Kent who needs architectural advice, and we see him making his way to the house of horror where his dream will begin again.

Brain damage

Despite the blitz, the people of the British Isles probably emerged saner from the Second World War than they had from the First. Blitz victims suffered from shock, tiredness, and profound discomfort even when they escaped physical injury. But the danger was shared by all and, for some people at least, it gave them the opportunity to use talents and energies which had hitherto lain dormant. Nella Last, a fifty-one-year-old Cumbrian housewife, underwent something of a transformation:

> 'When I contrast the rather retiring woman who had such headaches, and used to lie down so many afternoons, with the woman of today who can keep on and *will not think*, who coaxes pennies where once she would have *died* rather than ask favours, who uses too bright lipstick and on dim days makes the corners turn up when lips will not keep smiling . . .'[6]

For those in the armed services, there were woundings, mutilations, and the horrific burns suffered by airforcemen who survived their planes crashing. But there was nothing to compare with the nightmare of trench warfare in the 1914–18 War.

Men damaged by the war figured quite frequently in American film noir: Robert Ryan as an anti-semitic psychopath in *Crossfire*, William Bendix with the metal plate in his head which makes him hear 'monkey music' wherever he goes in *The Blue Dahlia*, for example. In Britain they tended

33 Sammy Rice (David Farrar) with his tin foot. Knucksie (Sid James) and Susan (Kathleen Byron) offer moral support, but what he really wants is whisky. *The Small Back Room* (1949).

to turn up less predictably. Nigel Patrick plays a man supposed to be a dead hero but who in fact deserted and became a black marketeer in *Silent Dust*. Deserters feature in *Man on the Run* and *Good Time Girl*. Dennis Webb in *The Flamingo Affair*, Trevor Howard in *They Made Me a Fugitive*, Ronald Howard in *Night Beat*, all have problems adjusting to civilian life, as does David Farrar with his German wife in *Frieda*. David Niven in *A Matter of Life and Death* is brain-damaged by his parachute-less drop into the sea, but his visions appear plausible enough to us, and it is difficult to regard him as psychologically disturbed. More obviously war-damaged protagonists appear in two films based on novels by Nigel Balchin, *The Small Back Room*, Powell and Pressburger's first film after leaving the Rank Organization, and *Mine Own Executioner*, directed by Anthony Kimmins and scripted by Balchin himself.

Both qualify as morbid films in their lighting style and general atmosphere, though *The Small Back Room* has no femme fatale and, except for an expressionist sequence with a giant whisky bottle, is one of Powell and Pressburger's most restrained films (and the only one between 1947 and 1956 not made in colour). They return again to the blacked-out London of *Contraband* but this time they have a much more exacting and sophisticated story to tell. Sammy Rice (David Farrar), a civilian explosives expert, tries not to get involved in the office politics which plague government-funded research units, a task made more difficult by the fact that the woman he is secretly engaged to, Susan (Kathleen Byron), is personal assistant to the unit's ambitious political attaché (Jack Hawkins). Life for Sammy is further problematized by the fact that he has had his right foot blown off and the metal replacement causes him constant pain which is only satisfactorily relieved by whisky. After a traumatic night when he falls out with Susan and gets very drunk, he is called to offer advice on a pair of bombs of a type which have been causing unexploded bomb units particular trouble. By the time he arrives a young officer has already blown himself to pieces trying to defuse one of the bombs. Sammy re-establishes his self-respect by successfully defusing the other one. When he returns, he finds that Susan still loves him and that he is to be offered his own research unit. It sounds like a happy ending, but it is a very long haul through a dark tunnel to get to it.

The Small Back Room was well received by the critics, though less commercially successful than Powell and Pressburger's Technicolor films. *Mine Own Executioner*, despite being a clumsy, unconvincing film, was more popular. For the critics there was Burgess Meredith, a talented left-wing actor noted for his vigorous anti-Nazi stance, and an attempt at a different and mature relationship between Meredith's character, Felix Milne, a psychiatrist, and his wife (Dulcie Gray). For audiences there was the morbidly attractive area of psychiatric disorder, Felix's relationship with a femme fatale (Christine Norden), and a big, handsome, manic-depressive character, Adam Lucien (Kieron Moore), whose experience in a Japanese Prisoner-of-War camp impels him to murderous attacks on his loving wife.

In *The Small Back Room*, Powell and Pressburger capture the edgyness, the claustrophobia of Balchin's novel – tension-ridden journeys on the Underground; a pneumatic drill gnawing away at concentration during a vital meeting – and Kathleen Byron and David Farrar's restrained romantic feeling for each other (an ironic sequel to their unfortunate relationship in *Black Narcissus*) seems an integrally downbeat element of this dark, melancholy, world. Balchin and Anthony Kimmins are less successful in integrating Felix's marital difficulties and the politicking around his position at the clinic with the test he has to face – to rescue Adam Lucien from his nightmares and stop him from murdering his wife.

The flaw, though, is not just one of adaptation. With sympathy and attention divided between the psychiatrist and the psychopath, and only the most clichéd and conventional relationship between them, the film lacks the resonance and ambiguity which a skilfully constructed potboiler such as *The Night Has Eyes* manages to pack in.

Hunted heroes

One of the recurring motifs of film noir is that of a man accused of a crime of which he is innocent, pursued through a hostile and indifferent world while he himself searches for the real killer. It was a common enough theme in British thrillers in the thirties – Hitchcock's *The Thirty-Nine Steps*, and *Young and Innocent*, Arthur Woods' *They Drive by Night* – but in the forties it occurred less frequently and when it did the men on the run were sometimes guilty.

Escape, based on a play by Galsworthy which had already been filmed by Basil Dean in 1930, was made by Norman Lee for Twentieth Century-Fox, with Rex Harrison in the role of the ex-officer who accidently kills a policeman while defending the honour of a Hyde Park prostitute and is sent to Dartmoor for his pains. He escapes and stays at large long enough to meet a girl who falls in love with him. In 1930 – and no doubt in 1920 when the play was written – the exposé of a brutal prison system and the sympathy shown to an escaped convict had a certain radical edge, but the antics of Galsworthy's gentleman convict seemed out of place in post-war Britain.

Two of the spiv films – Cavalcanti's *They Made Me a Fugitive* (1947) and Lawrence Huntington's *Man on the Run* (1948) – follow the thirties pattern quite closely, though both Clem Morgan, an RAF officer who has drifted into black-marketeering, and Peter Burdon, an army deserter, are less than innocent heroes. *Take My Life* (d. Ronald Neame, 1948), with its complex plot, simple emotions, and set-piece suspense sequence in a deserted school, is very much a throwback to the Hitchcock films of the thirties. Its hero (Hugh Williams) – accused of murdering a girlfriend who might have troubled his prosperous marriage – is entirely innocent. But Williams, who specialized in pleasant but rather ineffectual husbands, spends most of the film in prison awaiting trial for the murder and it is his wife, a glamorous opera singer played by Greta Gynt, who undertakes the dangerous task of finding the real murderer.

Two other films, Gainsborough's *My Brother's Keeper* (1948) and Carol Reed's *Odd Man Out*, contributed more original elements to the morbid cycle. *My Brother's Keeper*, directed by Alfred Roome, a distinguished Gainsborough editor, is marred by a silly sub-plot involving David Tomlinson as a reporter roused from his honeymoon, but the main story is

34 George (Jack Warner) is sceptical about the value of remaining chained to
Willie (George Cole). *My Brother's Keeper* (1948).

original and significant. George Martin (Jack Warner), a hardened
criminal, escapes from the prison van taking him to court, dragging with
him the snivelling youth to whom he is handcuffed (George Cole). They
eventually reach the home of Martin's ex-mistress (Jane Hylton), who
reluctantly offers them shelter. But the next morning Martin kills a man
who stumbles upon their hideout, and, freeing himself from the youth
whom he regards as spineless and stupid, he arranges a rendezvous with
his wife. But before she can give him the clothes, money, and food he needs
to effect his escape, he is trapped by the police.

Warner's George Dixon/Joe Huggett persona has obscured the fact that
he played some memorable villains in forties films. Here he is a complex
mixture of good and bad, a clever, resourceful man warped by his years in
gaol. 'There's something in his mind that's not quite right. He's just a

misfit if you know what I mean,' his long-suffering wife (Beatrice Varley) tells his mistress as they wait for the final denouement. In *Escape* the gentleman hero gives himself up once he finds a woman who will stand by him and a policeman he can respect. George Martin, a dyed-in-the-wool convict, has no faith at all in the workings of English justice. 'Fair trial!' he snorts, 'There's no such thing. I've had twenty trials so I should know.' Confronted by an inquisitive farmer, he bludgeons him to death; cornered by the police, he prefers to take his chance across a minefield rather than give himself up.

For all its flaws, *My Brother's Keeper* is a remarkable film. Martin's relationships with his two women, and with the young and probably innocent man he drags along with him, are explored with an unusual lack of sentimentality. 'Don't give me that stuff', he tells the tearful Cole after sawing through the chains which bind them together. 'There's no such things as friends. People are either useful or useless. You're useless.' We are never allowed to feel sorry for this ill-fated and desperate man, just a tinge of horror and regret as he goes out to meet his maker.

Basil Wright described *Odd Man Out* as 'That rarest of things – a film about human feelings and thoughts and motives, all of which are real and recognizable, and touched with true pity and terror.'[7] What is perhaps rarer for a British film is that *Odd Man Out* is deliberately artistic. It is organized as a classical tragody: there are no sub-plots and the camera rarely leaves the suffering, wounded hero, and everything happens within a compact time-span and in a narrowly defined geographical area.

Johnny (James Mason), an Irish gunman, leads a bank raid to raise funds for his organization. His heart is not really in it, his attention wanders, he is shot, and he falls from the getaway car. For the next eight hours he searches for a safe haven but he becomes increasingly delirious and is gunned down trying to board the ship which was to have taken him away from Ireland. Most critics agreed with Wright that the film was a masterpiece and – partly no doubt because of the popularity of James Mason – it was a big box-office success. However Edgar Anstey, Wright's colleague on the *Documentary Newsletter*, had serious reservations, arguing that: 'It can scarcely be denied that at a time when the country is exhausted by war the film wallows in the hopeless plight of almost all its characters.' He concludes that:

The idea that *Odd Man Out* can be regarded as a sort of Hymn to Charity is so much mumbo-jumbo concealing the real truth that it is an 'escape' film in the profoundest sense. In itself that is not important. But let us watch carefully to see that in periods of cold, discouraging weather we do not too readily accept the view that the defeat of all humanity's aspirations is not only inevitable but aesthetically admirable.[8]

It is Anstey who developed that comparison with the 'morbid' German Expressionist films of the twenties which Arthur Vesselo picked up to use against *They Made Me a Fugitive*. He is a less sophisticated writer than Basil Wright but his attack on *Odd Man Out* is useful in exposing critical double standards. As he indignantly points out:

> the fact must be faced that the rather alarming sympathy which most critics have felt with the mood of this picture, has blinded them to an exasperating unevenness. There is some extraordinarily poor acting (notably from the policemen) and levels of characterisation and accents of speech are so variegated that we have no consistent atmosphere of Belfast or any other real place.[9]

As no subsequent 'morbid' film received such a warm welcome, it would be more accurate to argue that the critics' admiration for the artistic pretensions of the film blinded them to its mood.

The murderers are among us

In 1946 George Orwell wrote his essay on the 'Decline of the English Murder', expressing nostalgia for a golden age of English murder when the most famous murderers were respectable men and women who killed as a means of escaping an intolerable social situation.[10] These murderers – Dr Crippen, Mrs Maybrick, Bywaters and Thompson – nourished guilty passions which could only be fulfilled if some human obstacle, generally a wife or a husband, was removed. They were sympathetic, even tragic figures, and their crimes were carried out with intelligence and ingenuity. Orwell compares them to Elizabeth Jones and Karl Hulten, the perpetrators of the 'Cleft Chin Murder', who achieved notoriety in the dying days of the war. Their violence was unmotivated, futile, senseless, their case merely sordid, a symptom of a society made sick by political double-think and the false values of films and pulp novels.

If the war strengthened communal, sociable attitudes in many people, it fostered a dangerous introversion in others. Though little more than overgrown juvenile delinquents, Jones and Hulten inhabited a fantasy world of gangsters and casual violence where murder was an enjoyable form of self-expression. This divorce from reality was a characteristic shared by three other murderers who caught the public imagination in the 1940s: Neville Heath, the psychopathic charmer who posed as an RAF hero and murdered two women in 1946; John George Haigh who courted a teenage virgin while inveigling himself into the lives of at least six lonely middle-aged women and murdering them; and Donald Hume the failed flyer and small-time spiv who murdered thirteen-stone 'Honest Stan' Setty in 1949 and dropped his headless torso into the Essex marshes.

Paradoxically, as real-life murders became more fantastic, those in films became more subdued. Screen murderers in post-war films tended to be good men led astray, closer to Orwell's tragic victims of circumstance than Heath, Haigh, and Hume. Robert Newton's signalman in *Temptation Harbour*, James Mason's embittered surgeon in *The Upturned Glass* and Eric Portman's barber in *Daybreak* arouse pity and compassion rather than horror and disgust. Even when the murderers have more dubious motives – Portman and Newton's jealous husbands' in *Dear Murderer* and *Obsession*, for example – they are shown as suffering human beings at pains to explain to their victims why they must die. Psychologically disturbed murderers (or potential murderers) appear in *Wanted for Murder, Mine Own Executioner, Take My Life*, and *The October Man*, but they too are afforded sympathy where earlier they might have been regarded as monsters.

Films which took real-life crimes as their source tended to humanize or at least neutralize their murderers. Jean Kent makes Elizabeth Jones a jolly, vivacious good-time girl; and the Heath-like character played by Dennis Price in *Holiday Camp* is an ineffectual bluffer, a pretentiously middle-class fly-in-the-ointment of working-class harmony, who proves less successful with the ladies than nobbly, unglamorous Jimmy Hanley. Had he been played by James Mason, who had something approximating more closely to Heath's murderous charm, he might have posed a more serious threat.

Comparisons were drawn between Haigh – who habitually drank a glass of his victims' blood before dissolving their bodies in sulphuric acid – and Robert Newton's acid-bath killer in *Obsession*, but Newton's Dr Riordan is a sad character trapped in a loveless marriage and his attempt at a perfect murder never looks like succeeding. Riordan returns early from a business trip in order to expose his wife's infidelity, abducts her lover and imprisons him in a bombed-out building to which he returns every day with food and a hot-water bottle filled with acid. His plan is to wait until the hue and cry has died down before actually carrying out his murder, so that if suspicion should fall upon him he can produce the victim alive. Meanwhile he fills a bath with the contents of the hot-water bottle in order to dispose of the body should things go according to plan. The plot doesn't stand up to severe scrutiny but the relationships between Riordan and his wife, his victim, and the oddball Scotland Yard detective (Naunton Wayne) who finds him out are nicely realized and the film works well as a study of sexual repression. Though it is directed by Edward Dmytryk and the part of the unfortunate victim is played by an American (Phil Brown), it is all very politely English with Sally Gray superb as the petulant, unhappy wife who causes all the trouble and the hero of the film turning out to be a small and undistinguished dog.

The October Man has no explicit links with Haigh, indeed it was made

35 Dr Riordan (Robert Newton) puts on rubber gloves before emptying his acid-filled hot-water bottle. Bill (Phil Brown) despairs of ever understanding the English upper classes. *Obsession* (1949).

before his crimes were uncovered, but it is set in the shabbily respectable lodging-houses of West London where Haigh operated. Jim Ackland (John Mills), a young chemical engineer, is involved in a road accident in which his niece is killed. He blames himself for her death and sinks into amnesia. Released from hospital a year later, he gets a job in an aircraft factory and takes a room in a lodging-house. He is reluctant to involve himself in the social life of the house and his 'odd behaviour' is soon commented on by his gossipy neighbours. He gets on well at work and forms an attachment with Jenny Carden (Joan Greenwood), the sister of a colleague, but when a girl is found murdered in the lodging-house Jim is suspected of her murder. He isn't sure himself that he doesn't have psychopathic tendencies and his relationship with Jenny falters under this strain. However, she is not a woman to be easily repulsed and she is able to convince Jim of his sanity and help him find the real murderer.

The similarities with *The Night Has Eyes* are apparent, but the trappings of Gothic horror – a sadistic hero/villain, a persecuted heroine, an isolated and mysterious setting – are exchanged for a grubby, atmospheric realism. The hero is unsure of himself, the villain (Edward Chapman) is a rather pathetic middle-aged businessman, and the setting a drab, battered society very slowly recovering from the effects of war.

Male tormentors

In British films of the forties evil women tend to be sexually unattractive – the housekeepers played by Mary Clare, Beatrix Lehmann, and Katina Paxinou in *The Night Has Eyes*, *Candles at Nine*, and *Uncle Silus*. Where femmes fatales do appear – Camelia in *Temptation Harbour*, Frankie in

36 'Gentle as he appears, he may be suspected of the murder in the park'. John Mills' troubled hero. *The October Man* (1947).

Daybreak, Storm in *Obsession*, Kate in *The Upturned Glass*, Molly in *The October Man*, Liz in *Take My Life* – they generally pay a heavier price than the men to whom they bring trouble. Martha Wolfenstein and Nathan Leites, in their psychological analysis of British, French, and American films of the late forties, come to the conclusion that:

> British films in contrast to both American and French tend to see women more as possible victims of men's violence or betrayal. Correspondingly they give more emphasis to the dual potentialities of men, as attackers or rescuers. The unexciting good man who stands by is a more valued character in British than in American films because he is more needed. The cautionary images of the beautiful girl found strangled in the park, of a girl about to jump off a moonlit bridge because she is driven to distraction by a violent and moody man, or simply of a beautiful blond head bowed in suffering, are recurrent motifs in British films. The tenderness of the hero is given depth since it guards against his potentiality for causing such suffering; gentle as he appears, he may be suspected of the murder in the park, and his image is enhanced by the suggestion of this possibility. . . . In British films the male character bears the interesting ambiguity which in American films is associated with the good-bad girl.[11]

Whereas female stars tend to appear only in one or at most two of these 'morbid' films, four interestingly ambiguous men – James Mason, Robert Newton, David Farrar, and Eric Portman – make repeated appearances.

Broodingly handsome Mason got sick of the juvenile-lead-type characters he was expected to play in the thirties (such as Bunny Barnes of the Secret Service in Adrian Brunel's *Prison Breaker*), and cast himself as a sympathetic murderer on the run in his own co-production *I Met a Murderer* in 1939. But the industry took little notice and even after *The Night Has Eyes* he continued to play unambiguously wholesome characters in *Alibi, Thunder Rock*, and *The Bells Go Down*. After *The Man in Grey, Fanny by Gaslight, The Seventh Veil*, and *Odd Man Out*, he became the most popular screen actor in Britain. But with the exception of a few individuals like Ted Black, Sydney Box, and Lawrence Huntington, he had nothing but contempt for the British film industry and was happy to move to Hollywood in 1947.

Before he went, Mason and his wife Pamela Kellino made a low-budget film for Huntington and the Boxes. Though it lacks the artistry of *Odd Man Out, The Upturned Glass*, a moody revenge tragedy, has a single-mindend intensity which more than makes up for its infelicities in plot and characterization. Mason plays a brilliant but unhappy surgeon who is about to seize the opportunity for love and marriage when his prospective bride (Rosamund John) is murdered by her sister-in-law (Kellino). Stoically accepting this cruel blow dealt him by the fates, Mason sets out

37 Broodingly handsome brain surgeon Michael Joyce (James Mason) works out how to murder Kate Howard (Pamela Kellino/Mason). *The Upturned Glass* (1947).

to woo the murderess in order to establish her guilt and kill her. He succeeds, but in the process loses his sanity.

Robert Newton was more of a character actor than a star. During the late thirties he played smart but ill-fated underworld figures in *The Squeaker* and *The Green Cockatoo*, a penniless writer accused of murder in *Dead Men Are Dangerous*, and rolling-eyed heavies in *Jamaica Inn* and *Poison Pen*. During the war he re-worked his rough villain character for *Major Barbara* and *Hatter's Castle* and his lightweight cad for *They Flew Alone*, but gained most fame as Frank Gibbons, the ordinary, strike-breaking man-on-a-Clapham-omnibus in *This Happy Breed*. It is this decent, respectable working man who re-appears in *Temptation Harbour*, though here there is an undertone of suppressed violence, similar in its menace to the hysteria bubbling under the surface of Dr Riordan's smooth exterior in *Obsession*.

38 From his signal-box high above Folkestone harbour, signalman Bert Mallinson
(Robert Newton) surveys old-fashioned and untidy Welwyn studio. *Temptation
Harbour* (1947).

Temptation Harbour, directed by Lance Comfort for ABPC in 1947,
shared many of the characteristics of the traditional Welwyn crime
thrillers but it was made with a much higher budget and solidly situated
in a realistic setting. It was based on a Georges Simenon story, *Newhaven –
Dieppe*, and was unflatteringly compared to gloomy French melodramas
like *Quai des Brumes* and *La Bête Humaine*, but it is very English and one
of the few films between *Waterloo Road* and *Room at the Top* to have a
convincing working-class character as its main protagonist.

From his perch high above Folkestone harbour, signalman Bert
Mallinson (Robert Newton) sees two men struggling for possession of a
suitcase. One of them falls into the water and the other runs off. Bert dives
into the harbour to save the man but finds only the suitcase – which is full

of money. A series of incidents frustrates his attempts to report the incident
and return the money, and he is tempted to spend some of it on his
motherless teenage daughter. Before long he falls for a sulky French
femme fatale and begins to dream of a new life in France. Nemesis in the
form of a sinister cat-burglar (William Hartnell) stalks him and a tragic
climax ends his hopes of a life of luxury and romance.

Arthur Vesselo accused the film of morbid pessimism:

> There is no multicoloured fancy-dress business about *Temptation
> Harbour*, which is in the sombrest blacks and whites, and takes the line
> of being extremely down-to-earth. In so far as this means using the
> generous resources of the cinema to present us with a realistic picture of
> life as it is lived by poor and simple people in a big harbour town, it is
> more than acceptable. In so far as it means portraying their life as
> something degraded and vicious – or at best, ignorant, weak, and utterly
> helpless against evil – it is merely depressing. Nor is it a valid defence
> to say that the film is factual and points no morals, for indeed it does
> appear to point a moral, which is that small-scale and hesitant wrong-
> doing does not pay (implying that large-scale and determined wrong-
> doing might).[12]

This is unnecessarily supercilious. There is nothing degraded or vicious
about Newton's Bert Mallinson and the film's morality is impeccably
conventional. What appears striking now is not his wish to escape from
the grim, grey existence he leads, but the strength of the bonds which tie
him to austerity-wracked Britain. He admonishes his daughter for taking
meat from the butcher's where she works, despite the fact that she is
underpaid and overworked, and his dreams of the good life in France with
Camelia (Simone Simon) are disturbed by thoughts of what his next-door
neighbour – appropriately played by Kathleen Harrison, who as Mrs
Huggett was to become an icon of working-class honesty and resilience –
would think of him.

Mallinson has a strong sense of right and wrong and his falls from grace
stem, ironically, from acts of kindness and generosity. He dives into the
harbour, with no thought of his own gain, to save a man's life; he breaks
into the stolen money to give his hardworking daughter a taste of the
pleasures she has missed because of poverty and war; even his interest in
Camelia is initially that of a kindly, fatherly man offering sympathy and
support. But it is a strength of the film that he is no cardboard innocent. In
dealing with gold-digging Camelia – a fairground mermaid with 'enough
atomic energy in the lobes of her ears to flatten London' – and the
haunted, nervy Hartnell, Mallinson discovers that he has interests,
abilities, passions, not normally associated with railway signalmen. He
thinks he is in love and finds himself capable of murder, but once he has
rid himself of his rival he resumes his solid, honest identity and after

comforting his daughter ('You don't want to let them see you've been crying') takes the long, slow walk to the police station.

David Farrar, a rugged, good-looking actor who never gained the sort of recognition due to him, showed evidence of his potential for ambiguity during the war, appearing as a British officer who is in reality a German commando in *Went the Day Well?*, and a German officer who is really a British spy in *The Night Invader*. Whereas Newton was essentially a melodramatic actor capable of toning himself down sufficiently to play realist roles, Farrar was essentially a realist actor capable of exploding into melodrama. Thus he came across well as the dogged, casually brave sea-captain in Ealing's drama-documentary *For Those in Peril*, but made a one-dimensional wicked squire in Powell and Pressburger's *Gone to Earth*. As with Mason and Newton, though, his best roles – Sid Nichols in *The Trojan Brothers*, Mr Dean in *Black Narcissus*, Robert Dawson in *Frieda*, Sammy Rice in *The Small Back Room* – are neurotic, troubled men, at odds with the world.

Eric Portman, the most morbidly prolific of the four, began his film career as Carlos the gypsy, the necessarily overshadowed hero of *The Murder in the Red Barn*, from whom Maria Marten is tempted by the wicked squire (Tod Slaughter). Significantly, in view of his later roles, he re-appears at the end as the mystery hangman who ensures that Slaughter has a timely and just dispatch. During the war he played the ruthless, fanatical U-Boat officer in *49th Parallel*, one of the gallant, resourceful RAF men in *One of Our Aircraft is Missing*, and the blunt northern foreman in *Millions Like Us*, but it was the eccentric English gentleman Thomas Colpeper of *A Canterbury Tale*, 'with bees in the bonnet and blue bottles in the belfry', who set the tone for Portman's post-war screen persona.

Lance Comfort's *Great Day* (1945), Lawrence Huntington's *Wanted for Murder* (1946), and Terence Young's *Corridor of Mirrors* (1948) explicitly re-use elements of the Colpeper character. In *Great Day* Portman plays a retired army captain with a deep love of the English countryside who feels bitter and frustrated at being unable to contribute to the war effort. Whereas Colpeper reassesses his views about women, succeeds in bringing the three pilgrims to a state of grace and retains his status as a mysterious, charismatic figure, Captain Ellis is overshadowed by his wife and daughter (Flora Robson and Sheila Sim) and attempts suicide after disgracing himself. *Wanted for Murder*, co-scripted by Rodney Acland and Emeric Pressburger, stresses the more dangerous aspects of the Colpeper character. Colpeper is a farmer, in love with England's rural heritage, Victor Colebrooke, the wealthy, unmarried businessman Portman plays in *Wanted for Murder*, is obsessed by his great-grandfather, a nineteenth-century public hangman. Whereas Colpeper is haunted by something real, if intangible, Colebrooke is caught up in a psychopathic fantasy, and his misogyny expresses itself not in glue-throwing but in murder.

Paul Mangin, Portman's character in *Corridor of Mirrors*, is equally fantasy-ridden and is accused, tried, and hanged for the murder of a woman found strangled with her own hair in his home. He had imagined himself the reincarnation of a Renaissance aristocrat and used his wealth to recreate an unreal world, but he is innocent of the girl's death and the real murderer is his mad, jealous housekeeper (Barbara Mullen). His only chance of avoiding execution is to admit his own insanity but he prefers to accept his fate.

The Portman characters in *The Mark of Cain* (1948), *Dear Murderer* (1947), and *Daybreak* (1948) are equally angst-ridden but their problems are more easily traced to jealousy. In *The Mark of Cain* Portman's character loves his brother's wife, murders him and allows her to take the blame when she refuses to reciprocate his passion. But he is a wholly unpleasant character, and our sympathies are vested in the ill-done-by wife (Sally Gray). Portman's character in *Daybreak* is more sympathetic. Like Newton's Bert Mallinson, Eddie Tribe, despite being the public hangman, is an ordinary middle-aged working man, but when he chivalrously tries to help a beautiful, enigmatic woman (Ann Todd) he finds himself caught in a maelstrom of emotion which destroys his orderly world. *Dear Murderer* is more conventional but the emotional pattern is more complex. Portman's Lee Warren kills one of his wife's lovers and frames another for the murder only to find that she seems to care little for either of them and still less for him. Greta Gynt's glitteringly evil Vivienne twists her suave, clever husband round her finger and eventually kills him, but the impact of the film is reduced by conventional courtroom dramatics and a wholly uninteresting hero (Maxwell Reed). *Dear Murderer* was based on a play by St John Legh Clowes, a now-forgotten figure whose career in films began and ended with the most sensational contribution to the morbid cycle, *No Orchids for Miss Blandish*.

D for disgusting

René Raymond, a commercial traveller for a large firm of book wholesalers, had adopted the pseudonym James Hadley Chase and written a pseudo-American gangster story, *No Orchids for Miss Blandish*, in 1939. The book was a huge and unexpected success and in 1942 was turned into a popular play with Robert Newton as the gangster Slim Grissom and Linden Travers as Miss Blandish. Sydney Box acquired the rights and early in 1945 announced he would make a big-budget film with an all-American cast. But it was a subject unlikely to meet with the approval of J. Arthur Rank and when Box took over at Gainsborough he discreetly passed on the project to Renown, a small but enterprising distribution company which was trying to move into film production. Renown invited in St John Legh Clowes to direct a modestly budgeted adaptation of the play with Linden Travers and the American 'B' movie star Jack La Rue taking over Newton's role.

When it was released early in 1948 the critics excelled themselves in heaping hysterical abuse on the film. 'The most sickening display of brutality, perversion, sex and sadism ever to be shown on a cinema screen', squawked the *Monthly Film Bulletin*; 'repellent . . . all the morals of an alleycat and all the sweetness of a sewer', thundered C.A. Lejeune; the *Daily Mirror* found it 'about as fragrant as a cesspool'; the *Evening Standard*, 'a most sickening display of sadism, brutality and suggestiveness'; the *Sunday Pictorial* 'a piece of nauseating muck'; the *Daily Express* 'a wicked disgrace to the British film industry', and Dilys Powell thought the film should be given 'a "D" certificate – for disgusting'.

Incredulity was expressed that the BBFC had granted the film a certificate. It was not unknown for Mrs Crouzet the examiner to misread the sexual connotations of a scene, though she tended to err on the side of caution, finding obscenity where none was intended, but in *No Orchids* she found nothing to object to at all, and it is not just an eighties tolerance of higher levels of sex and violence in films which makes *No Orchids* seem innocuous. In the book Miss Blandish is kidnapped, beaten up, raped, and kept in a state of drugged submission for three months by the sexual psychopath Slim Grissom. In the film Slim Grissom courts Miss Blandish anonymously, rescues her from the small-time riff-raff who have kidnapped her, and, risking the anger of his gang who want their share of her ransom, offers her her freedom. She chooses to stay with him, seeing it as an escape from the claustrophobic conformity of upper-class life. Slim's reputation is enough to strike terror into his fellow gangsters and there are hints in La Rue's fine, restrained performance of suppressed violence which might explode at any minute. But with Miss Blandish he acts the perfect gentleman – like a shy, polite Humphrey Bogart – and risks, and loses, everything in a bid to save their doomed romance.

No Orchids is not a film which stands up to detailed critical scrutiny. As with most low-budget films there are flaws and longeurs which make it irritatingly shoddy in parts and inevitably the film compares unfavourably with the American films noirs which explore the gangster milieu with more resources, expertise, and conviction. Sid James looks out of place as an American barman, South African singer Zoe Gail hardly compares with Lauren Bacall or Rita Hayworth. But the film is an interesting experiment and its huge popularity in those areas where it was not banned suggests that it offered audiences pleasures which the critics were immune to.

George Orwell, in his essay on 'Raffles and Miss Blandish', compares the gentlemanly Raffles stories of E. W. Hornung with the explicitly sensational writing of James Hadley Chase, Peter Cheyney, and the

39 Doomed romance with 'all the morals of an alleycat and all the sweetness of a sewer'. Jack la Rue and Linden Travers. *No Orchids for Miss Blandish* (1948).

American pulp writers from whom they drew their inspiration. He obviously finds their descriptions of violence distasteful, but what he really objects to is what he sees as the Fascistic idealization of power underlying this sort of writing:

> In a book like *No Orchids* one is not, as in the old-style crime story simply escaping from dull reality into an imaginary world of action. One's escape is essentially into cruelty and sexual perversion. . . . It is a daydream appropriate to a totalitarian age. In his imagined world of gangsters Chase is presenting, as it were, a distilled version of the modern political scene, in which such things as mass bombing of civilians, the use of torture to obtain confessions, secret prisons, executions without trial, floggings with rubber truncheons, drownings in cesspools, systematic falsification of records and statistics, treachery, bribery and quislingism are normal and morally neutral, even admirable

when they are done in a large and bold way. The average man is not directly interested in politics and, when he reads, he wants the current struggles of the world to be translated into a simple story about individuals. He can take an interest in Slim and Fenner as he could not in the G.P.U. and the Gestapo. People worship power in the form in which they are able to understand it.[13]

Despite the hysteria of the critics this was not a characteristic of St John Legh Clowes' *No Orchids*, nor of any of the unjustly neglected or maligned films which shed light on the darker side of forties society.

10   Nothing to Laugh at at All

Dan Young: 'I say, there's pink rats running all over my room.'
Frank Randle: 'That's nowt, this place is full of blue elephants.'
                                                    (*Somewhere on Leave*)

Teddy Knox (as Hitler) to assembled Nazi dignitaries: 'We'll see the burgomaster now, but the other burghers can wait.'
                                                                (*Gasbags*)

Harry Korris (as Napoleon) to Lisa Lee (as Josephine): 'Don't call me Nappy or my generals will think I'm a wet blanket.'
                                                             (*Happidrome*)

'There were no wrecks and nobody drownded. In fact nothing to laugh at at all.'
                                       (Stanley Holloway. *Albert and the Lion*)

The disparity between critical assessment and popular appreciation apparent in reactions to spiv films and melodramas is even more evident in attitudes to British comedies which from the *Pimple* films of the pre-sound era to the *Carry Ons* of the sixties and seventies attracted big audiences but were ignored or disparaged by the critics. Most British comedies were cheaply and sometimes shoddily made and as far as the critics were concerned there was no valid tradition of British comedy until the advent of the Ealing comedies in the late forties. But these bastard children of the film studio and various branches of live entertainment are too numerous to pass over in silence: more than a quarter of the British films released between September 1939 and December 1949 were comedies, and many of them were commercially more successful than the culturally esteemed realist films.

The war provided new comedy situations which the industry was quick to exploit. The excitement and upheaval of being conscripted into the armed services inspired a series of 'joining-up' comedies – *Pack up Your Troubles* (with Wylie Watson and Reginald Purdell), *Somewhere in England* (with Frank Randle and Harry Korris), *Laugh It Off* (with Tommy Trinder), *Old Bill and Son* (with John Mills and Morland Graham), *Garrison Follies* (with Barry Lupino), and *Old Mother Riley Joins Up* (with Arthur Lucan and Kitty MacShane) – which dealt with life in the services among the new recruits. Those comedians who stayed in civilian life – Jack Hulbert and Cicely Courtneidge (*Under Your Hat*), Duggie Wakefield (*Spy for a Day*), George Formby (*Let George Do It* and *Spare a Copper*), Arthur Askey (*Band Waggon* and *Back Room Boy*), Basil Radford and Naunton Wayne (*Crooks Tour*), Will Hay and Claude Hulbert (*The Ghost of St Michaels*), and Sid Field (*That's the Ticket*) – found themselves embroiled with spies, fifth columnists, and saboteurs.

The picture of Britain these comedies present is grotesque but fascinating. Officers are stiff and stuffy although they sometimes have a pretty daughter, and some upper-class characters end up in the ranks alongside the chummy, good-natured working-class types who prove adept at rooting out fifth columnists and putting on concerts. Cheeky, inquisitive evacuees plague civilian life and funny things go on during the black-out, but most people grin and bear it cheerfully and those few who do complain generally turn out to be in league with spies and saboteurs. *Spare a Copper* (1940, d. John Paddy Carstairs), for example, has George Formby as a war reserve policeman on the trail of a gang of Birkenhead saboteurs. His superiors pick one of the saboteurs, in preference to George, to be promoted to the Flying Squad, and invite the gang-leader, the proprietor of the local variety hall, to the policeman's ball. But the omnipresence of spies and saboteurs hardly betokens paranoia. George rarely stops smiling, emerging from one narrow escape after another, saving the ship which was to have been blown sky high, and making sure all the villains get their just deserts.

In terms of style and personnel there was no radical break between the war years and the 1930s. Most of the stars recruited for war comedies had already seen service in low-budget thirties comedies. Sandy Powell made nine films before he accidentally joined the navy in *All at Sea*, Leslie Fuller made twenty-one before joining Fred Emney and Jack Buchanan on *The Middle Watch*. Where new blood was introduced it tended to be poured into old bottles. Arthur Askey, after a successful debut in *Band Waggon*, starred in a version of Brandon Thomas' Edwardian farce *Charley's Aunt*, a re-make of Arnold Ridley's much-filmed play *The Ghost Train*, and two more films with very familiar plots: *I Thank You* (penniless actors struggling to put on a show) and *Back Room Boy* (spies employing ghosts to ward off inquisitive visitors). Frank Randle, most successful of the music-hall comedians to move into films during the war years, not only retained his stage persona but repeatedly used material from the handful of sketches for which he was famous. Two of the surviving *Somewhere* films he made with Dan Young, Robbie Vincent, and Harry Korris – *Somewhere in Camp* and *Somewhere on Leave* – both feature concerts where Randle plays his lecherous and much-married octogenarian anxious to 'get to the point' with his new sweetheart.

The music-hall tradition

Despite being regarded as old-fashioned, parochial, and unpolished, comedy films had been the one unequivocal success of the British film industry in the thirties. At a time when many British films were being booed off the screen, the cinema-going public showed a tolerant affection for their native comedians despite the fact that the films they appeared in were technically inferior to the slick, wise-cracking American comedies. With the exception of Hitchcock's *Blackmail*, the first British talkie to be a commercial success was Herbert Wilcox's *Rookery Nook*, a cheaply made adaptation of a Ben Travers farce starring Ralph Lynn, Tom Walls, and Robertson Hare. According to Wilcox it cost £14,000 and in England alone yielded £150,000; not surprisingly, seven similar farces followed in quick succession.[1] Promising variety entertainers like Ernie Lotinga, Will Hay, Sydney Howard, Sandy Powell, Max Miller, and Albert Modley were eagerly recruited along with more up-market performers such as Leslie Henson, Bobby Howes, Jack Buchanan, Jack Hulbert, and Cicely Court-neidge. Most of them remained committed to their various forms of live entertainment, but George Formby and Gracie Fields proved so successful that they were transformed into British film stars, as popular – in Britain at least – as the gods and goddesses of Hollywood.[2]

Formby had begun his career on the northern music-hall circuit by copying the act of his father, George Formby Senior, 'the Wigan Nightingale'. Formby Junior developed into a broader comedian, his cheeky grin and jangling banjolele dispersing the cloud of tragic pathos which had hovered over his father's head. In 1934 he made a low-budget comedy – *Boots! Boots!* – for John E. Blakeley, a Manchester businessman with extensive interests in the film business. It was a success and another – *Off the Dole* – followed. Blakeley deliberately restricted the budgets of the two films to ensure that healthy profits could be made in the north of England along. The south tended to prefer witty, fast-talking 'wide-boy' comics like Max Miller to the clowns and drolls beloved in the North. Nevertheless, Basil Dean, who found that the films he made with Gracie Fields were far more profitable than anything else made at Ealing, was struck by George's vitality and presence ('another personality that seems to bounce off the screen') and signed him up.[3] By 1938 he was Britain's most popular film star, a position he maintained until 1944 (when he was toppled by James Mason).

Basil Dean, superciliously biting the hand that fed him, comments that Formby 'didn't act gormless as many successful Lancashire comedians have done, he was gormless'.[4] But George was not as daft as he looked. Phyllis Calvert, while expressing reservations about his personality, had nothing but praise for his professionalism:

'Technically, in front of the camera he was infallible. . . . There's a scene in *Let George Do It* where he goes to five doors in a nightclub, finding his way blocked by the villains and he's singing and playing his uke all the time. The song ends when he gets to the last door. He had to do this several times during shooting and on each occasion he finished the song at the exact moment he reached the final door. He was just as effective in another scene in which he gets out of bed singing, shaves, brushes his hair, dresses . . . and hits the last note as he buttons his coat. This was absolutely perfect timing – all in one camera take. It's incredibly difficult to do, but he did it instinctively without having to rehearse.'[5]

Formby adapted to film much better than most of his comic contemporaries. Max Miller had a phenomenal reputation as a live performer, but his films fed off rather than enhanced that reputation. As a verbal comedian whose talent lay in the rapport he built up with an audience, much more was lost than for Formby, whose songs and slapstick worked as well on film as they did on stage.[6] Moreover, though his appeal to women might now seem resistible enough, his ability to play the innocent, cheerful underdog made romance at least feasible. Most British comedians were too old or too ugly or too peculiar to make their pursuit of beautiful women anything more than risible. Will Hay eschewed romance altogether, Flanagan and Allen seemed happiest in each other's company; Trinder, Randle, Askey, and Old Mother Riley tended to pass the romantic buck to someone more suitable; and Miller looked disconcertingly lecherous wooing women young enough to be his daughters.

Formby, with his catchy songs and indefatigable optimism, became a national figure. The Lancashire accent remained to enhance his homely comic appeal but the cloth-cap image was quickly discarded and there was none of the 'baghum owd lad's and 'a goo t' buckabury' that peppered the speech of uncompromisingly regional comedians like Frank Randle. Formby's sunny, vacant optimism made him appear a childish but lovable figure. Even a high-brow theatre critic like Harold Hobson was prepared to concede that he could be very appealing:

'With a carp-like face, a mouth outrageously full of teeth, a walk that seems normally to be that of a flustered hen and a smile of perpetual wonder at the joyous incomprehensibility of the universe and the people in it, Mr Formby has that foolish simplicity which one would like to think is a better protection from harm than all the wisdom of the worldly.'[7]

One might expect that such an icon of gullible naivety would hardly survive the harsh reality of war, yet if anything Formby's popularity increased and his last four films for Ealing – *Come on George, Let George Do It, Spare a Copper*, and *Turned Out Nice Again* were all big box-office successes.

This enduring popularity was partly due to Formby's own behaviour. Innocence can easily turn into priggishness and simpleness into stupidity, but in Formby's case they manifested themselves in an admirable desire to pay for his fame and fortune by dispensing goodwill and entertainment. Throughout the war he tirelessly toured camps, bases, and outposts to put on concerts for the troops. Sincerity transformed gullibility into determined idealism. The ease with which George exposed traitors, unmasked spies, and prevented saboteurs from doing their dirty work in *Let George Do It* and *Spare a Copper* could be laughed at rather than sneered at by audiences who knew that their comic hero was sharing with them the real dangers of war. Formby's career declined after leaving Ealing in 1941, but this had more to do with the inadequate vehicles which he subsequently appeared in than in any diminution of his personal popularity.

Though relations with Basil Dean and his successor at Ealing, Michael Balcon, were not always amicable, Formby worked well there and he had been served by good scripts and talented leading ladies (Florence Desmond, Polly Ward, Kay Walsh, Googie Withers, Pat Kirkwood, Dorothy Hyson, Phyllis Calvert). Columbia, Formby's new company, proved less adept at getting the formula right.

Walter Greenwood, who had scripted Formby's first Ealing film, *No Limit*, supplied a weak story for his first Columbia film, *Much too Shy*, and matters were made worse by landing him with an insipid heroine and the scene-stealing Jimmy Clitheroe. Jeffrey Richards talks of Formby combining 'the appeal of the proletarian little man' with that of 'the lost child at large in the world'.[8] But the introduction of Jimmy Clitheroe, twenty-six at the time but looking like an eleven-year-old (as he was to for the next thirty years), inevitably spoils that appeal and George comes across as merely a fool. *South American George*, scripted by Leslie Arliss and Norman Lee, was equally unsatisfactory, despite the presence of Linden Travers, Enid Stamp Taylor, and Felix Aylmer, and though there was a return to form in *Get Cracking* (1943) and *Bell-Bottom George* (1944), the decline continued with two more banal films, *He Snoops to Conquer* (1944) and *I Didn't Do It* (1945) before coming to an abrupt halt with *George in Civvy Street* in 1946. This last film does have its good moments and three of the songs – 'We've Been a Long Time Gone', sung to a liner-load of disgruntled sailors, 'Madder than the Mad March Hare', part of a peculiar dream sequence with Formby as the Hare at the Mad Hatter's tea party, and 'You Don't Need a Licence for That', with Formby enthusiastically accompanied by a 'hot' jazz band – almost make up for the dire script and the weak supporting cast. Nevertheless it was disliked by the public and failed at the box-office.[9]

Formby's popularity as a film star was not equalled by another British comedian until the rise of Norman Wisdom in the fifties. His closest rivals during the war were Arthur Askey and Frank Randle, who come from almost opposite ends of the comedy spectrum from one another. Askey was born into a lower-middle-class Liverpool family and served his apprenticeship as a comedian in concert parties, seaside summer shows, and Christmas pantomimes before coming to national attention in *Band Waggon*, the first of the BBC's regularly scheduled radio comedy shows. Askey and his accomplice Richard 'Stinker' Murdoch, created a fantasy world populated by weird people and even weirder animals which caught the public imagination. By the time war broke out the country was awash with their catch-lines – 'Before your very eyes', 'Don't be filthy', 'Hello Playmates', and 'Ay-thang-yew'.

A stage show based on *Band Waggon* did not prove a great success, but Gainsborough decided that Askey was popular enough to replace Will Hay, who had followed Michael Balcon to Ealing. The film version of *Band Waggon*, begun at Islington just before war broke out and completed at Shepherd's Bush, is a clever amalgam of the characters and motifs of the radio show and a typical Gainsborough plot cooked up by resident scriptwriters J.O.C. Orton, Val Guest, and Marriott Edgar. Stinker and Arthur are driven from their haunt on the roof of Broadcasting House, and take up residence in a castle which they are able to rent very cheaply because it is haunted. The ghost turns out to be old Moore Marriott, paid by a ring of spies to scare away inquisitive visitors. They unmask him and recruit his help in taking over the gang's transmitter, which they use to launch a pirate television station and at last win recognition from the BBC.

It is a neat, amusing film and was successful enough to launch Askey's film career. By 1940 the *Motion Picture Herald* poll showed he was Britain's fourth most popular star (behind George Formby, Robert Donat, and Gracie Fields) and seven more films followed in quick succession. Divested of the huge horn-rimmed glasses which seemed an integral part of his face, he made a convincingly feminine Charley's Aunt, though the film as a whole is disappointing. Director Walter Forde was happier with comedy thrillers than with farce and *The Ghost Train*, which he also directed, is much more satisfying despite the fact that Askey's character is superfluous to the plot. The next film, *I Thank You* (1941 d. Marcel Varnel), Askey regarded as a 'stinker', but it has a fascinating finale where old music-hall star Lily Morris comes out of aristocratic retirement to sing to the crowds in a tube station bomb shelter. *Back Room Boy* (1942, d. Herbert Mason) returns again to the *Ghost Train* plot but gives Askey a central role as a lovelorn lighthouse-keeper whose isolation is disturbed by a disrespectful evacuee, a troupe of shipwrecked chorus girls, and a gang of German spies. This, the funniest if the least original of the Askey comedies, was followed by three films which broke completely with the old Gainsborough plots and personnel and teamed Askey with Max Bacon, Jack Train, Anne Shelton, and Evelyn Dall, all of whom had made their reputation in wartime radio. After a reasonably promising start with *King Arthur Was a Gentleman* (1942, d. Marcel Varnel) there was a rapid decline into bathos with *Miss London Ltd* (1943, d. Val Guest) and *Bees in Paradise* (1944, d. Val Guest).

J.B. Priestley, in his *English Journey*, discerned as well as the expected two nations – an England of thatched cottages and leafy lanes and an England of slag heaps and heavy industry – a new England of:

> arterial and by-pass roads, of filling stations and factories that look like exhibition buildings, of giant cinemas and dance-halls and cafés, bungalows with tiny garages, cocktail bars, Woolworths, motor-coaches, wireless, hiking, factory girls looking like actresses, greyhound racing and dirt tracks, swimming pools, and everything given away for cigarette coupons.[10]

If Max Miller and George Formby occasionally strayed into this new England, they did so bringing with them the familiar virtues and vices of traditional working-class culture. But Askey, with his background in seaside pierrot troupes like the Fol-de-Rols and the Jovial Jesters, belonged very much to that third England, more extinct now that the arterial roads have become motorways and the giant cinemas and dance-halls have been pulled down, than the older two Englands.

At the height of his success as a radio performer, Askey was booked for the Shepherd's Bush Empire at a hundred pounds a night. He approached the engagement with some trepidation:

> I had always been scared of playing the Halls, for I never thought I was 'broad' enough. I was still essentially concert party in my approach and I had seen some popular radio artistes who had 'died' on the Halls. . . . Was it to be my turn now?[11]

The little man hopping about the stage like a demented gnome singing silly songs about seagulls and busy-busy bees was ideal for the light, airy world of the seaside concert party, but the variety halls kept their roots in a darker, proletarian culture which required something more earthy. In the event all went well, not because Askey broadened his style to win over the music-hall habitués, but because he attracted his own audience of *Band Waggon* fans many of whom 'had never been in a Music Hall in their lives'.[12]

It is easy to forget the importance of live entertainment in the first half of the twentieth century. The golden age of the music hall might have ended with Marie Lloyd and Dan Leno, but in the more commercial form of 'variety' it enjoyed a long Indian summer which only came to a close in the 1950s. Max Miller was the darling of the southern halls, the highest-paid variety act ever known by the early forties, but Frank Randle was pre-eminent in the north, 'the King of Blackpool'. He was born, like

Formby, in Wigan, though much lower down the social scale. He began his career as an entertainer busking to the crowds in Blackpool and progressed via a trampoline act (the 'Bouncing Randles') to become an immensely popular music-hall comic with the ability to reduce an audience to helpless hysteria. Unlike Miller or Formby who would talk and sing directly to the audience, Randle worked through sketches, generally assuming the identity of a cunning, lecherous old man, most famously the 'old hiker', a belligerent, unstoppable octogenarian ('I'm eighty-two and full of vim!') whose encounters with bulls, 'hottuns', and ale kept audiences enthralled. In contrast to the strict discipline exercised by the other great sketch comedians, Sid Field, Robb Wilton, and Jimmy James, Randle would sometimes indulge in wild improvisation, drawing in his audience, defying the strict time schedule set by managements on variety acts, and returning to the free and easy interaction between audience and performer which had characterized the early music hall.

George Orwell, in his essay 'The Lion and the Unicorn', comments that

> The genuinely popular culture of England is something that goes on beneath the surface, unofficially and more or less frowned on by the authorities. One thing one notices if one looks directly at the common people, especially in the big towns, is that they are not puritanical. They are inveterate gamblers, drink as much beer as their wages will permit, are devoted to bawdy jokes, and use probably the foulest language in the world. . . . One can learn a good deal about the spirit of England from the comic coloured postcards that you see in the windows of cheap stationers' shops. These things are a sort of diary upon which the English people have unconsciously recorded themselves. Their old-fashioned outlook, their graded snobberies, their mixture of bawdiness and hypocrisy, their extreme gentleness, their deeply moral attitude to life are all mirrored there.[13]

Randle's world is exactly that of the seaside postcards, a primitive world of misshapen bodies and stunted passions. To transfer it onto film was virtually impossible. John E. Blakeley, having lost Formby to Ealing, was eager to turn Randle into a profitable substitute, but efforts to emulate the relative sophistication of the Formby films were soon abandoned:

> There were perpetual attempts at scripting, direction, introduction of outside talent, at pretending that the films were, in fact, film. Basically, as far as idiom went, they were not film. They were music hall. The cameraman, Ernie Palmer, and the director, Johnny Blakeley, took no identity on themselves other than the identity normally taken by audience and theatre producer. The picture frame was static as a proscenium arch. The camera angle was eye-level frontal throughout. There was no zooming, little panning, no dollying and no change of

angle. The camera was in fact a man in a music hall. Blakeley's job was to see that the stars didn't move out of picture. He didn't do much else.[14]

Leslie Halliwell, himself from Bolton and a Randle enthusiast, labels the *Somewhere* films 'a series of misshapen and badly made regional comedies which afflicted British cinema in the forties'.[15] But like the Tod Slaughter melodramas, the aesthetic failings of the Randle films hardly obscure the view they allow into a lost world. Significantly, the one film Randle made which does have pretensions to proper production values – *When You Come Home*, directed by John Baxter in 1947 – is much less funny that the *Somewhere* films where the jokes come thick and fast and the stories are too daft to be much of a distraction.

Somewhere in Camp (1942) has Frank Randle, Dan Young, and Robbie Vincent as privates giving their kindly, long-suffering sergeant, Harry Korris, a permanent headache. Their comrade-at-arms, private Jack Trevor (John Singer) – who looks as if he has been drafted straight from the boy scouts to the army – is in love with the Colonel's daughter (Toni Lupino), and as a keen, educated young man with an upper-class accent, he has every hope of winning her hand. However the Adjutant is also in love with her and a series of obstacles have to be overcome before Jack receives his commission and gets the girl. As in a pantomime, the high-flown romantic story is continually interrupted by vulgar clowning. Thus it hardly matters that the antics of Randle and company are irrelevant to the story. The plot becomes merely a frame to hold together various funny sketches.

A more legitimate complaint could be made that several of the sketches used in *Somewhere in Camp* are repeated with only minor variations in the next film *Somewhere on Leave*. Randle and Dan Young systematically mutilate the grand piano Sergeant Korris has asked them to move in the same way that they wreck the billiard table in the sergeants' mess in the previous film; Randle's randy old man again tries to seduce his middle-aged sweetheart, though this time she is played by Dan Young instead of Harry Korris; and Randle once again subjects a languorously hoity-toity young woman (Edna Wood) to a series of indignities on the dance floor. Fortunately the sketches are good enough to bear repetition and each film has its own unique central sequence which makes it easy to forgive the other weaknesses. In *Somewhere in Camp* it involves Randle in a desperate tussle with a lumbago patch and then – toothless though he is – with a sadistic dentist. In *Somewhere on Leave* he gives a virtuoso performance as a drunk, moving from jovial inebriation to paralytic incoherence with impressive dignity, and ending up in a bath, washing himself thoroughly, oblivious to the fact that he still has his vest and long-johns on.

Though Randle's films never achieved the sort of box-office success won by George Formby, in northern towns like Macclesfield they attracted bigger audiences than Hollywood blockbusters and it would be wrong to suppose that they had no appeal to audiences south of the Trent.[16] John Montgomery points out: 'Randle's films always did well in working class districts simply because his appeal was entirely to the working classes and he made no pretensions to be posh or (as he would say) "la-di-dah".'[17]

After *Somewhere on Leave* the team split up, Harry Korris and Robbie Vincent rejoining their radio partner Cecil Frederick for *Happidrome* (produced by Jack Buchanan for MGM-British); Dan Young teaming up with Nat Jackley and Norman Evans to make two films for Mancunian, *Demobbed* (1944) and *Under New Management* (1946); and Randle using a variety of partners – from Tessie O'Shea to Diana Dors – to make another seven films: *Somewhere in Civvies* (1943); *Home Sweet Home* (1945), *When You Come Home* (1947), *Holidays With Pay* (1948), *Somewhere in Politics* (1949), *School for Randle* (1949), and *It's a Grand Life* (1953). Apart from John Baxter's *When You Come Home* all of these films were directed by John E. Blakeley.[18]

Baxter had a deep affection for the music hall tradition. Two films he made in the thirties – *Say it with Flowers* and *Music Hall* – captured on film famous old performers like Florrie Forde, Charles Coborn, and Marie Kendall (the originators of, respectively, 'Oh! Oh! Antonio!', 'The Man Who Broke the Bank at Monte Carlo', and 'Just Like the Ivy'), and when he joined British National he was able to entice Old Mother Riley away from Butchers and Flanagan and Allen from Gainsborough. He directed three of British National's eight Old Mother Riley pictures and produced and directed four Flanagan and Allen films – *We'll Smile Again* (1942), *Theatre Royal* (1943), *Dreaming* (1944), *Here Comes the Sun* (1945) – the last two after he had left British National to work as an independent producer/director. It was in this capacity that he made *When You Come Home* for Butchers.

It is a bigger budget production than Randle's Mancunian films and Baxter makes a real effort to enforce the normal rules of film grammar. Like *London Town*, the vastly more expensive musical created by Rank for Sid Field, it doesn't come off, but Baxter's film is much more adventurous than *London Town* and there are moments when Randle demonstrates a hitherto unseen subtlety. The film starts with Randle's 'granpa's birthday' sketch with the old buffer coming in drunk to find the family assembled round an impressive birthday cake, but this is merely the frame for a story set forty years earlier when Randle, the odd-job man in a music hall, joins forces with the daughter of the hall manager, a newspaper reporter, and a host of small-time entertainers to prevent the hall being taken over by property developers. The theme had already served Baxter well in earlier films like *Let the People Sing* and *Theatre Royal*, but he never quite manages to integrate it with his second theme, that of the put-upon little man who – inspired by a loquacious ventriloquist's dummy – learns to stand up for himself.[19]

Although the Randle films are the most interesting of the films relying on variety comedians, they are by no means the only ones. Mancunian put together a very able second string in Norman Evans, a monkey-faced Rochdale comedian best known for his caricature of a working-class housewife in his famous sketch 'Over the Garden Wall', and Nat Jackley, a giraffe-like comedian from Liverpool. They were teamed with Dan Young (the monocled toff, Private Basher, from the *Somewhere* films) and a tough little Lancashire woman, Betty Jumel, in two films – *Demobbed*, a bizarre farce set in a Lancashire factory, and *Under New Management*, where Evans, a chimney sweep, inherits a hotel beset, like Formby's pub in *George in Civvy Street*, by spivs and speculators. In 1950 Evans reappeared in female guise in *Over the Garden Wall* with Jimmy James as his husband, after which the cycle ended. Mancunian's post-war films had been produced at their own studios, a converted chapel in the Rusholme district of Manchester. In 1954, after Randle's last film – *It's a Grand Life* – was completed, the studio was sold to the BBC.

Mancunian's films were distributed outside Lancashire by the small but venerable company Butchers, which had launched into production in the early days of the war when more prestigious companies were cutting back. They had relied heavily on variety artists for their cheap, cheerful films – Barry Lupino in *Garrison Follies*, Albert Burdon in *Jailbirds*, Albert Modley in *Bob's Your Uncle*, Bunny Doyle and Betty Driver in *Facing the Music*, Leslie Fuller in *Front Line Kids*, Elsie and Doris Waters in *Gert and Daisy's Weekend*, *Gert and Daisy Clean Up*, and *It's in the Bag* – with considerable success. But they seem to have had difficulties with studio space and after 1944 came increasingly to rely on Mancunian for their films. One of their last ventures, *Variety Jubilee* (directed by Maclean Rogers who directed the great majority of their films), was about a successful attempt to revive the music-hall tradition. Reginald Purdell, Marie Lloyd Jr, George Robey, Betty Warren, Wilson. Keppel, and Betty, the Plantation Girls, and the Band of the Coldstream Guards, together made it look a viable enough proposition, but in the real world music hall was nearing the end of its life. The war had closed many of the halls and in the austere economic climate of the late forties few showmen had the resources to renovate and re-open them. By the early fifties even top entertainers like Max Miller and George Formby were finding fewer and fewer outlets for their talents.

As far as most of the other studios were concerned music hall was very old-fashioned, down-market stuff. ABPC preferred to rely on adaptations of West End stage successes such as Ian Hay's much-filmed *The Middle Watch* and the Ben Travers farce *Banana Ridge*. British National, once it had parted company with Baxter, lost interest in variety performers except for the ever-popular Old Mother Riley, and, after experiments with transatlantic humour (*Don Chicago*, directed ironically by Maclean Rogers) and upper-class whimsy (*The Ghosts of Berkeley Square* with Robert Morley and Claude Hulbert), gave up comedy entirely.[20]

Gainsborough and Ealing, which had enjoyed considerable commercial success with Will Hay, Gracie Fields, and George Formby in the thirties, concentrated on different sorts of comedies in the forties. Gainsborough brought in the new radio comedians – Askey and Murdoch from *Band Waggon*, Ben Lyon, Bebe Daniels, and Vic Oliver from *Hi Gang*, and Tommy Handley and assorted members of his team from *ITMA*. Ealing made four films with Formby – by far the most successful of the studio's films during the war years – but Balcon seems to have had few regrets about losing their major star to Columbia.[21] Balcon's espousal of documentary realism made him impatient of the frivolity of the Formby films, though he retained his respect for the studio's other comic mainstay Will Hay and made good use of the up-and-coming Cockney comedian Tommy Trinder in serious war films like *The Foreman Went to France* and *The Bells Go Down*.

Towards the end of the war both Gainsborough and Ealing made films about the 'golden age' of the music hall. Gainsborough's *I'll Be Your Sweetheart* (scripted and directed by Val Guest) looked behind the scenes at the men who wrote famous turn-of-the-century songs like 'I Wouldn't Leave My Little Wooden Hut', 'Oh Mr Porter', and 'The Honeysuckle and the Bee', and their battle for a copyright law which would prevent pirates from stealing their songs. Vic Oliver and Moore Marriott as the songwriters, Margaret Lockwood as a leading music-hall singer, and Michael Rennie as a crusading song publisher, made an unusual team. But the film is too wordy to be a proper musical, not funny enough to be a comedy, and not dramatic enough to be a melodrama.

Ealing's *Champagne Charlie* is set further back, in the 1860s, and concentrates on the rivalry between two famous 'lions comiques', George Leybourne (Tommy Trinder) and The Great Vance (Stanley Holloway). Cavalcanti's sure-footed direction and Michael Relph's bold production design create a glitteringly attractive view of the old music hall and Trinder and Holloway re-create the old songs with great flair and enthusiasm.[22] Andy Medhurst in his article on 'Music Hall and British Cinema' complains that the music-hall performances we see in *Champagne Charlie* are 'not able to sustain the same level of intensity, or provide single images of breathtaking iconographic power, such as can be found in *Millions Like Us* or even *I Thank You*.'[23] This is unfair as Trinder, without ever attempting to sink his Cockney persona into that of Midlander George Leybourne, gives a superb performance and his rendering of 'When the Pigs Begin to Fly' is as good as anything by the 'genuine' music hall artists. But Medhurst is right in commenting on the absence of that incandescent resonance one gets from Bertha Wilmott (in *Millions Like Us*) or Lily Morris (in *I Thank You*) as they sing their respective versions of 'Waiting at the Church'. It is this documentary quality, shared by all those low budget films made to showcase the talents of variety artists, which even the great documentarist Cavalcanti finds it impossible to recapture in *Champagne Charlie*.

Upper-class comedy

West End revues, farces, musicals, and drawing-room comedies had been filmed regularly in the thirties, making film stars of Jessie Matthews, Jack Buchanan, Jack and Claude Hulbert, Cicely Courtneidge, Leslie Henson, and the Aldwych farce team of Ralph Lynn, Tom Walls, and Robertson Hare. The war provided a less favourable climate for this sort of comedy than it did for the low-brow varieties. Jack Buchanan, the debonair song-and-dance man, acquired the Riverside studios in 1940 and turned to production; Jessie Matthews appeared only in a low-budget thriller, *Candles at Nine*; Jack Hulbert and Cicely Courtneidge made only *Under Your Hat*, based on their successful stage show; Leslie Henson stuck to live performance (though he makes a guest appearance as himself in *The Demi-Paradise*); the Aldwych farce team split up before war broke out but Robertson Hare appeared in a couple of farces – *Banana Ridge* and *Women Aren't Angels* – and then teamed up with George Formby in *He Snoops to Conquer*. However, if these traditional forms of upper-class comedy were gradually being extinguished, the gap was to some extent made good by a new type of comedy celebrating the character and lifestyle of the rich.

The first manifestation of the new trend is discernible only in retrospect. Despite being based on a very successful play by Terence Rattigan and directed by Anthony Asquith, *French Without Tears*, made by Two Cities for Paramount in 1939, is an undistinguished comedy. Four young men at a French crammer college compete for the favours of their friend's sister (Ellen Drew), and after the usual complications the most cynical and worldly of them (Ray Milland) wins her. Nevertheless the film was successful enough to launch Two Cities as a production company and Rattigan as a screenwriter.

The next, and much more significant, film in the cycle is *Quiet Wedding*, produced by Paul Soskin for Paramount early in 1940 while Two Cities' two Italian principals, Mario Zampi and Filippo del Giudice, were interned. It was directed by Anthony Asquith and scripted by Rattigan and Anatole de Grunwald from a play by Esther MacCracken. The story – about a young couple (Margaret Lockwood and Derek Farr) who get fed up with the fuss about their forthcoming marriage, run off to spend a night together and arrive back almost too late for their own wedding – is no more substantial than that of *French Without Tears*, but the film is enormously enriched by its array of British character actors: Marjorie Fielding, A.E. Matthews, Bernard Miles, Athene Seyler, Frank Cellier, O.B. Clarence, Wally Patch, Roland Culver, Margaret Rutherford, Hay Petrie, Jean Cadell, Esma Cannon, Ivor Barnard, Roddy Hughes, Peter Bull, Martitia Hunt, and Muriel George. Whether or not one likes or agrees with the values of the film, it is difficult not to be drawn into its charmingly dotty world. Instead of the cardboard playboys of *French Without Tears*, *Quiet Wedding* is populated by a bewildering variety of eccentrics, from Bernard Miles' obstinately incorruptible village policeman to Peggy Ashcroft's free-loving Freudian femme fatale.

In a much-quoted passage George Orwell compares England to a family,

a rather stuffy Victorian family, with not many black sheep in it but with all its cupboards bursting with skeletons. It has rich relations who have to be kow-towed to and poor relations who are horribly sat upon, and there is a deep conspiracy of silence about the source of the family income. It is a family in which the young are generally thwarted and most of the power is in the hands of irresponsible uncles and bed-ridden aunts. Still, it is a family. It has its private language and its common memories, and at the approach of an enemy it closes its ranks.[24]

Quiet Wedding is much less sardonic than this – the young lovers are smothered by crazy relatives and friends and Lockwood's discontented heroine makes a stab at rebellion, but doubts about the necessity or wisdom of conforming to expectations are banished by kindly advice from a worldly aunt and an understanding father.

Asquith's next comedy, *The Demi-Paradise*, written and produced by de Grunwald for Two Cities, seems to start from a more critical view of this England of dotty eccentrics. Its hero, the Russian engineer Ivan Kouznetsoff (Laurence Olivier), initially has his suspicions confirmed that the English are cold, unfriendly, inefficient, lazy, class-ridden, xenophobic and stupid. However, by the end of the film he has changed his mind. As he tells the crowd waiting to launch the icebreaker they have built for Russia:

'My friends, and you really are my friends all of you. When I came to your country I was filled with misconceptions and prejudices. But now that I have got to know you I know that you are a grand, a great people. No don't blush now, don't look embarrassed. I must tell you that much of the world thinks that you care only about money and you care much more about cricket, or nightingales or a good job well done. Much of the world thinks that you are perfidious and hypocritical and you are warm and friendly. And do you know why the world thinks these things?

Because you want it to. It amuses you. It pleases that dreadful sense of humour of yours.'

The Demi-Paradise's exploration of the notion of Englishness means that it can usefully be bracketed with those films which celebrate the English heritage like *This England, This Happy Breed, The Life and Death of Colonel Blimp*, and *A Canterbury Tale*. But the characters – Olivier's Kouznetsoff, Felix Aylmer's Bradshaw-quoting shipping magnate, Margaret Rutherford's magnificently regal pageant-organizer, and most of the other denizens of this toytown England – are not intended to be taken wholly seriously.

For Asquith and de Grunwald Anglo-Russian friendship seems to be inextricably bound up with the English sense of humour. On both of Ivan's visits to Britain he accompanies Ann, the shipbuilder's daughter (Penelope Dudley Ward), to a West End show, the star attraction of which is that most esoteric of English comedians, Leslie Henson. On the first occasion Ivan is completely bemused, on the second he laughs heartily, though one suspects he is being polite. He cannot share completely this English sense of humour, but at least he has come to understand its importance in British culture:

'that, that sense of humour, is perhaps the guiding factor of your lives. If you can laugh at life and at yourselves, you can be tolerant. If you can laugh, you must hate persecution, you must love democracy. Above all you must love freedom. For there is no laughter where there is no freedom. Now my people, the people of Russia they also love to laugh. And they will fight to the death rather than surrender their right to laugh. Today we are allies, friends. Let us remain friends. Let us fight together in the years to come and then laugh together in the years afterwards. Fight selfishness and greed and violence and then laugh them out of existence.'

Spoken by Olivier this is very moving and it is easy to be persuaded that *The Demi-Paradise* does express something which is essentially English, at least of that old England, 'the country of the cathedrals and minsters and manor houses and inns, of Parson and Squire', which Priestley still found existed in 1933 and which is celebrated in the upper-class comedies.[25] One can object that credibility is stretched to breaking point by housing a major shipbuilding concern with a large industrial work-force in a quaint little one-street town populated by lovable eccentrics, but it is a strength of the film that such objections arise only as afterthoughts. Subsequent upper-class comedies found it increasingly difficult to convincingly hold together this myth of an idyllic, countrified England where God was in his heaven and everyone happily adjusted to their place in society.

Gainsborough's *Dear Octopus*, released a few months earlier than *The*

Demi-Paradise, is very much a follow-up to *Quiet Wedding* but it has a much more sombre, bitter-sweet character. Directed by Harold French (who had directed the stage version of *French Without Tears*) and based on a play by Dodie Smith, it centres on the golden wedding celebrations of an upper-middle-class couple (Helen Haye and Frederick Leister) which bring their far-flung family (the dear octopus) home to the nest. Margaret Lockwood, well cast as a declassé secretary/governess/companion, agrees to marry the favourite son of the family (Michael Wilding), but their romance is pushed into the shade by that of the old couple and the return of a black sheep (Celia Johnson) who has defied her mother and made a mess of her love life. It is a much less funny film than *Quiet Wedding* or even *The Demi-Paradise*, without the sense of the ridiculous which permeates the Asquith films. But the characters (the upper-class characters at least) have more depth and the film has a real quality of pathos, a yearning affection for a way of life which had been ended by the war and was never to return

Three more films in this tradition surfaced during the war, *English Without Tears* and *Tawny Pipit*, both for Two Cities, and *On Approval*, a 1920s play by Freddie Lonsdale about a penniless duke and an American heiress testing each other's suitability for marriage in an isolated Scottish castle. It was directed and produced by Clive Brook, who also starred in it along with Beatrice Lillie, Roland Culver, and Googie Withers. Sydney and Muriel Box were closely involved in the initial stages and it was they who suggested shifting the setting from the 1920s to the Edwardian period. It is very much a throwback to an earlier form of drawing-room comedy, and Brook reinforced the self-conscious escapism of his film by devising an introductory montage sequence which whisks us away from wartime austerity to the never-never land before the First World War. The film won almost universal critical approval (Lindsay Anderson was to claim that it was 'the funniest British comedy ever made'), though its appeal was limited to what the *Kine Weekly* called 'good and high class halls'. It is unlikely that there were enough sophisticated patrons to make it a very profitable film, and Brook's interesting film career ended here.

On Approval steadfastly turned from contemporary society and buried itself in a past where the only problems the aristocracy had involved choosing between wealthy heiresses who wanted to pour their money into recklessly emptied coffers. *English Without Tears*, scripted by Rattigan and de Grunwald and directed by Harold French, makes a humorous attempt to deal with the changes wrought by the war on the role and lifestyle of the upper classes. Gilbey (Michael Wilding), butler to Lady Christabel Beauclerc, an eccentric bird-lover, is the son and grandson of a butler. His stiff decorum and remote detachment pierce the heart of his mistress' niece Jean (Penelope Dudley Ward). When war comes and Gilbey prepares to join up, Jean is moved to declare her love. Gilbey is flattered

but cannot contemplate such a misalliance. A year or two later he returns
as a second lieutenant, feeling he is now in a position to claim her hand.
However, life has changed for the upper classes too. Lady Beauclerc has
shifted her sympathy from migrating birds to human refugees, and with
Jean's help she has turned her London house into a centre where foreign
soldiers can learn about the English language and culture. Surrounded by
officers of all ranks and nationalities, Jean has grown out of her
fascination with butlers and is very blasé about second lieutenants. The
plot becomes impossibly complicated by amorous French and Dutch
officers and the class issues get lost. But at times it is a witty and moving
film.

Tawny Pipit falls somewhere between the upper-class comedies and the
post-war Ealing and Gainsborough films which celebrate English life
lower down the social scale. A nurse (Rosamund John), a convalescing
airman (Niall MacGinnis), a village parson (Christopher Steele), and a
retired Colonel (Bernard Miles) mobilize the inhabitants of a rural
community in support of a couple of rare birds under threat from egg-
stealers, busybodies, and the army. As with Lady Christabel in *English
Without Tears*, a clear parallel is drawn between the English love of birds
and their hospitality to persecuted foreigners. In whipping up support
from the villagers the Colonel tells them:

'We've welcomed to our country thousands of foreigners at one time or
another – French, Dutch, Czechs and Poles and a lot of them are jolly
decent people and anyway they can't help being foreigners. Well that's
what these little pipits are you see and we're jolly well going to see to it
that they get fair play or we shall want to know the reason why.'

Miles, who co-directed, wrote, and produced the film, was never one to
shirk direct messages, and *Tawny Pipit* is more broadly drawn than the
Ealing films and more radical than the Asquith/Rattigan films. It was only
modestly successful in Britain, but it was later to become a favourite on
the American art-house cinema circuit.

After the war there were half-hearted attempts to continue the cycle.
ABPC, which had persevered with old-style upper-class comedies – *The
Middle Watch, Spring Meeting, My Wife's Family, Banana Ridge, Women
Aren't Angels* – up to 1943, belatedly recruited Harold French to direct
Esther McCracken's *Quiet Weekend* (1946) and Asquith and de Grunwald
to adapt Rattigan's *While the Sun Shines* (1947). Both had been popular
stage plays, but as films they were much less successful than Herbert
Wilcox's 'Mayfair' series which imaginatively re-worked the formula,
shifting the emphasis away from comedy towards music and romance. *I
Live in Grosvenor Square* has Robert Morley as an eccentric duke and Rex
Harrison as an aristocratic army officer who stands for the Parliamentary
constituency held by his family for generations and loses, though the main

action centres on the tragic romance between the duke's daughter (Anna Neagle) and an American airman (Dean Jagger). *Piccadilly Incident* has a showgirl (Anna Neagle) falling in love with and marrying a scion of the aristocracy (Michael Wilding) before being tragically separated by the war. *The Courtneys of Curzon Street* explores relationships between lords and commoners over three generations. *Spring in Park Lane* and *Maytime in Mayfair*, the last two in the series, are much lighter, comedies about diamond merchants, West End couturiers, and lords disguised as footmen, with an abundance of singing and dancing by Neagle and Wilding.

Two Cities, which had begun the cycle with *French Without Tears*, brought it to a close with *Woman Hater* (1948, d. Terence Young), *The Weaker Sex* (1948, d. Roy Baker), and *The Chiltern Hundreds* (1949, d. John Paddy Carstairs) which was one of the top box-office films of 1949 – making more of a stir at the time than *Whisky Galore* and *Kind Hearts and Coronets*. Based on a play by William Douglas Home, it re-unites

40 Post-war austerity among the aristocracy. Lord and Lady Lister (A. E. Matthews and Marjorie Fielding) prepare the dinner. Beecham the butler (Cecil Parker) waits to serve it. *The Chiltern Hundreds* (1949).

Marjorie Fielding and A.E. Matthews as an upper-class couple and David
Tomlinson as their son. Now, though, they are no longer rich. Death duties
have swallowed up their wealth and their stately home is run by a
harassed butler (Cecil Parker) and a maid with ideas above her station
(Lana Morris). The romance, between Tony Pym (Tomlinson) and an
American millionaire's daughter, is almost on the level of that of the
juvenile leads in a Frank Randle film, and the main interest centres on
Pym's attempt to get into Parliament. Returning from the army to fight
for the seat which his family have held for hundreds of years, he finds the
political climate less predictable than he expected. Cleghorn, his Labour
opponent, dubs Tony 'the last in a long line of plutocrats, peers and
parasites' and sweeps to victory on a popular tide of democratic
indignation. When Cleghorn is promoted to the House of Lords, Tony is
persuaded to stand as the Labour candidate, expecting to be unopposed.
But Beecham, the butler, by far the most competent and articulate
member of the Pym household, feels it his duty to uphold the family
honour and stands as a Tory. After several re-counts he wins.

In the wartime comedies the upper-class characters, eccentric though
they are, come across as something more than caricatures, but A.E
Matthews' rabbit-obsessed lord is played strictly for laughs. In Labour
party Britain the sort of character he represented no longer had a part to
play and could only be regarded as a funny old relic of the past. As such he
could be bracketed with those old cars and steam engines which play such
an important part in fifties comedies. But the future lay with a more
mundane middle-class sort of comedy.

Ealing comedy

Considering how Ealing has become synonymous with comedy, it is
surprising how few comedies were made at the studio in the forties.
During the war there were eleven (twelve if one counts *Champagne
Charlie*), few of which bear much resemblance to the later Ealing
comedies. An exception is *Saloon Bar*, released in May 1940. Scripted by
Ealing stalwarts John Dighton and Angus MacPhail and directed by
Walter Forde it is a modest but very charming film about a group of pub
regulars teaming up to save their barmaid's boyfriend who has been
sentenced to death for murder. Led by a loquacious bookie (Gordon
Harker), they turn detective and find the real murderer. As in *Passport to
Pimlico*, *Whisky Galore*, and *The Titfield Thunderbolt*, the film is set in a
close-knit community which is suspicious of outsiders. At a point when the
three main protagonists are working out details of how the murder was
done, they are interrupted by a meek, friendly little man (Eliot Makeham
– who was to reappear as a fifth columnist a couple of months later in

41 Looking for clues. Barmaid Anna Konstam and regulars Mervyn Johns, Gordon Harker and Joyce Barbour. *Saloon Bar* (1940).

Spare a Copper) who tries to engage them in conversation. He is made to feel so unwelcome that he quickly dries up, swallows his drink, and leaves. There is another intrusion later on when the pub is invaded by a party of theatre-goers. They are frightfully posh and obviously used to being treated with deference and respect. But the clientele of the Cap and Bells show them neither, and they leave in a huff with Harker mimicking their complaint 'No tomato juice! What a fearful pub!'

Gordon Harker's Inspector Hornleigh, a boastful but likeable character not dissimilar to Honest Joe Harris, the *Saloon Bar* bookie, appeared in three films made by Gainsborough for Twentieth Century-Fox. But none of the other wartime comedies made at Ealing – the George Formby films, the jovial knockabout comedies *Sailors Three* and *Fiddles Three*, and the Will Hay films – have much in common with what subsequently became known as Ealing comedy.[26] Will Hay's *The Ghost of St Michaels* (scripted by Dighton and MacPhail and directed by Marcel Varnel), is a spirited re-working of the *Ghost Train* theme, with Hay and his schoolboys evacuated to a Scottish castle haunted by enemy agents. Teamed with silly-ass comedian Claude Hulbert, it looked as if Hay had made a successful break with his scene-stealing collaborators Moore Marriott and Graham Moffatt. But the next two films – *The Black Sheep of Whitehall* and *The Goose Steps Out* (made without Hulbert) – are tiresomely overladen with propaganda, and it is only when he re-joined Hulbert in the rich black comedy *My Learned Friend* that he made a film equal to his best work at Gainsborough. Unfortunately Hay's health began to fail while he was working on the film and cancer was diagnosed. Though he lived until 1949 he never made another film.[27]

Between January 1945 and December 1947 only twenty-one British comedies were released. Of the wartime comedy stars – Randle, Hay, Askey, Formby, Lucan, Handley, Flanagan and Allen, Trinder – only Randle survived into the late forties (although Old Mother Riley was to reappear briefly in the fifties and Askey and Trinder became television stars).[28] Ealing released no comedies at all in 1945 or 1946, despite the fact that they had recruited a new scriptwriter, T.E.B. Clarke, with a background in humorous journalism. Use had been made of his book *What's Yours?* for *Saloon Bar*, but Balcon didn't think Clarke's writing was very funny and put him to work on serious projects like *The Halfway House*, *Johnny Frenchman*, and *Dead of Night*. However, in 1946, with the support of producer Henry Cornelius and director Charles Crichton, he was able to push through an idea for a comedy about schoolboys unmasking a gang of black-market racketeers.

Hue and Cry, released in February 1947, was the first of the post-war Ealing comedies and set their tone of whimsical realism. Like *Saloon Bar*, it is a comedy thriller, though shot mostly on location and with a cast of schoolboys it has a more outdoor feel and bears a family resemblance to the Italian Neo-Realist films of Vittorio de Sica and Cesare Zavattini. Clarke's scripts – which include *Passport to Pimlico*, *The Blue Lamp*, *The Lavender Hill Mob*, and the *Titfield Thunderbolt* – now look rather quaint and contrived, but his affection for everyday realism, which he shared with Zavattini, gives his writing a distinctive quality rare among British screenwriters. *Hue and Cry* was warmly received by the critics and the public, but Balcon was not convinced that Ealing's future lay in comedy and set Clarke and Crichton to work on a wartime resistance drama, *Against the Wind*. It failed dismally at the box-office – more because its theme had become unfashionable than because it was a bad film – and director and writer were separated to work on different projects, both of them comedies.

Crichton's *Another Shore*, scripted by Walter Meade from a novel by Kenneth Reddin, was the only comedy Ealing released in 1948. With extensive location shooting in Dublin, the film was given a bigger budget than *Hue and Cry*, and apart from some poor back-projection it is visually impressive. The story is unusually improbable for post-war Ealing – a late manifestation of that retreat into fantasy that characterized the comedies of 1944–5. A Dublin civil servant (Robert Beatty), obsessed with the idea of escaping to the South Sea island of Raratonga, gives up work, refuses all involvement with women, and diligently waits for a road accident to occur from which he can rescue a millionaire who will make his dream come true. When an opportunity does arise he fails to take it, having been brought back to reality by a persistently seductive young woman (Moira Lister). Given such an unpromising plot the film is remarkably enjoyable. Robert Beatty – a Canadian – is an unsentimental hero, a good straight man to Stanley Holloway's eccentric drunk, Moira Lister's vamp, and a string of Irish character actors. But its fantasies were too fey for the critics and too esoteric for the public and it was not a commercial success.

1949 was a boom year for comedies, a total of thirty-three being released that year and, despite the poor reception afforded *Another Shore,* Ealing made its contribution with four films – *Whisky Galore, Passport to Pimlico, Kind Hearts and Coronets* and *A Run for Your Money* – which were to firmly establish the studio's reputation for comedy. Like *Hue and Cry, Whisky Galore* was made outside the studio as something of an experiment. Monja Danischewsky, Ealing's publicity director, pushed Balcon into giving him a break as a producer and was teamed with Alexander Mackendrick, who had worked at Ealing as a sketch artist and then a writer and was being given his first chance as a director. *Whisky Galore*, scripted by Compton Mackenzie from his own novel, is based on a real event which occurred in the early years of the war when a ship laden with whisky was wrecked off a Scottish island where whisky was in short supply. The enterprising islanders braved the excise men and the sea and retrieved part of the cargo for themselves. In Mackendrick's film the main obstacle between the islanders and the whisky is the English Captain of the Home Guard, played with a certain stuffy dignity by Basil Radford. Outwitted and betrayed – even his wife refuses to back him up wholeheartedly – he nevertheless remains so pig-headedly convinced that what he is doing is right that he remains a formidable and worthy opponent.

Mackendrick's humour is more universal and unsentimental than Clarke's and he resists the temptation to rely on Celtic whimsy. *Whisky Galore* has its share of eccentric characters, beautiful scenery, and Scottish dances, but they are never allowed to get out of hand. This tight little community, like that of the *Saloon Bar,* won't be patronized and doesn't ask to be indulged. The measure of Mackendrick's achievement can be seen if *Whisky Galore* is compared to the last film of this Celtic cycle, *A Run for Your Money*, a weak comedy directed and partly scripted by Charles Frend about innocent Welshmen (Donald Houston, Meredith

Edwards, and Hugh Griffith) abroad in the big city, with Moira Lister on the prowl and only an ineffectual gardening correspondent (Alec Guinness) to protect them.

Robert Hamer's *Kind Hearts and Coronets* tends to be seen as a unique and inexplicable masterpiece with no antecedents and no decendants. In fact at least two brilliant black comedies preceded it in the forties – Will Hay's *My Learned Friend* and Launder and Gilliat's *Green for Danger*. However, with its urbane middle-class murderer (Dennis Price) and its remarkably sensual anti-heroine (Joan Greenwood), it is hardly a typical Ealing comedy. (The coy, optimistic eccentricities of John Mills' *Mr Polly* seem more appropriate to Ealing.) Several critics applauded the film's sophistication, though others dogmatically objected to its reliance on a narrator, and even the audacious gimmick of having Alec Guinness play all eight members of the ill-fated d'Ascoyne family failed to set the box-office tills alight. Like *Whisky Galore* it is not mentioned by any of the trade papers as being notably successful and it was only after being warmly received in Europe and America that it began to be considered something out of the ordinary. By contrast, T.E.B. Clarke's *Passport to Pimlico* was one of the most popular films of 1949.

The film evolved from Clarke's characteristically quirkish interest in long-outdated laws which had never been repealed. Here he found an ideal starting point for his practice of spinning out a plausible thread from an improbable, but not impossible, premise. A gang of kids accidentally detonates an unexploded bomb, revealing a treasure chest containing a horde of valuables and a document which shows that this small area of Pimlico is part of the state of Burgundy. Though Burgundy itself was long ago dismembered, this forgotten outpost of the Duchy is not subject to English laws – which means that its inhabitants can dispense with rationing, coupons, licensing laws, and all the trappings of austerity.

Michael Balcon claims that

> In the immediate post-war years there was as yet no mood of cynicism; the bloodless revolution of 1945 had taken place, but I think our first desire was to get rid of as many wartime restrictions as possible and get going. The country was tired of regulations and regimentation, and there was a mild anarchy in the air. In a sense our comedies were a reflection of this mood ... a safety valve for our more anti-social impulses.[29]

Surprisingly, then, the freedom from restrictions enjoyed by the 'Burgundians' is extremely short-lived. After a riotous night when ration cards are torn up and singing, drinking, and dancing go on till the early hours in the local pub, the community wakes up to find itself invaded by spivs, black marketeers and all sorts of outsiders. This doesn't last long, as Whitehall erects an 'iron curtain' around Pimlico, and what the film really celebrates is the wartime spirit revived in 'plucky little Burgundy'. With the sort of paradoxical common sense which characterizes the film, Mrs Pemberton the grocer's wife (Betty Warren) explains: 'We always were English and we always will be English and it's just because we are English that we're sticking up for our right to be Burgundian.'

Charles Barr argues that, whereas Robert Hamer and Alexander Mackendrick were maverick directors whose comedies (*Kind Hearts and Coronets*, *Whisky Galore*, *The Man in the White Suit*, *The Maggie*, and *The Ladykillers*) were tangential to the Ealing tradition, those scripted by T.E.B. Clarke were its sentimental core.[30] However, Clarke's early films at least, which root their fantasies firmly in contemporary society, have as much in common with some of the comedies emerging from Gainsborough as they have with the other Ealing films.

Ken Annakin's *Holiday Camp* was the most successful of the Gainsborough films produced under the Box regime and was a major box-office success in 1947. Scripted by Sydney and Muriel Box, Mabel and Denis Constanduros, and Ted Willis (then a young left-wing dramatist), *Holiday Camp* combines the squabbling but respectable working-class family of *Millions Like Us* with the Prisoner-of-War-camp possibilities of *2,000 Women* and *The Captive Heart*. The holiday camp habit had begun to be exploited commercially in the thirties but it reached its peak in the immediate post-war years. The 1938 Holidays With Pay Act meant that the great majority of the working class was allowed two weeks' holiday a year, and all-in deals offered by holiday camps provided an attractive alternative to the traditional seaside lodging-house to a population acclimatized to communal living.[31]

Godfrey Winn's short story, which provided the starting point for the film's script, centred on Esther Harman, a middle-class spinster (Flora Robson in the film), who at last freed of a possessive old mother comes to the holiday camp as a change from the stifling boredom of the south coast resorts she had visited with her mother. She is disturbed by the voice of the camp announcer, not only because it intrudes into her privacy but because it is remotely familiar to her. Unable to contain her curiosity, she makes her way to the control tower and discovers he is the man she loved during the Great War. He is blind and has lost all memory of his life before he was wounded, and thus fails to recognize her. He talks happily about his present life, how fortunate he has been in his marriage, and how much he enjoys bringing happiness into people's lives at the camp. She slips away somehow purged by the experience.

The Gainsborough scriptwriters interweave this story with several others, shifting the focus from Miss Harman to a boisterous working-class family, the Huggetts. Joe Huggett (Jack Warner) is virtually the same character as Corporal Horsfall of *The Captive Heart*, a no-nonsense bus-driver who easily outsmarts the card sharps who have diddled his son out of his holiday money. But his family is a much more modern one than that seen in *The Captive Heart*. In place of the homely old bird played by Gladys Henson he now has pert, dizzy Kathleen Harrison and two teenage children. Gainsborough was much more ready to embrace the present on its own terms than was Ealing.

The critics were fascinated – if rather appalled – by this glimpse into a world of determined working-class jollity. Their objections centred not on the Huggetts but on a new element introduced into Godfrey Winn's story, the character of 'Binkie' Hardwicke (Dennis Price), an RAF type with an eye for the girls who, after failing to entice an attractive good-time girl out on to the moonlit dunes, settles for poor little Esma Cannon and murders her. 'Binkie' is obviously modelled on sex-murderer Neville Heath, whose case filled the headlines in 1946, and the critics considered this an unnecessarily morbid intrusion into an otherwise light-hearted film. However, the holiday camp is treated very much as a microcosm of British society and Dennis Price's irrational, war-obsessed killer functions effectively as an embodiment of post-war anxiety, jolting the film out of cosy complacency and acting as a sinister antidote to Jack Warner and the Huggetts.

The Boxes were quick to exploit the popularity of *Holiday Camp* and three follow-up films – *Here Come the Huggetts*, *Vote for Huggett*, and *The Huggetts Abroad* – were made over the next two years, 'Huggetry' became a term of derision for working-class domestic comedy, though the films now form an interesting bridge between John Baxter's sentimental dramas of working-class life and television soap operas like *Coronation Street* and *East Enders*. *Vote for Huggett* (1948, d. Ken Annakin), for example, has Joe taking on the political establishment of his London suburb and with the help of the kids from the local youth club, three eccentric old ladies, and his own native horse-sense, exposing their corrupt property deals and winning popular approval for his people's pleasure garden. The plot could be from a John Baxter film, but the tone of the Huggett films is very different. With a Labour government in power there was no longer any need to feel sorry for the working class. Joe and Ethel Huggett and their relatives, neighbours, and friends show no sign of being poor and oppressed, and though Joe says 'Sir' to his social superiors and dresses like Sid Field when invited to the Golf Club, he is quick enough to let the world know that working men have brains too.

In accordance with earlier Ealing films like *Saloon Bar*, the main protagonists of T.E.B. Clarke's films tend to be lower-middle-class, whereas Gainsborough was more prepared to present working-class characters. However, the gap between Stanley Holloway's Pimlico grocer Arthur Pemberton and Jack Warner's ordinary working man, Joe Huggett, is quite small. Pemberton is already ensconced on the local council whereas Joe's aspirations to such a position are considered very

42 Joe Huggett (Jack Warner) upholding 'that progressive egalitarian co-operative spirit which had developed during the war'. *Vote for Huggett* (1949).

audacious. But both men fight against selfish business interests to implement schemes which will benefit the whole community and, without being explicitly associated with the Labour party, they are both upholders of that progressive, egalitarian, co-operative spirit which had developed during the war and swept the Labour party to victory in 1945. Though much of that enthusiasm and idealism may have been dissipated by the end of the decade, a small group of films which maintain that ethos – the *Huggett* films and *Passport to Pimlico*, Jeffrey Dell's *It's Hard to be Good*, Derek Twist's *All Over the Town*, Ralph Smart's *A Boy, a Girl and a Bike*, and Henry Cass' *Last Holiday* – can be discerned among the comedies which flooded the market in the last years of the forties.

In J.B. Priestley's novel, *Bright Day*, published in 1946, a writer goes to a seaside hotel to work on a film script but enters into a deep reverie which takes him back to his adolescence in Bradford and his relationship with a warm, colourful, middle-class family. As one might expect with

Priestley, the golden vision disintegrates and turns to dust. But as the reverie ends so does the writer's illusions about his script. He abandons it and joins a group of young enthusiasts determined to make films of some social significance. In reality things didn't work out so neatly. Priestley did form a production company – Watergate – and invited Henry Cass, who had recently directed the exotic weepy *The Glass Mountain*, to direct the first film script he wrote single-handedly, *Last Holiday*.[32]

A salesman for an agricultural implements company (Alec Guinness), told he has only six weeks to live, blows his savings on a seaside holiday. As a 'mystery man' with plenty of money he soon attracts friends and admirers. With nothing to lose he acts in an honest and outspoken way and breaks down the snobbery and isolation of the guests and staff at the hotel, imbuing it with a spirit of harmony and co-operation. Though the film fared better than Bernard Miles' *Chance of a Lifetime* which projects the same sort of ideals, it was not liked by the circuit bosses and didn't get

43 Alec Guinness teaches the necessity of everyone pulling together to inventor Wilfred Hyde White, consultant Ernest Thesiger, and industrialist Moultrie Kelsall. *Last Holiday* (1950).

a proper West End release. Unsurprisingly it was a commercial failure and had no successors. No doubt a certain amount of political bias was at work here, but the film is not as good as it should be. The performances – particularly of Alex Guinness, Kay Walsh, and Sid James – are excellent, but production values are shabby and Priestley's trick ending is disastrously inappropriate.

Last Holiday was not quite the last attempt to evolve a radical, sophisticated form of comedy; Sandy Mackendrick's *The Man in the White Suit* and T.E.B. Clarke's *The Lavender Hill Mob* gave evidence of Ealing's continued fertility in the early fifties, though by the end of the decade the tradition had been superseded by the more amoral satires of the Boulting brothers. Upper-class comedy was replaced by comedies with more ordinary middle-class characters like the *Doctor* series produced by Betty Box. The low-brow tradition proved surprisingly resilient, spawning the popular television series *The Army Game*, with its characters not a million miles from the *Somewhere* stalwarts, and the enormously successful *Carry On* films.

11   Challenge to Hollywood

'We don't want much. All we want is to have our British films play to a fair proportion of the world's audiences. That is of course if they're good enough and entertaining enough. And I'm sure they will be. (J. Arthur Rank, *March of Time*, December 1945)[1]

Rank and the Americans

Despite the vital role that Anglo-American co-operation had played in winning the war, the partnership was not entirely a happy one. America seemed to have come out of the war rich and strong, Britain battered and poor. The British economy had been distorted by the war effort, massive losses had been sustained by bomb damage, a third of the merchant fleet had been sunk and overseas investments had been severely depleted. Lend-Lease – the provision of interest-free American loans – had been abruptly terminated once the war ended and though a $3,750 million loan had been negotiated by the end of 1945 there was considerable resentment at the terms on which it was offered. As the *Economist* commented:

> Our present needs are the direct consequences of the fact that we fought earliest, that we fought longest and that we fought hardest. In moral terms we are the creditors; and for that we shall pay $140 million a year for the rest of the twentieth century. It may be unavoidable; but it is not right.[2]

The loan was accepted but a number of factors – a deterioration in the terms of trade, a run on the pound, the winter 1946–7 fuel crisis – meant that it was used up much more quickly than expected. In July 1947 Attlee told Parliament that Britain was approaching a crisis and that emergency measures would have to be taken to stem the flow of dollars. Luxuries like tobacco and Hollywood films seemed obvious targets.

Hollywood was well aware of the dangers it faced in its most important overseas market. In March 1946, when Congress was debating the British loan, the influential trade paper *Variety* had warned:

> Britain, which provides by far the largest single share of the export market would be virtually cut off from American films in the event the

loan flops. Without the money, the English would have to tighten their belts still further and this would mean an end to all luxury imports, which includes films of course.[3]

It was a long-standing grievance of British film producers that whereas American films seemed to enjoy untrammelled access to British screens, British films only rarely reached an American mass audience. Attempts by Alexander Korda and the Ostrer brothers to penetrate the American market in the thirties had failed dismally and helped to induce the production crisis of 1937. But from 1944 onwards J. Arthur Rank launched a much more formidable campaign. He had strong business links with United Artists and Universal, a supply of quality films and, as a useful bargaining counter, control over two of the three major cinema circuits on which American films were shown in Britain. When Rank came to America in May 1947 he found the American film industry surprisingly co-operative. As *Variety* explained:

> most film moguls have figured it would be good business to help English pix in any way possible to find a market here since the income taken from the U.S. by British films is inconsequential compared to what Hollywood product gets out of England. Any British retaliation for alleged injustices here could be very serious for American income from abroad.[4]

He left, with an agreement that each of the big five US majors would provide his films with $2 million worth of play-dates on their affiliated circuits.[5]

Up to this point Britain's economic plight had helped rather than hindered Rank's ambitions. Cinema attendance remained high with so few alternative recreations available to the public, and fear of government action to restrict the import of films had persuaded the Hollywood moguls to consider sympathetically Rank's demands for a fair showing for British films in America. Though subject to harassment for their monopolistic practices by the Justice Department, the Hollywood companies enjoyed the wholehearted support of the American government for their overseas efforts. They assumed that Rank had a similarly close relationship with the British government and by making concessions to him they were staving off discriminatory measures against the import of Hollywood films into Britain. In this they were mistaken. Rank, a staunch Tory under suspicion of exercising monopoly power over the British film industry, was not regarded with any favour by Labour politicians and he was not taken into the confidence of the government as to their plans for the film industry. On 6 August, to the surprise of Rank as much as the Americans, Hugh Dalton, the Chancellor of the Exchequer, imposed a seventy-five per cent *ad valorem* tax on the import of foreign films. Two days later the

Motion Picture Export Association (MPEA), representing the major Hollywood companies, announced a total boycott of the British market.

Such drastic measures were viewed with disfavour on both sides of the Atlantic and an early settlement to the dispute was expected. Throughout August *Variety* was able to report that American exhibitors were 'leaning over backwards to avoid any resemblance of reprisals'. On the British side exhibitors were dismayed at the possibility of an end to cheap Hollywood films and prophesied doom and destruction unless the Americans were mollified. British producers, who had worked for so long under the shadow of Hollywood, were left confused and uncertain by the withdrawal of their great competitor. On 2 October the *Kine Weekly* reported that:

> the Import Duty and other causes have seriously upset plans announced at the beginning of the year and have brought about many sudden changes of schedule, the shelving of some subjects and the last-minute introduction of others. The result is a state of flux in the production industry, and a strong indication that this year's output will be very little in excess of 1946. This fact coupled with uncertainty about the future, means that we have reached a crisis.[6]

Harold Wilson, who was appointed President of the Board of Trade later that month, did his best to overcome the crisis by exhorting British producers to make more films and grab a larger share of their own home market, and by the end of the year, with the dispute still unsettled, producers were beginning to take up the challenge. Alexander Korda reactivated his old company, London Films, took over British Lion, a small distribution company which had acquired unexpected prestige by backing *In Which We Serve*, and moved in to de-requisitioned studios at Isleworth and Shepperton. However, he faced problems raising finance for his ambitious programme of films. As a confidential Board of Trade minute put it:

> The film industry is not one which normal financial channels look upon with favour. Its habits are peculiar, most of the people engaged in it are rogues of one kind or another, and a good deal of money has been lost by unwise investment in it, or by the uncontrolled behaviour of producers.[7]

This reluctance of private financial interests to invest in the film industry eventually led the government to loan money to British producers – to Alexander Korda in particular – but the initial expansion came from within the Rank Organization.[8]

The import duty and the subsequent embargo had put Rank in something of a dilemma. He had pushed to get into the American market because his big-budget films, even when successful, were not recouping enough of their costs in the British market alone. After buying a chain of cinemas in Canada he had had some success in persuading Canadian audiences to accept British films. With guaranteed play-dates for his films in America, there was at least a chance that the notoriously insular American audience might also be won over. But as box-office results proved disappointing and relations between Britain and America soured, fewer and fewer cinemas were prepared to show British films. By the end of the year Rank had decided on a radical change of policy: instead of trying to carve out a share of the US market, he would attempt to squeeze the Americans out of the British market which they had dominated for so long. A production programme of thirty-six films was announced which would be funded by a major restructuring of the Rank empire.

Rank and the British market

The companies Rank had taken over from Gaumont-British had remained independent of, indeed were often in competition with, the companies Rank had taken over from Odeon. Rank's holding company, the General Cinema Finance Corporation, which controlled Gaumont-British, Two Cities, Independent Producers, and Denham and Pinewood studios, had hitherto borne the burden of film production; henceforth it was to be shared by the profitable Odeon side of the organization. This attempt at rationalization aroused considerable suspicion. Film production was regarded as a risky business, and one that the founders of Odeon Theatres had explicitly vowed to abstain from. United Artists, which held a substantial but non-voting share in the company, threatened legal action, and the reaction of the English financial press was equally hostile.[9] Nevertheless the deal went ahead and a serious attempt was made to make British films the mainstay of the two Rank circuits.

Had the embargo been likely to continue this would have been a sensible move. But in March 1948 Wilson reached agreement with the Americans. In 1946 Hollywood films had cost Britain sixty-eight million dollars; the import duty had been designed to reduce this figure to around seventeen million dollars, but as no new films had been imported only minor savings had been made. For six months the Americans had relied on films imported before the embargo and reissued old favourites; now these supplies were drying up. If it was just a matter of helping British producers, Wilson had only to wait till the Americans capitulated, but there were other interests to consider. The Rank circuits might be adequately supplied with British films but this left four thousand other cinemas dependent on a very meagre ration of non-Rank British films. Angry exhibitors insisted that if the embargo was not lifted they would be forced to close their doors. Wilson agreed to scrap the import duty in return for a deal whereby only seventeen million dollars of the earnings of Hollywood films in Britain were remitted. This sum was to be supplemented by an equivalent amount to whatever was earned in America by British films, and with the funds that remained 'blocked' in Britain the Americans were permitted to invest in film production and to buy the foreign rights to British films.

Wilson's enemies and Rank's apologists have presented the Anglo-American agreement as an American victory with disastrous consequences for British film interests, but in retrospect it appears an adroit settlement of what had developed into a futile and mutually harmful dispute. In view of the close political, military, and economic relations between Britain and America, an attempt to exclude American films permanently from the British market was unthinkable, especially as British film producers had revealed themselves as totally incapable of filling the vacuum which would exist if there were no more imports from Hollywood. And Wilson did contrive to protect those producers – notably Rank and Korda – who had significantly increased their output.

During the period of the boycott a new Cinematograph Films Bill had passed through Parliament. Though it provoked vigorous debate its provisions were relatively uncontentious: the 'renters quota' was dropped, the composition of the Cinematograph Films Council was changed, and the 'exhibitors quota' was to be fixed at six-monthly intervals by Parliamentary Statutory Instrument rather than fixed in advance by the Act. This latter provision, however, enabled Wilson to conceal from the American negotiators his intention of setting an unprecedentedly high quota to protect British producers. It was not until June 1948 that he announced that it would be raised from seventeen-and-a-half to forty-five per cent.

Rank felt confident enough to sever the links between his circuits and the American companies – Fox, Paramount, RKO, and United Artists – which before the embargo had supplied the Odeons and Gaumonts with over a hundred films a year. In June he informed them that he would be unable to find space for more than twenty-five Hollywood pictures for the remainder of 1948, and then added insult to injury by offering them playing-time as supports for his British films.[10] With the Rank circuits virtually closed to them, the Americans had to find other, less suitable outlets for their films among the small circuits and independents. An attempt was made to put together a fourth national circuit, but the independents, convinced that the feud with Rank wouldn't last, were reluctant to commit themselves. United Artists' Arthur Kelly, after several weeks' negotiations, was gloomily pessimistic. He reported that with the market glutted with surplus American films, 'rentals on top-budget pictures have taken a tumble and because of the number of American pix the indies can lay their hands on, it's practically impossible for the Yanks to get extended playing time.'[11]

The independent exhibitors, on the other hand, though spoilt for choice with top-class American films, found themselves in the galling position of having to devote almost half their screening time to poor quality British films. As *Variety* reported with some satisfaction:

> Hike in the quota act last year was followed by such a quantity of inferior British product that the net value of theatre property, including that of the circuits, has deteriorated by one-third. So said Theo H. Fligelstone, newly elected vice-chairman of the London Branch of the Cinematograph Exhibitors Assn. recently at the organisation's annual meeting. Two years ago, Fligelstone added, exhibitors had declared there was no need of a quota act as they were only too pleased to show British pictures which were drawing a large public. In contrast, he said, exhibitor contribution to loyalty at the present time was playing to empty houses with British pix.[12]

Rank, with a programme of sixty new features which included expensive pictures like *The Blue Lagoon, The Passionate Friends, Eureka Stockade, Saraband for Dead Lovers*, and *Scott of the Antarctic*, ten re-issues, nine 'curtain raisers', half-a-dozen episodes of *This Modern Age*, and several films from Universal and Eagle-Lion, American companies in which Rank had substantial shareholdings, insisted that his policy was paying off and produced figures for average weekly takings from Odeon cinemas which showed that British films took more than American films.[13] But by the end of the year *Variety*, sensing that the challenge to Hollywood was faltering, announced that:

> The big British film bubble appears to have all but burst. Hollywood's fears of a year ago that it would be forced into a worldwide duel with the British for screen domination are rapidly fading. Neither as producers of film in the volume or quality sufficient to capture international markets, nor as salesmen of their product to the exhibitors of the world – their own included – have the British 'caught on' in the opinion of American film men.[14]

1948 was not a bad year for British films at the box-office. According to the *Kine Weekly*, William Wyler's *The Best Years of Our Lives* was the top film of the year but nine of the fourteen runners up were British. Some of the more successful British films – *Spring in Park Lane, It Always Rains on Sunday, Miranda, The Weaker Sex, No Orchids for Miss Blandish, When the Bough Breaks, Good Time Girl, Noose, No Room at the Inn* – were made economically enough to recoup their costs in the British market alone. But Rank's attempt to switch his production programme to this sort of modest-budget film-making had unfortunate consequences.

Until the embargo Rank productions had been geared towards a world market. Even companies like Gainsborough and Ealing (which became tied to the Rank Organization in 1945 after accepting a distribution contract which effectively bought Ealing's films in advance of production) were encouraged to make uncharacteristically big-budget films, while the costs of the films made by Two Cities and the Independent Producers group were exceptionally high even by Hollywood standards. When profits in America failed to materialize and the decision was taken to concentrate on the home market, budgetary constraints were introduced. Rank, who had acted like a Renaissance prince dispensing lavish funds to his talented but extravagant teams of film-makers, was transformed into an apostle of scientific management, organizing production on factory lines and ruthlessly pruning anything which failed to be cost-effective. During 1949 small, old-fashioned studios at Islington, Highbury, and Shepherd's Bush were closed down, the work-force at Denham drastically reduced and production concentrated at Pinewood where producers were encouraged to make use of the 'independent frame' facilities which enabled a film to be shot using miniaturized, mobile sets and back-projection.

Such crude economies alienated Rank's most talented film-makers. Powell and Pressburger, dismayed at the lack of sympathy and understanding shown *The Red Shoes*, left to join Alexander Korda; Launder and Gilliat, equally disgruntled over *The Blue Lagoon*, soon followed. Ian Dalrymple and Jack Lee, at Wessex, stayed to make *Dear Mr Prohack* and *All Over the Town*, but it was only after they too joined Korda that they had their first big success with the Prisoner-of-War-camp drama *The Wooden Horse*. David Lean and Cineguild remained loyal longer, but the lack of commercial success afforded *The Passionate Friends* and *Madeleine* eventually led to a rift. Two Cities, Gainsborough, and the new units set up specifically to make low-budget films fared little better. Two Cities failed to find an identity after the departure of Giudice and came to rely increasingly on ineffectual comedies like *The Perfect Woman* and soggy melodramas like *Madness of the Heart*. Gainsborough under the Boxes received an unfairly bad press considering their achievement in turning out large numbers of cheap and watchable films, but even so, standards declined as output was increased. The 'curtain raisers' produced by John Croydon at Highbury, and the films bought in from the independent production company Aquila, were little better than the 'quota quickies' of the thirties. Rank cinema programmes which relied upon such inadequate productions alienated audiences and there was a gradual drift away from the Odeons and Gaumonts. In November 1949, at the annual general meeting of Odeon Theatres where a total loss for the year of £3,528,615 was declared, Rank admitted that:

'many of the films we produced were not of the quality to ensure reasonable returns. It can now be seen that our plans to meet an unexpected and critical situation were too ambitious, that we made demands on the creative talent in the industry that were beyond its resources, and that as a result, we spread our production capacity, in which I still have unshaken faith, too thinly over the films we made.'[15]

Extravagance in production

The failure of the challenge to Hollywood finally dissolved the optimism about British film-making which had built up during the war. The quota was reduced to forty per cent in 1949 and thirty per cent the following year and attempts were made to discover what had gone wrong. At the end of 1948 two committees were appointed by Harold Wilson: the Working Party on Film Production Costs under the chairmanship of Sir George Gater, and the Committee of Enquiry into the Distribution and Exhibition of Cinematograph Films chaired by Lord Portal – and after his death by Sir Arnold Plant.

Since the Palache Report of 1944 there had been persistent accusations that British film production was unnecessarily profligate and wasteful. Criticism reached a climax during 1945–6 when two big-budget Rank films, *Caesar and Cleopatra* and *London Town*, went heavily over their already generous budgets. In many ways these two films were special cases – *Caesar and Cleopatra* was directed and produced by Gabriel Pascal, a Hungarian adventurer with little ability or experience as a film-maker, while *London Town* was directed and produced by American veteran Wesley Ruggles, totally at sea in trying to make a British musical on Hollywood lines at the recently de-requisitioned and run-down Shepperton studios. The mainstay of Rank's Independent Producers – Powell and Pressburger, Launder and Gilliat, David Lean, Ronald Neame, and Anthony Havelock-Allan – had served a thorough apprenticeship in the thirties and were hardened professionals whose films for Rank were expensive because they were complex and ambitious not because they were poorly planned and badly executed.

There was no doubt though that production costs had risen alarmingly since 1939 and the economies Rank introduced in the late forties seemed to have been of dubious value. According to the PEP Report:

> The fact is that part of the expanded programme was carried out by an organisation mainly accustomed to, and adjusted to high cost productions. This can be seen clearly in the financial records of many of those films made in the immediate post-war years. As well as films which were conceived as 'prestige' productions, there were others which were planned more modestly but which ended up, from the cost point of view at least, near the 'prestige' class.[16]

Frank Launder pointed out that in making *The Blue Lagoon* a good deal of money could have been saved if he had been allowed to shoot more of the film on location, rather than returning to Pinewood to keep the studio working at full capacity.[17] And an even more jaundiced ex-Rank producer,

R.J. Minney of Gainsborough, complained to the press that the Rank Organization was top heavy,

> 'and being over centralised all the films cost more to make because they have to carry the very large overheads. For example, a film which I could produce for £100,000 costs £40–50,000 more when made under the Rank Organization.'[18]

The Gater Committee, which reported in October 1949, was scathingly critical of the general ethos under which the industry operated:

> it lives in a general atmosphere of extravagance and unreality, leading to a disregard of expense which would not be tolerated in other forms of business. This is a problem which is inherent in any industry concerned with the provision of entertainment. . . . We are bound to say, however, that even when due allowance has been made for the artistic element in the film industry, there is evidence that towards the end of the war and in the years immediately following it extravagance in the British film industry was allowed to go beyond all reasonable bounds. During this period many people were attracted to the industry who lacked experience in film-making, and, encouraged by the exceptional success of certain British films and the boom in cinema attendances, films were made with an ever increasing disregard of cost.[19]

Predictable recommendations were made about the need for better labour relations and more efficient production planning, but with its house in such disorder the film production industry appeared undeserving of any sort of government subsidy.

The NFFC

However, before the Gater Committee delivered its report the government had already decided that independent producers, at least, must be provided with additional financial facilities if they were to survive. In July 1948, after attempting unsuccessfully to channel private capital into the industry, Wilson announced his intention of setting up a film fund with money provided by the Treasury.[20] Interim legislation was passed and in October a company soon to be known as the National Film Finance Corporation was established with a capital of two-and-a-half million pounds. Its managing director James Lawrie, who had been general manager of the Industrial and Commercial Finance Corporation where he had been unsullied by any previous contact with film finance, was faced with the immediate problem of choosing which producers he should entrust with the Treasury's money. As the most common method of financing a film was through a distribution contract, Lawrie decided it would be sensible to let a distribution company act as intermediary between the NFFC and the producers. Korda's British Lion was the obvious candidate and was granted a loan of one million pounds with another two million to follow. Korda's unfortunate record of financial mismanagement was ignored.

British Lion took up and seemed initially to have lost three million pounds of the NFFC's budget, and there was much jeering in the press at the government's incompetence in dealing with the wily Korda. Subsequently the NFFC was to take the bull by the horns and lend directly to producers – instituting strict budgetary controls as a condition of its involvement and introducing a salutary discipline to British film production. But the British Lion experiment was not quite the disaster it has been painted. Many of Korda's films – *The Third Man, The Small Back Room, Maytime in Mayfair, The Wooden Horse, The Happiest Days of Your Life* – were to prove extremely successful and most of the NFFC money was eventually recuperated. Had the loan not been made, British Lion and the cluster of talented producers which sheltered under its wing would have barely survived. In a judicious assessment of the performance of the NFFC in its first two years the PEP Report points out that:

> By March 31, 1951, the Corporation had made loans to five distributing companies and forty production companies for the making of 101 films. Because the Corporation can make loans 'only if money cannot be obtained on reasonable terms from an appropriate source', it is reasonable to suppose that many of the 101 films would never have been made without the Corporation's financial help.[21]

The NFFC was to continue to play an important role for the next thirty-five years before falling victim to government misconceptions about the ability of the British film industry to survive without government assistance.

The Plant Report and the Eady Levy

The survival of British Lion was considered so important because it was the only production and distribution company of any size which was independent of both the Americans and the cinema-owning combines. There were fears that, without the force of a major distributor behind them, those producers not associated with Rank or ABC would have difficulty getting a fair showing for their films in the circuit cinemas. The Plant Committee was set up in December 1948 to prepare a detailed survey of the distribution and exhibition side of the industry, and to suggest remedies for any inequities it found there. Wilson favoured government intervention to curb the powers of the circuits and was worried that Plant, 'a laissez-faire economist', would come down heavily against such an interference with market forces.[22] In fact, Plant's free-market principles were offended by the prevalence of monopolistic and restrictive practices in the film industry and the report proposed a radical limitation of the barring system which gave particular cinemas the exclusive right to show a film within a particular area, and the introduction of competitive bidding for films in place of the rigid division between first, second, and subsequent-run cinemas. However the power of the distributors and exhibitors proved strong enough to withstand any proposals for change and the most important measure of reform to grow out of the Plant Report concerned production.

The Plant Committee accumulated a formidable barrage of statistics, and one of the important facts to emerge was that only a small percentage of box-office receipts were returned to the producer. In refutation of the claims of incompetence and extravagance, film-makers could henceforth argue that 'British films pay; they pay very well. But they pay the wrong people.'[23] Though their production methods left much to be desired, British film-makers did suffer from a serious structural disadvantage: cinema owners and cinema audiences had grown used to a regular supply of quality American films which could be shown relatively cheaply in Britain because they had recovered most of their costs in their own home market. British producers had to content themselves with a similar share of box-office profits to their American counterparts while drawing on a much smaller market for their films.

This situation might have been expected to benefit exhibitors and there are indications that in the late twenties and early thirties cinema owning was a highly profitable business.[24] But until the last years of the thirties new cinemas were built at such a rate that competition was fierce and it was the public who benefited in terms of low prices, luxurious decor, and elaborate showmanship. The gap between what people had to pay and what they were prepared to pay was exploited by the government during the war by massive increases in Entertainment Tax on the sale of cinema tickets. Though attendance rose dramatically during the forties, the profits of cinema owners took a smaller percentage of box-office receipts in 1947–8 than they did in 1938–9, while Entertainment Tax had increased from eleven-and-a-half to thirty-six per cent.[25] Of the £109 millions taken at the box-office in 1948, £39 millions were paid to the Inland Revenue in Entertainment Tax.[26] Ironically it was the government which now benefited most from the import of cheap American films.

In their evidence to the Plant Committee the Cinematograph Exhibitors Association asked for a straightforward reduction in Entertainment Tax, while the British Film Producers Association wanted fifty per cent of the amount taken by the government to be given back to British film producers as a subsidy. Wilson agreed to a compromise plan worked out by the Treasury official Sir Wilfred Eady, involving a small reduction in Entertainment Tax and an increase in seat prices which was expected to bring in an additional three million pounds to the industry. The exhibitors would be allowed to keep half of this sum but the other half would go into a British Film Fund and be distributed at the end of the year to the producers of British films. Americans who made films in Britain would also participate in the share-out and, as it was paid in proportion to the box-office earnings of a film, there was a built-in incentive for them to make popular big-budget films. The Eady Levy was brought into effect by the Finance Bill of July 1950, initially as a temporary measure, but in 1951 it was extended for three years and in 1957 it became statutory and remained in force until 1985.

The British film industry continued to suffer crises, but in the fifties film production enjoyed greater health and stability than might have been expected given the competition from television. British films like *A Queen is Crowned, Doctor in the House, Genevieve, The Dambusters*, and *Reach for the Sky* continued to do very well at the box-office. In America the last of the Rank prestige films (*Hamlet, The Blue Lagoon*, and *The Red Shoes*) enjoyed surprising success and throughout the fifties a variety of British films – from Ealing comedies to Hammer horror films – found a market in America. The bid to make Britain's film industry a serious rival to Hollywood failed, but there was a long and relatively prosperous Indian summer before serious disintegration set in at the end of the 1960s.

Conclusion

'I would think nothing of spending nine hours in a cinema (or rather three different ones). To me there were only two types of film, the good and the very good.' (J.P. Mayer, *British Cinemas and their Audiences*, 1948)[1]

It is true that many products of our contemporary film industry represent for our age what the Roman *circus* meant for the declining Roman Empire: the danger is real and imminent.

If we persist in our academic remoteness from film as mass-influence, the doom of our civilization is certain. Film is symptom *and* cause. But this pessimistic trend is only a warning. It only illustrates the power of the film medium – as popular art and educational instrument – to serve *positive* ends if *responsibly* developed. (J.P. Mayer, *Sociology of Film*, (1946)[2]

'I cannot express on paper the wild thrilled feeling that runs through me during a film I am enjoying terrifically, especially during love scenes. (J.P. Mayer, *British Cinemas and their Audiences*, 1948)[3]

In 1945 the sociologist J.P. Mayer attempted an investigation of the extent and effect of the cinema's influence. He was given the freedom of the Odeon circuit and interviewed managers, doormen, and usherettes, as well as observing and questioning audiences. But after nine months of such painstaking research, the Rank Organization withdrew its co-operation and Mayer was forced to try another tack. Over the next year he put a series of questions to the readers of the popular film magazine *Picturegoer*, asking them to write in detail on whether films had influenced their decisions and behaviour, whether films had seeped into their dreams, and, finally, to write 'motion picture autobiographies' tracing the history of their interest in films and how they thought it had affected their lives.

A substantial selection of these replies are reproduced verbatim in Mayer's two books – *Sociology of Film* (1946) and *British Cinemas and their Audiences* (1948) – and they bear fascinating and sometimes frightening witness to the huge influence cinema exercised over people's lives: the unemployed Irish shop assistant with bad teeth who insisted he would make an ideal husband for Deanna Durbin ('if ever we are married it will not be one for the divorce court to wreck, but one of happiness'); the women nursing unrequited passions for Errol Flynn or Tyrone Power.[4] Mayer dismissed out of hand the possibility that films enriched people's lives: 'Many of my contributors attribute to film that it helps them to discover their "personalities". In fact just the opposite is true.' And gloomily concluded 'that the majority of films we see are pernicious to our nervous system. They are a mere drug which undermines our health, physical and spiritual.'[5]

Mayer was a member of that liberal intelligentsia which deplored the threat an exploitative, irresponsible cinema seemed to pose to the new dawn of a truly democratic society. As he points out:

> Western civilization can only remain healthy when a synthesis between cultural and mass standards can be brought about. In this sense democracy is still, despite the Education Act of 1944 and the Nationalization of the Coal Mines in 1947, a task, but not yet a fact.[6]

His noble intentions, however, are vitiated by an arrogantly condescending attitude to his source material and towards cinema in general. The hapless *Picturegoer* respondents, their spelling and grammatical mistakes preserved for posterity (did he really think working-class people went around talking about 'flims' and 'skyscrappers'?) are treated like retarded schoolchildren. In this Mayer was not untypical of the critical establishment. Lindsay Anderson, for example, one of the most promising young left-wing critics, was even more contemptuous of the ordinary cinema-goer, declaring in 1948, 'It is today impossible to make films which will appeal to a moronic mass audience (critics should be compelled to spend their Sunday evenings sitting in front of cinema queues, just looking at them), and at the same time be good.'[7]

Mayer and Anderson operated from a left-wing standpoint which asserted that what was good and natural and healthy in popular culture was being undermined by an artificial 'mass culture' which reduced its victims to passive, manipulable morons. For those of us who religiously attended Saturday morning pictures and mis-spent our youth watching X films, this seems an unnecessarily pessimistic outlook and in practice difficult to distinguish from high art contempt for all aspects of popular culture. It meant that in the forties films were accepted by critics and intellectuals for their progressive intentions (most of the realist films) or for their adherence to high art criteria of harmony and good taste (films made from Coward's or Rattigan's or Shakespeare's plays, and self-consciously 'filmic' films like *Odd Man Out* and *The Queen of Spades*). Films which fell into neither category – most melodramas, costume pictures, low-brow comedies, films dealing with the underworld and the darker side of life – were condemned as 'sordid', 'morbid', or 'horrid'.

Strictures against moronic audiences and soppy, artificial films derived from a didactic tradition which contended that what is pleasurable should also be instructional, and consequently that films which seemed to make no serious statement about life were trivial, time-wasting, and in the long run pernicious. The fantasy life of the masses, it was feared, was becoming morbidly infected, and films which overwhelmed the audience with sensations or encouraged them to become uncritically absorbed were necessarily bad. Hence the appeal of sober, responsible realism which seemed to have an educational as well as an entertainment value.

The essential task of any proper history of British cinema is to explore the extensive hinterland put out of bounds by this combination of well-intentioned puritanism, snobbery, and timid, derivative aesthetics. I would gladly contend that *The Man in Grey* is a better and more interesting film than *San Demetrio–London*, that *They Made Me a Fugitive* is a more original and convincing film than *Odd Man Out*, but the aim of this book is not to uncover a new selection of masterpieces of British cinema. With film, aesthetics are never enough. Viewed in isolation *In Which We Serve*, *Brief Encounter*, even *The Red Shoes*, degenerate into kitsch. Films need a context, whether as the work of a particular director, the product of a studio or – as I have preferred to discuss them here – as part of a cycle of films emerging from a particular society over a particular period.

Such a process might incidentally overturn the pantheon of acknowledged classics but it would be churlish to deny the impact of realism on British cinema. Dramatized documentaries like *Target for Tonight*, compilation films like *Desert Victory*, films heavily influenced by documentary ideas and attitudes such as *The Way Ahead* were genuinely popular and, though after forty years their realism has worn thin, they introduced new themes, broke with old stereotypes, encouraged the use of location shooting and more natural dialogue and encouraged film-makers to look beyond stage and literary adaptations for the raw materials of their films. But the advance in technique and inventiveness didn't manifest itself just in greater realism. The romantic, escapist, fantastic side of British cinema benefited too: *The Man in Grey* and *Fanny by Gaslight* are much more resonant, complex, atmospheric films than thirties predecessors like *The Lilac Domino* or *Nell Gwynn*.

After the war, though the critics believed that realism was being squeezed out of British cinema, its lessons were absorbed and ambitious films like *Madeleine* and *The Passionate Friends*, *The Red Shoes* and *Black Narcissus*, *Blanche Fury* and *So Evil My Love*, *They Made Me a Fugitive* and *It Always Rains on Sunday* successfully transcended the division between realism and tinsel.

Chronology: Cinema and Society in the Forties

1939

In March Czechoslovakia was invaded by Germany, and Britain made its alliance with Poland. In August Russia signed a non-aggression pact with Germany. On 3 September Chamberlain announced that a state of war existed between Britain and Germany. In December British battleships sank the *Graf Spee* in the Battle of the River Plate.

The outbreak of war brought production to a virtual standstill. Six films which were in an advanced stage of production were completed (*Blind Folly* for RKO at Walton on Thames, *Band Waggon* at Islington and Shepherd's Bush, *Dr O'Dowd* at Teddington, *Old Mother Riley Joins Up* for British National at Elstree, *The Proud Valley* at Ealing, and *Traitor Spy* at Welwyn). Only another eleven films were made in the rest of the year, none of them very lavish productions: *The Lion Has Wings* (Korda), *Busman's Honeymoon* (MGM-British); *Contraband* (British National) at Denham; *The Briggs Family* at Teddington; *Charley's Big-Hearted Aunt* at Shepherd's Bush; *Bulldog Sees It Through* at Welwyn; *Crimes at the Dark House* at the old Whitehall studio, Elstree; *Convoy* and *Let George Do It* at Ealing; *Jailbirds* and *Laugh it Off* at Walton; and *Law and Disorder* (for RKO) at Highbury.

According to the *Kinematograph Weekly* the top film of the year was *The Citadel*, directed by King Vidor, produced by Victor Saville for MGM-British in Britain.[1] The other British films mentioned as successful at the box-office were: *Pygmalion*, (George Bernard Shaw's comedy adapted by Anthony Asquith and Gabriel Pascal); *The Lady Vanishes* (Hitchcock's thinly-veiled anti-Nazi thriller); *St Martin's Lane* (a sentimental backstage melodrama with Charles Laughton and Vivien Leigh); the George Formby vehicles *It's In the Air* and *Trouble Brewing*; *Yellow Sands* (a comedy with Wilfrid Lawson, Robert Newton, Belle Chrystall, and Marie Tempest); *Keep Smiling*, (Gracie Fields); *Old Bones of the River* and *Ask a Policeman* (Will Hay); *A Stolen Life* (a melodrama with Elizabeth Bergner and Michael Redgrave); *The Ware Case* (an Ealing courtroom drama directed by Robert Stevenson); *Q Planes* (a lightweight spy thriller with Ralph Richardson and Laurence Olivier); and *The Outsider* (a melodrama directed by Paul Stein for ABPC). After war broke out fewer British films are mentioned: Korda's Technicolor extravaganza *The Four Feathers*; the

Tod Slaughter melodrama *The Face at the Window*; Hitchcock's last film before departing for Hollywood, *Jamaica Inn*; MGM-British's *Goodbye Mr Chips*; Powell and Pressburger's *The Spy in Black*; *Shipyard Sally* (Gracie Fields for Twentieth Century-Fox); *The Four Just Men* (Ealing); and two comedy-thrillers directed by David Macdonald, *This Man in Paris* and *Spies of the Air*.

1940

In April Germany invaded Norway. In May Churchill replaced Chamberlain as Prime Minister, Germany invaded Holland and Belgium, and British troops were evacuated from Dunkirk (28 May–3 June). On 22 June France surrendered. On 15 September the RAF sealed their victory over the Luftwaffe, but the Battle of Britain was followed by the bombing blitz on British towns and cities (September 1940–May 1941). In December British troops began to drive back the Italians in North Africa.

Of the fifty-one films released in 1940, twenty-four were comedies or comedy thrillers, and of these, seventeen dealt with the war in one way or another.[2] Of the six serious war films, four dealt with the war at sea and the dilemma neutral vessels found themselves caught in, while the other two (*Pastor Hall* and *Night Train to Munich*) extended British sympathy to mid-European victims of Nazi oppression.

Two thirds of the films released came from just six companies – Gainsborough (eight, including the three produced under the Twentieth Century Productions banner for Fox), Ealing (seven), British National (six), Warner Brothers (six), Butchers (five), and ABPC/Pathé (four).

According to the *Kine Weekly*, *Gone With the Wind* was the top film followed by Hitchcock's first Hollywood films *Rebecca* and *Foreign Correspondent* and Greta Garbo's *Ninotchka*, directed by Ernst Lubitsch for MGM. The only British films mentioned as successful were: *Come On George* (George Formby); *The Frozen Limits* (the Crazy Gang); *The Stars Look Down* (Carol Reed's film about injustice and social aspiration in a mining community, like *The Citadel* an adaptation of a novel by A. J. Cronin); and *French Without Tears* (directed by Anthony Asquith from a play by Terence Rattigan); all of which were completed before war broke out. *Band Waggon* and *Charley's Big-Hearted Aunt* (Gainsborough's first two Arthur Askey films); Powell and Pressburger's *Contraband*; *For Freedom* (a Gainsborough war drama set during the Battle of the River Plate, directed by Maurice Elvey); *Ten Days in Paris* (a comedy thriller directed by Tim Whelan for Columbia); Formby's *Let George Do It*; *Gaslight* (a Victorian melodrama directed by Thorold Dickinson); and *Night Train to Munich* (directed by Carol Reed for Twentieth Century Productions), were made in the first uncertain days of the war.

1941

In March Rommel began to push back the British army in North Africa. On 27 May the German battleship *Bismarck* was sunk after a 1,750 mile chase and the loss of the British battle-cruiser *HMS Hood*. On 1 June British forces were evacuated from Crete. On 22 June Germany invaded Russia. In November the British aircraft carrier the *Ark Royal* was sunk in the Mediterranean. On 7 December Japanese planes sank the American fleet in Pearl Harbor.

Only forty-seven British films were released, almost half of them comedies. Those with war themes continued to concentrate on the unmasking of spies and saboteurs, but Butchers introduced new themes in *Facing the Music* (fun in a munitions factory), *Gert and Daisy's Weekend* (mischievous evacuees), and *Bob's Your Uncle* (the Home Guard). The serious war films include *Target for Tonight, Dangerous Moonlight, 49th Parallel*, four spy thrillers, *Ships with Wings*, and the first clearly defined resistance film, *Freedom Radio*, made by Two Cities for Columbia. There was a distinct tendency to mobilize the past for propaganda purposes – *The Prime Minister, This England, Atlantic Ferry, Penn of Pennsylvania* – and with John Baxter's *Love on the Dole* and *The Common Touch*, the first manifestations of a concern for a new and better post-war society.

Gainsborough, Ealing, British National, Butchers, ABPC, and Warners managed thirty-one films between them, although Warners switched from low-budget comedies and thrillers to more prestigious pictures it could distribute in America as well as Britain and released only two films compared to the previous year's five. British National with *This England, Pimpernel Smith, Love on the Dole*, and *The Common Touch* emerged as the trail-blazer of the new war culture. Ealing, Gainsborough, and Butchers continued to rely on comedies with a topical wartime setting. ABPC concentrated on non-war comedies and thrillers.

The most popular film of the year was Powell and Pressburger's *49th Parallel* followed by Chaplin's *The Great Dictator*, Leslie Howard's *Pimpernel Smith*, Anatole Litvak's *All This and Heaven Too* (a Warner Brothers Hollywood costume melodrama with Charles Boyer and Bette Davis), and Korda's *Lady Hamilton* (made in Hollywood but with a pronounced British bias). Other successful British films were: *Gasbags* (Gainsborough's last Crazy Gang film); *Spare A Copper* and *Turned Out Nice Again* (Ealing's last two Formby films); *The Ghost Train* and *I Thank You* (Arthur Askey); *The Ghost of St Michaels* (Will Hay and Claude Hulbert); *Quiet Wedding* (an Asquith/Rattigan comedy adapted from a play by Esther McCracken); John Baxter's *Love on the Dole* and *The Common Touch*; *Kipps* (directed by Carol Reed at Shepherd's Bush for Twentieth Century Productions); Harry Watt's *Target for Tonight*; *Major*

Barbara (Gabriel Pascal's big-budget adaptation of Shaw's play about the eccentric daughter of an arms manufacturer); *Dangerous Moonlight* (directed by Brian Desmond Hurst for RKO); *Jeannie* (an offbeat comedy directed by Harold French, with Barbara Mullen and Michael Redgrave); and *Hi Gang!* (starring Ben Lyons, Bebe Daniels, and Vic Oliver).

1942

In February Singapore fell to the Japanese. In May the RAF organized its first thousand-bomber raid (on Cologne), the Germans bombed Bath, Norwich, York, Canterbury, and Exeter in retaliation. In August Churchill flew to Moscow to meet Stalin; the failure of the Dieppe raid dampened any hope of a second front; the Russians began the long and bitter battle of Stalingrad. In November Montgomery won the first decisive British victory of the war at El Alamein. In December the Beveridge Report was published; and the Russians began pushing back the German invaders.

Only forty-five films were released but for the first time there was an overwhelming predominance of war films. Thirteen of the sixteen comedies had war themes and the number of serious war films was boosted to fifteen by the flourishing resistance cycle. Many of the films not dealing directly with the war either contributed to the 'England's heritage' cycle (*The Young Mr Pitt* and *The Great Mr Handel*), dealt with subjects closely related to the war (*They Flew Alone*, *The First of the Few*), or with life on the home front (*We'll Meet Again* and *Salute John Citizen*).

Gainsborough (five films), Ealing (five films), British National (seven films), ABPC (four films), Butchers (five films), and Warners (three films) continued to handle an overwhelming proportion of the industry's output, though a number of small independent production units began to make their presence felt – Two Cities with *In Which We Serve*, British Aviation with *Tomorrow We Live* and *The First of the Few*, Norman Walker with *Hard Steel* and *The Great Mr Handel*, Excelsior with *Secret Mission*, Paul Soskin with *The Day Will Dawn* – indicating that it was becoming easier to raise money for film production.

It was not a very good year for British films at the box-office, though *In Which We Serve*, released at the end of the year (and thus included in the 1943 results), was extremely popular. The top film was MGM's syrupy *Mrs Miniver*, and the only British film which came any way near equalling its popularity was Leslie Howard's *The First of the Few*. The other British films mentioned as successful were: Ealing's *Ships with Wings* and *The Foreman Went to France*; Carol Reed's *The Young Mr Pitt*; Powell and Pressburger's *One of Our Aircraft is Missing*, made for British National which also enjoyed some success with *We'll Smile Again* (Flanagan and

Allen), *Old Mother Riley's Circus*, *Those Kids From Town* (an evacuees' comedy directed by Lance Comfort), and *Salute John Citizen* (a home front drama directed by Maurice Elvey); *Much Too Shy* (George Formby for Columbia); *Backroom Boy* (Arthur Askey); *Hatter's Castle* (an adaptation of another A. J. Cronin novel, with Robert Newton as a tyrannical Victorian patriarch, directed by Lance Comfort for Paramount-British); two low-budget films from Butchers, *Somewhere in Camp* (Frank Randle, Harry Korris, and Robbie Vincent), and *Front Line Kids* were also noted as doing well.

1943

In January Churchill and Roosevelt met at Casablanca. On 2 February the Russians formally announced their victory at Stalingrad. On 3 March one-hundred-and-seventy-eight people were killed in the Bethnal Green tube station disaster. In May the Allies launched a successful offensive in Tunisia. In July Sicily was invaded. At the end of November Churchill, Roosevelt, and Stalin met in Tehran.

The number of films was up slightly to fifty, with eighteen serious war films and seventeen comedies, most of them with a wartime setting. Documentary-influenced realism was increasingly apparent, most obviously in Ealing's films – *San Demetrio–London*, *Nine Men*, and *The Bells Go Down* – but also in Gainsborough's *Millions Like Us* and *We Dive at Dawn*. The success of *The Man in Grey*, however, indicated that the public hankered for something richer and more flamboyant.

Gainsborough, Ealing, and British National each released six films and Butchers, despite having their Walton-on-Thames studio requisitioned, managed four. Warner Brothers and Columbia each released three films but ABPC lost its most active producer, John Argyle, to the Navy and only released two films. Independent producers, now increasingly associated with J. Arthur Rank, remained important and Two Cities emerged as a dynamic and successful production company releasing four very popular films: *The Gentle Sex*, *The Flemish Farm*, *The Lamp Still Burns*, and *The Demi-Paradise*.

The top box-office film was MGM's *Random Harvest*, followed by *In Which We Serve*, *Casablanca*, *The Life and Death of Colonel Blimp*, *Hello Frisco Hello* (a Twentieth Century-Fox period musical with Alice Faye), *The Black Swan* (another Technicolor Fox extravaganza), and *The Man in Grey*. The other successful British films were: *We'll Meet Again* and *Rhythm Serenade* (Vera Lynn for Columbia); *Women Aren't Angels* and *Warn That Man* (two uncharacteristic comedies made by Lawrence Huntington at Welwyn); the Boultings' *Thunder Rock*; Leslie Howard's *The Gentle Sex* and Launder and Gilliat's *Millions Like Us*; six resistance dramas – *The Silver Fleet, Tomorrow We Live, The Flemish Farm, Escape to Danger, The Adventures of Tartu*, and *The Night Invader*; Asquith's *We Dive at Dawn* and Jack Lee's *Close Quarters* (both of them concerned with life on a British submarine); *Desert Victory* (the first of the documentary compilation films); three comedies from British National – *Old Mother Riley, Detective, When We Are Married* (Priestley's Yorkshire comedy directed by Lance Comfort) and *Theatre Royal* (a Flanagan and Allen backstage musical directed by John Baxter); Harry Watt's *Nine Men* (made at Ealing); Asquith's *The Demi-Paradise* and Maurice Elvey's *The Lamp Still Burns* (like *The Gentle Sex* and *The Flemish Farm* made for Two Cities); *My Learned Friend* (the last of the Claude Hulbert/Will Hay films); *The Yellow Canary* (Anna Neagle/Herbert Wilcox); *The Dark Tower* (a Warners morbid melodrama directed by John Harlow); Gainsborough's *Dear Octopus* (directed by Harold French in the same vein as Asquith's *Quiet Wedding*); and a Butchers melodrama about the return of an amnesiac naval officer, *I'll Walk Beside You*.

1944

In January the Russian Army advanced into Poland and British forces landed behind German lines in Italy to begin the battle of Anzio. On 4 June Rome fell to the Americans; on 6 June Allied forces began the invasion of Normandy; on 13 June the first V1 flying bomb hit London. On 23 August Paris was liberated. On 8 September the first V2 rocket hit London. In December the Germans launched their counter-attack in the Ardennes.

Only thirty-six films were released, the lowest number since 1926. This was partly because of an almost complete absence of activity on the part of the Americans: between them they managed only four films (three from Columbia, one from RKO). ABPC also released only one film. Butchers, still continuing the unequal struggle to produce films without a studio of their own, released four films, including the documentary, *Tunisian Victory*, but apart from a handful of independents, almost the whole of Britain's production efforts were concentrated on Ealing (five films), Gainsborough (seven films), British National (eleven films), and Two Cities (seven films).

There was a marked turning away from the war. Only Ealing's dramatized documentary *For Those in Peril*, Gainsborough's Prisoner-of-War-camp drama *2,000 Women*, RKO's spy thriller *Hotel Reserve*, and Two Cities' *The Way Ahead* qualifying as serious war films, while many of the comedies – *Time Flies, Bees in Paradise, On Approval, Demobbed, Tawny Pipit, English Without Tears, Fiddlers Three, Dreaming, He Snoops to Conquer* – pushed the war firmly into the background.

A group of twelve films were awarded equal top box-office honours, but only two of them were British – *This Happy Breed* and *Fanny By Gaslight*. The American films included *For Whom the Bell Tolls*, *The Song of Bernadette*, *Jane Eyre*, and *The White Cliffs of Dover*. the only other British films mentioned as successes were: *Bell Bottom George* (George Formby); *San Demetrio–London* (Ealing); *The Way Ahead* (Carol Reed for Two Cities); Powell and Pressburger's *A Canterbury Tale*; Gainsborough's *Love Story* and *2,000 Women*; and George King's spy thriller *Candlelight in Algeria*.

1945

Saturation bombing of German cities culminated in the attack on Dresden on 14 February. VE Day was 8 May. The General Election on 5 July gave Labour a majority of 146. On 6 August an Atom bomb was dropped on Hiroshima, and a second on Nagasaki on the 9th; the war ended five days later. In September British design and manufacturing expertise was celebrated in the 'Britain Can Make It' exhibition. On 4 December and again on the 14th the Metropolitan Police launched 'dragnet' operations in London to try to catch some of the 20,000 deserters who were contributing to the crime wave.

Forty-two films were released. There was a slight increase in the number of films coming from the American companies – three from Columbia, two each from Warners and RKO, and the first (and only) fruit of MGM's collaboration with Alexander Korda, *Perfect Strangers*. Once again there were very few war films: ABPC's *The Man from Morocco*, an interestingly offbeat film starring Anton Walbrook as a Spanish Civil War veteran imprisoned by the Vichy French, and three films dealing with flyers and Anglo-American relations – *The Way to the Stars*, *Journey Together*, and *I Live in Grosvenor Square*. There were only nine comedies.

1945 was Gainsborough's best year, its five films – *Waterloo Road*, *A Place of One's Own*, *They Were Sisters*, *I'll Be Your Sweetheart*, and *The Wicked Lady* – achieving Ted Black's aim of a popular, balanced programme of films, though by this time he had left the company. Ealing, by contrast, seemed to be uncertain whether to continue with wartime realism (*Johnny Frenchman* and *Painted Boats*) or follow Gainsborough's lead into the exotic and mysterious (*Dead of Night* and *Pink String and Sealing Wax*). Two Cities released only two films – *Blithe Spirit* and *The Way to the Stars* – though both were successful prestige productions. This was in marked contrast to British National which released another ten films, ranging from a Ruritanian musical, *Waltz Time*, through low-budget crime thrillers such as *The Echo Murders* and *Murder in Reverse* to post-war social problem films – *The Agitator* and *The World Owes Me a Living*

– only a minority of which were successful at the box-office.

The top box-office film was, for the first time since 1941, a British film – *The Seventh Veil*. Of the twenty-two runners-up, four were British – Gainsborough's *Madonna of the Seven Moons* (released late in 1944) and *They Were Sisters*, Korda's *Perfect Strangers* and the first of the Wilcox/Neagle 'Mayfair' cycle, *I Live in Grosvenor Square*. The American films included *Arsenic and Old Lace*, *Meet Me in St Louis*, *A Song to Remember*, *Frenchman's Creek*, *Since You Went Away*, *Hollywood Canteen*, *National Velvet*, and *The Valley of Decision*. Other British films mentioned as doing well were: Pat Jackson's Technicolor drama-documentary *Western Approaches*; Sidney Gilliat's *Waterloo Road*; three ghost stories – David Lean's adaptation of Coward's *Blithe Spirit*, Gainsborough's *A Place of One's Own* and Ealing's *Dead of Night*; Asquith's *The Way to the Stars*, which, like *I Live in Grosvenor Square*, featured an American airman in love with an Englishwoman, and like *Journey Together*, another successful air-war picture, written by Terence Rattigan; two musicals – Gainsborough's *I'll Be Your Sweetheart* (directed by Val Guest) and British National's *Waltz Time* (directed by Paul Stein); the documentary compilation films, *Burma Victory* and *The True Glory*; *Murder in Reverse* (a British National crime thriller with William Hartnell); the Boxes' *29 Acacia Avenue*, and *Henry V* (released in 1944) which is mentioned ambiguously as 'the class horse but found the going uneven'.

1946

In March the Bank of England was nationalized. In April the Labour government launched its ambitious Groundnut Scheme in East Africa. On 21 July bread rationing was introduced. In August squatters occupied recently vacated Army/RAF camps. Throughout the year the war crimes trials of leading Nazis were held in Nuremburg.

Thirty-nine films were released. They can be divided roughly into six comedies, seven crime thrillers, eight musicals, six war films, two contemporary melodramas concerned with post-war adjustment, and two overseas adventure films, and British National's sheep-dog film, *Loyal Heart*. The Americans released only four films between them – Columbia's *George in Civvy Street*, their last Formby film, and *This Man is Mine*, a comedy about a Canadian soldier billeted on an English family with two eligible daughters; Fox backed Excelsior's *Wanted for Murder*, and Warners backed George King's *Gaiety George*, a musical starring Ann Todd and Richard Greene. Ealing released only *The Captive Heart* and *The Overlanders*, both of them shot mainly on location. British National remained remarkably prolific, releasing eight films, but Gainsborough managed only *The Magic Bow* and *Caravan*. In terms of the money spent on their films, the year's output was completely dominated by the independents working under the Rank banner: Launder and Gilliat's *I See a Dark Stranger* and *Green for Danger*; Wesley Ruggles' *London Town*; Pascal's *Caesar and Cleopatra*; Cineguild's *Great Expectations*; and the Archers' *A Matter of Life and Death*. Two Cities, still trying to fill the gap left by the departure of the Cineguild team, recruited Thorold Dickinson to direct *Men of Two Worlds*, gave Maurice Elvey the chance to direct the biggest budget picture of his amazingly prolific career, *Beware of Pity*, and allowed David Lean's script editor, Stanley Haynes, to make his debut as a director with *Carnival* and Peter Ustinov to make his with *School for Secrets*.

It was again a good year for British films with *The Wicked Lady* (released at the end of 1944) the top film and *Piccadilly Incident* one of the two runners-up (the other was *The Bells of St Mary's*). A list of 'Other Notable Box-office Attractions' included the following British films: *Brief Encounter*, *The Captive Heart*, *Caravan*, *Bedelia*, *The Years Between*, *London Town*, *Caesar and Cleopatra*, *Men of Two Worlds*, *Theirs is the Glory*, and *The Overlanders*.

1947

1 January was Vesting Day for the National Coal Board. By the end of the month the severe cold spell had brought power cuts; roads were closed by blizzards and in March greyhound racing, television and the Third Programme were suspended to conserve energy. When the thaw came it led to widespread flooding. In April the school-leaving age was raised to fifteen. In August a divided Indian sub-continent was granted its independence; Dior's second collection introduced the New Look to Britain. The autumn financial crisis led to severe petrol rationing and the abolition of the foreign travel allowance; the tax on the import of films into Britain led to Hollywood's embargo. In November Princess Elizabeth married Philip Mountbatten.

Fifty-eight films were released, most of them of some interest. War films had almost completely disappeared and the field is dominated by spiv films and morbid thrillers (fifteen films), costume pictures (sixteen films), and contemporary melodramas (twelve films). There were only six comedies but two of them, *Hue and Cry* and *Holiday Camp*, were to start a new and fruitful vein of 'situation' comedy.

Ealing enjoyed a good year with *Hue and Cry*, *Nicholas Nickleby*, *The Loves of Joanna Godden*, *Frieda*, and *It Always Rains on Sunday*, as did the revamped Gainsborough under Sydney Box (eight films including those going out under Box's own Triton label). British National, having parted from John Baxter, began its slide towards oblivion. It wound up its distribution organization, Anglo-American, and released only four films. The Rank independents seemed to be stabilizing: the worst offenders for extravagance – Pascal and Ruggles – were banished, Cineguild, the Archers, and Launder and Gilliat's company Individual, undertook more economical projects and they were joined by a new company, Wessex, headed by Ian Dalrymple. Both ABPC and Two Cities appeared healthy. ABPC recruited the Boultings to make *Brighton Rock* and backed Lance Comfort's *Temptation Harbour*. Two Cities, not yet suffering from the departure of Giudice, released *Hungry Hill, Odd Man Out, The October Man, Fame is the Spur* and *Uncle Silas*. The Quota requirements of the American companies were satisfied largely by Alliance, which had been set up to undertake joint Rank/RKO productions but had broken free of its ill-matched parents.

For the third year running the most successful box-office film – *The Courtneys of Curzon Street* – was British. Of the six runners-up two were American *(The Jolson Story* and *Duel in the Sun)* and four British *(Great Expectations, Odd Man Out, Frieda,* and *Holiday Camp)*. More than half the 'Other Notable Box-office Attractions' were British too: Powell and Pressburger's *A Matter of Life and Death* and *Black Narcissus*, Launder and Gilliat's *Green for Danger* and *Captain Boycott*, Cavalcanti's *Nicholas Nickleby* and *They Made Me a Fugitive*, Bernard Knowles' *Jassy* and *The White Unicorn*, Roy Baker's *The October Man*, Ealing's *Hue and Cry*, the Boxes' pre-Galnsborough *The Upturned Glass*, and *So Well Remembered*, an RKO-Alliance family saga.

1948

In February the Criminal Justice Act abolished hard labour, penal servitude and flogging. In March Britain withdrew from Palestine. Spring was the hottest for a hundred years. In the summer the Olympic Games were held in London. On 5 July the National Health Service was inaugurated. On 21 July bread rationing was abolished. Throughout November and December the Lynskey Tribunal heard evidence about contact man Sidney Stanley's shady dealings with the Board of Trade. Between May 1948 and May 1949 the Berlin airlift took place.
took place.

In an attempt to compensate for the embargo on American films, production had been increased and seventy-seven films were released in 1948, though only fifty-three of them could be regarded as first features. Again there were large numbers of crime films (nineteen), contemporary melodramas (thirteen), and costume films (sixteen). There were only two war films – Charles Crichton's *Against the Wind* and Edmond T. Greville's *But Not in Vain* – both of them about resistance to the Nazis in the Low

Countries, but there was a huge increase in the numbers of comedies and light romances, twenty-two of them ranging from Alexander Korda's *An Ideal Husband* to *Here Come the Huggetts* and *William Comes to Town*.

The companies mainly responsible for the increased numbers of films were Gainsborough (eleven films), Two Cities (nine films), and British Lion (eleven films). Many of these films were hurried, low-budget productions, though British Lion's output included *An Ideal Husband*, *Anna Karenina*, *Spring in Park Lane*, *The Fallen Idol*, and *Bonnie Prince Charlie*. Ealing managed only four films, though two of them – *Saraband for Dead Lovers* and *Scott of the Antarctic* – were much bigger budgeted films than the studio had hitherto embarked upon. The Rank independents, unlike Gainsborough and Two Cities, were undeflected from their normal practice of leisurely production of quality films. Individual released *London Belongs to Me*, the Archers, *The Red Shoes*, Cineguild, *Blanche Fury*, and Wessex *Esther Waters* and *Once a Jolly Swagman*. British National continued its eclipse, managing to put out only four modest films. Alliance continued to make films for the American companies, though its most famous film, *No Orchids for Miss Blandish*, was released through the small independent distribution company, Renown. There were a number of other American-backed projects – Premiere's *Idol of Paris* for Warners, Excelsior's *This Was a Woman* for Fox; and three of the American companies resumed direct production in Britain – Paramount with *So Evil My Love*, Columbia with *The First Gentleman* (directed by Cavalcanti), and Fox with *Escape*.

The most popular film of the year was William Wyler's *The Best Years of Our Lives*, but nine of the fourteen runners-up were British: *Spring in Park Lane*, *It Always Rains on Sunday*, *My Brother Jonathan* (an ABPC social melodrama directed by Harold French, with Michael Denison and Dulcie Gray), *Miranda*, *An Ideal Husband*, *The Red Shoes*, *The Weaker Sex* (a light comedy based on a play by Esther McCracken, directed by Roy Baker for *Two Cities*), Anthony Asquith's *The Winslow Boy*, and Carol Reed's *The Fallen Idol*. *Hamlet* was included as 'Most Artistic Film', and it was pointed out that *No Orchids for Miss Blandish* had broken box-office records in those areas where it had not been banned. The American films were *Road to Rio*, *The Naked City*, *Green Dolphin Street*, *Forever Amber*, and *Life With Father*. Other British films mentioned as 'notable box-office attractions' were: *Brighton Rock*, *When the Bough Breaks*, *Blanche Fury*, *Good Time Girl*, *Bond Street* (a compendium film starring Jean Kent produced by Anatole de Grunwald for Associated British), *London Belongs to Me*, *Noose*, and *No Room at the Inn* (a sensational social problem film starring Freda Jackson, directed by Dan Birt for British National).

1949

In February the Gater Committee was set up. In March Harold Wilson announced his 'bonfire of controls'. In October Stanley Setty's headless torso was found in the Essex marshes and Donald Hume was arrested for his murder

Ninety-six films were released – the backlog of the boom in production which Rank and to a lesser extent Korda had sponsored to prove that Britain could manage without American films during the embargo – but at least forty-five of them were second features. There was a decrease in the number of expensive costume films, though the ten which were released were equally varied, ranging from Harry Watt's slice of Australian history, *Eureka Stockade*, to the Edwardian musical *Trottie True*. There was an increase in the number of crime films to twenty-three, but of those only *For Them That Trespass*, *Now Barabbas was a Robber*, *Obsession*, *The Third Man*, *The Spider and the Fly*, and arguably *The Boys in Brown* could be regarded as first features. The bulk of the increase was taken up by a huge expansion in the number of comedies and light romances (to forty-two). More than half of these were second features and of the remainder only the Ealing films (*Passport to Pimlico*, *Kind Hearts and Coronets*, *Whisky Galore* and *A Run for Your Money*), Wessex's *All Over the Town*, Two Cities' *It's Hard to be Good*, *The Chiltern Hundreds* and *Adam and Evelyne*, Gainsborough's two *Huggett* films, *Helter Skelter* and *A Boy, a Girl and a Bike*, Peter Ustinov's *Private Angelo*, Frank Randle's *Somewhere in Politics* and the talent-filled featurette *Date With a Dream* deserve much attention.

1949 was a bad year for British films. Although the Korda/Selznick co-production, *The Third Man*, was the top film at the box-office, the only other British films mentioned either as 'runners-up' or as 'notable box-office attractions' were: Ealing's *Scott of the Antarctic* and *Passport to Pimlico*; Launder and Gilliat's *The Blue Lagoon*; the last of the Wilcox/Neagle 'Mayfair' cycle, *Maytime in Mayfair*; Two Cities' *Trottie True* and *Madness of the Heart*; and *The Guinea Pig*, *Silent Dust*, and *The Hasty Heart*, all of which were made directly or indirectly for Associated British.

1950

In January Klaus Fuchs was arrested for disclosing secrets of Britain's Atom bomb to the Russians. In May petrol rationing was ended. In June the Korean war began. The General Election held in July reduced Labour's majority to five.

Surprisingly, in view of the climate of pessimism and the closure of Shepherd's Bush, Islington, and Highbury studios, eighty-two films were released, of which around fifty could be classed as first features. Comedies were down to the more sensible level of eighteen films. Though most of them were undistinguished, they included Launder and Gilliat's very successful *The Happiest Days of Your Life*, *The Magnet*, T.E.B. Clarke's follow-up to *Passport to Pimlico*, which flopped at the box-office, giving the erroneous impression that Ealing comedy was dead, and J.B. Priestley's *Last Holiday*. The largest single group of films were the crime films (twenty-five) which clearly divided into low-budget 'B' movies like *Paul Temple's Triumph*, *The Man in Black*, and *Dick Barton at Bay*, and prestigious productions like *The Blue Lamp*, *Night and the City*, and Hitchcock's *Stagefright*. There was a limited but successful return to the war film with *Odette*, *The Wooden Horse*, *They Were Not Divided*, *State Secret*, and *Morning Departure*. There were fifteen costume films ranging from *Madeleine* and *Gone to Earth* to a low-budget version of *The Fall of the House of Usher*; the films which were commercially the most successful though were Hollywood-British versions of the past – Disney's *Treasure Island* and Fox's *The Mudlark* and *The Black Rose*. Similarly, of the fourteen contemporary melodramas, MGM-British's *The Miniver Story*, with Greer Garson's Mrs Miniver expiring from a terminal illness in austerity-ridden Britain, was the most popular, though the native product covered an interestingly diverse range of subjects from the low-life films *The Gorbals Story* and *Waterfront*, through *Dance Hall*, *No Place for Jennifer*, *Chance of a Lifetime*, and *The Girl Who Couldn't Quite* to the glossy middle-class dramas *Prelude to Fame* and *The Astonished Heart*.

Gainsborough, now deprived of its studios, continued a sort of half-life at Pinewood where the Boxes made *So Long at the Fair*, *The Astonished Heart*, and *Trio*. Two Cities moved from Denham to Pinewood and released four films in 1950. Cineguild produced its last film for Rank, *Madeleine*, but new independent producers were recruited – Jay Lewis (*Morning Departure*), Betty Box (*The Clouded Yellow*), and Joseph Janni (*The Woman in Question*), with some succcess. ABPC, working more closely than ever with Warner Brothers, closed Welwyn, but its large and completely renovated Elstree studios were working at full capacity and ten films were released in 1950. The American companies themselves released five glossy films (*Treasure Island*, *The Black Rose*, *The Miniver Story*, *The Mudlark*, and *Night and the City*) that were almost indistinguishable from their big-budget Hollywood films.

Despite the failure of *The Magnet*, Ealing enjoyed a good year with *Cage of Gold*, *Dance Hall*, *The Blue Lamp*, and *Bitter Springs*; and British Lion, which had attracted the most prestigious independent production units, was rewarded with a certain number of successes – Wessex's *Wooden Horse*, the Boultings' *Seven Days to Noon*, and Launder and Gilliat's *The*

Happiest Days of Your Life, though the Archers were less fortunate with *Gone to Earth* and *The Elusive Pimpernel*.

The top box-office film of the year was *The Blue Lamp* but there were only eight British films among the twenty-eight runners-up. They were: *The Dancing Years* (an Ivor Novello operetta directed by Harold French for Associated British); *State Secret* (a Launder and Gilliat comedy thriller); *The Cure for Love* (Robert Donat's adaptation of a Lancashire farce by Walter Greenwood); *Trio* (a Gainsborough compendium of Somerset Maugham stories); *They Were Not Divided* (a Two Cities war film directed by Terence Young); *Morning Departure* (a war film produced by Jay Lewis and directed by Roy Baker for Rank); *The Black Rose* (the first of the Technicolor American costume pictures made in Britain); and Hitchcock's *Stagefright*.

Notes

Introduction

1 Dilys Powell, *Films Since 1939*, London, 1947, p. 22.
2 James Park, *Learning to Dream*, London, 1984, p. 115.

1 Britain Alone

1 P.L. Mannock, *Kinematograph Weekly*, 21 December 1939, p. 18.
2 Guy Morgan, *Red Roses Every Night*, London, 1948, p. 14. Morgan's account of the Granada circuit during the war gives a graphic picture of cinema-going during the Blitz.
3 *Kinematograph Weekly*, 7 September 1939, p. 4.
4 See Sarah Street and Margaret Dickinson, *Cinema and State*, London, 1985, pp. 103–19, for conflicting government attitudes.
5 Korda was one of those accused of having 'gone with the wind up', but in those early months of the war it is unlikely that he would have been able to find financial backing for film-making in Britain, and Churchill thought he would be more useful making pro-British films in Hollywood. In 1942 he was rewarded with a knighthood. See Karol Kulik, *Alexander Korda: The Man Who Could Work Miracles*, London, 1975, p. 254; and Michael Korda, *Charmed Lives*, London, 1980, p. 139.
6 For a more detailed analysis of *Let George Do It* see Tony Aldgate, 'Raise A Laugh' in *Britain Can Take it*, Tony Aldgate and Jeffrey Richards, Oxford, 1986, pp. 76–93.
7 Tom Harrisson, 'Films and the Home Front', in *Propaganda, Politics and Film, 1918–45*, Nicholas Pronay and D.W. Spring (eds), London, 1982, p. 229.
8 *The Cine-Technician*, February-March 1940, p. 10.
9 Ibid.
10 Angus Calder, *The People's War*, London, 1971, p. 159.
11 'The Other Side of the Atlantic', *Documentary Newsletter*, September 1940, p. 4.
12 A.J.P. Taylor, *English History 1914–1945*, Harmondsworth, 1976, p. 557.
13 His successor was Duff Cooper, who in turn was replaced by Brendan Bracken in July 1941. See Caroline Moorehead, *Lord Bernstein*, London, 1984, p. 117, for Reith's view of Churchill.
14 Harry Watt, *Don't Look at the Camera*, London, 1974, p. 128.
15 They are catalogued by Frances Thorpe and Nicholas Pronay in their useful *British Official Films in the Second World War*, Oxford, 1980.
16 Harry Watt, op. cit., p. 145.
17 Ibid., p. 152.
18 'The Other Side of the Atlantic', op. cit., p. 3.
19 Moorehead, op. cit., p. 130.

20 Sidney Bernstein, *The Film and International Relations*, London, 1945, p. 13.
21 Tony Aldgate examines *49th Parallel* in detail in 'Why We Fight', Aldgate and Richards, op. cit., pp. 21–43.
22 See Jeffrey Richards, 'Wartime British Cinema Audiences and the Class System', *Historical Journal of Film, Radio and Television*, vol. 7, no. 2, 1987, for the box-office success of *Ships With Wings*.
23 Morgan, op. cit., p. 69.
24 For Howard's contribution to the war effort and a detailed analysis of *Pimpernel Smith* and *The First of the Few* see Jeffrey Richards, 'The Englishman's Englishman', in Aldgate and Richards, op. cit., pp. 44–75.
25 *Kinematograph Weekly*, 8 January 1942, p. 42.

2 War Culture

1 George Orwell, 'The Lion and the Unicorn', *Collected Essays, Journalism and Letters*, vol.2, Harmondsworth, 1980, p. 99.
2 Dilys Powell, *Films Since 1939*, London, 1947, p. 23.
3 Angus Calder, *The People's War*, London, 1971, p. 159.
4 Sidney Bernstein, *The Film and International Relations*, London, 1945, p. 12. See also, James Robertson, *The British Board of Film Censors: Film Censorship in Britain 1896–1950*, London, 1985; and N. Pronay and J. Croft, 'British Film Censorship and Propaganda Policy During the Second World War', in J. Curran and V. Porter (eds), *British Cinema History*, London, 1983, pp. 144–63.
5 Elizabeth Sussex, *The Rise and Fall of British Documentary*, Berkeley and London, 1975, p. 140.
6 For a more detailed analysis of the film and the play it is based on, see Tony Aldgate, 'Signs of the Time' in A. Aldgate and J. Richards, *Britain Can Take It*, Oxford, 1986, pp. 168–86.
7 W. J. Speakman, in a paper given to a BFI conference, reported that: '*Love on the Dole*, whilst acclaimed by the critics, left all but better-class audiences cold. The chief reason for this was because it portrayed working-class life as it is, and therefore, did not take the masses out of themselves'. *Film Appreciation and Visual Education*, London, 1944, p. 42. This smacks of the timid, conservative, narrowly commercial prejudice which characterized the Cinematograph Exhibitors Association, and Mr Speakman also dismisses *San Demetrio–London* and *One of Our Aircraft is Missing* as flops. Josh Billings of the *Kine Weekly* mentions *Love on the Dole* as one of the more successful British films of 1941. *Kinematograph Weekly*, 8 January 1942, p. 41.
8 *Kinematograph Weekly*, 14 January 1943, p. 1030.
9 *New Statesman*, 2 May 1942.
10 See Mary-Lou Jenning (ed.), *Humphrey Jennings: Film-maker, Painter, Poet*, London, 1982, p. 25; and see also Jeffrey Richards, 'England, Their England', in Aldgate and Richards, op. cit., pp. 218–30 for an illuminating comparison between Humphrey Jennings and George Orwell.
11 Geoff Brown, *Walter Forde*, London, 1977, p. 47.
12 Angus Calder, op. cit., p. 417.
13 A. J. P. Taylor, *English History 1914–1945*, Harmondsworth, 1976, p. 616.
14 *Sunday Pictorial*, 26 July 1942.
15 See Basil Dean, *Mind's Eye*, London, 1973, pp. 284–5, for a spectacular pro-Russian pageant held at the Albert Hall; and Mike Raphael, *The Demi-Paradise*,

unpublished MA Thesis, Polytechnic of Central London, 1982. Ironically, while making the film, Asquith, despite his position as President of the ACT, had problems with his works committee who were worried that the Russian point of view was not being sympathetically enough represented. R. J. Minney, *Puffin Asquith*, London, 1973, p. 107.

16 *Observer*, 14 May 1944.

17 See Norman Longmate, *The G.I.s: The Americans in Britain 1942–1945*, London, 1975, for relations between GIs and British women.

3 Realism and Tinsel

1 Editorial, *Documentary Newsletter*, May 1943, p. 1.

2 *Kinematograph Weekly*, 8 January 1942, p. 87.

3 Ibid., p. 85.

4 Monja Danischewsky, *White Russian, Red Face*, London, 1966, p. 134.

5 Quoted by Jeffrey Richards, *Thorold Dickinson*, London, 1986, p. 104. Richards' book is a useful and long overdue assessment of a neglected director.

6 Tony Aldgate argues that the film's brutality was in line with MOI policy to shock people into realizing the consequences of a Nazi invasion. '*Went the Day Well?* sought to show just what those consequences might be, and in its violent depiction of those consequences, along with its arguments against complacency and for robust self-defence, it accorded quite neatly with MOI intent.' 'If the Invader Comes', A. Aldgate and J. Richards, *Britain Can Take It*, Oxford, 1986, p. 133.

7 Michael Balcon, *Realism and Tinsel*, London, 1944, p. 11.

8 See Charles Barr, *Ealing Studios*, London and Newton Abbot, 1977, pp. 13–38, for a perceptive analysis of Ealing's war films.

9 For detailed analyses of the film see Daniel Millar, 'Fires Were Started', *Sight and Sound*, Spring 1969, pp. 100–4; and Jeffrey Richards, 'England Their England' in A. Aldgate and J. Richards, op. cit., pp. 218–45.

10 See John Grigg, *1943: The Victory that Never Was*, London, 1985, for a critique of Churchill's strategy.

11 A. J. P. Taylor, *English History 1914–1945*, Harmondsworth, 1976, p. 687.

12 The only other films made at Ealing before the war ended were Basil Dearden's adaptation of Priestley's utopian play *They Came to a City*, Harry Watt's comedy *Fiddlers Three*, and Charles Frend's *Johnny Frenchman*, a poor film in itself but a good example of Ealing's enduring interest in the lives of small communities.

13 Dilys Powell, *Films Since 1939*, London, 1947, p. 36.

14 Alan Wood, *Mr Rank*, London, 1952, p. 145.

15 Geoff Brown, *Launder and Gilliat*, London, 1977, p. 111.

16 Quoted in Sue Aspinall and Robert Murphy (eds), *Gainsborough Melodrama*, London, 1983, p. 70.

17 *Time and Tide*, 14 October 1944.

18 *New Statesman*, 16 December 1944.

19 Pam Cook, 'Melodrama and the Women's Picture', and Sue Aspinall, 'Sexuality in Costume Melodrama', in Aspinall and Murphy, op. cit..

20 R. Broad and S. Fleming (eds), *Nella Last's War*, Bristol, 1981, p. 255.

21 See Margaret Lockwood, *Lucky Star*, London, 1955, p. 135, for her account of a confrontation with Rank over the part offered her in *The Magic Bow*.

22 See their articles in Aspinall and Murphy, op. cit.

23 Mass Observation painted a more pessimistic picture of the life of women working in war factories: 'Any journalist looking over the place for a few hours would have every excuse for going home and writing up a sunshine story about wartime hostel life in the most glowing terms he could conjure up for the occasion. And yet when one lives there, a different picture comes to light. A picture of endless grumbling and bickering; a picture of back-biting and tale-bearing; of feuds between girls and staff, and between one set of girls and another. The real excellence of material conditions is almost lost to sight amid the welter of ill-temper and discontent which characterises life here.' *War Factory – A Report by Mass Observation*, Tom Harrisson (ed.), London, 1943, p. 106.

4 The Rank Empire

1 J. Arthur Rank, *Methodist Recorder*, 26 March 1942. Quoted by Alan Wood, *Mr Rank*, London, 1952, p. 68.
2 *Economist*, 9 November 1940, p. 587.
3 Attendance rose from 990 million in 1939 to 1,541 million in 1943 to a peak of 1,635 million in 1946. *The Film Industry Statistical Digest*, no. 2, p. 17. British Film Producers Association, June 1955.
4 Alan Wood, *Mr Rank*, London 1952, p. 153.
5 Ian Christie, 'Blimp, Churchill and the State', in *Powell, Pressburger and Others*, London, 1973.
6 E.W. and M.W. Robson, *The Shame and Disgrace of Colonel Blimp*, London, 1943, for a fierce, if eccentric, attack on Powell and Pressburger's films. Nicholas Pronay and Jeremy Croft in their otherwise sensible article 'British Film Censorship and Propaganda Policy During the Second World War', V. Porter and J. Curran (eds), *British Cinema History*, London, 1983, pp. 144–63, suggest that with Machiavellian sophistication, the MOI fabricated the whole row about government hostility to *Colonel Blimp* in order to boost its credibility with American audiences. Subsequent explorations of the issue – Tony Aldgate's chapter 'What a Difference a War Makes' in A. Aldgate and J. Richards, *Best of British*, Oxford, 1983, and Michael Powell, *A Life in Movies*, London, 1986, pp. 399–404 – lend little support to this thesis.
7 The Archers were also responsible for *The Silver Fleet* (1943 d. Vernon Sewell) and *The End of the River* (1947 d. Derek Twist).
8 Mr F. L. Gilbert, *Production Facilities (Films) Ltd*, unpublished MS, p. 26.
9 *Kinematograph Weekly*, 19 April 1945.
10 See Jeffrey Richards, 'Naval Cavalcade', A. Aldgate and J. Richards, *Britain Can Take It*, Oxford, 1986, pp. 187–217, and Roger Martin, *The Moment of In Which We Serve*, unpublished MA thesis, Polytechnic of Central London, 1982, for detailed analysis of the film. Michael Powell, op. cit., pp. 379–83, attests to Lean's vital role in *49th Parallel*.
11 Jeffrey Richards, 'Naval Cavalcade', op. cit., pp. 192, 208. See also, Andrew Higson's abstruse but rewarding, 'Addressing the Nation: Five Films', G. Hurd (ed.), *National Fictions*, London, 1984, pp. 22–6.
12 Lindsay Anderson, 'Angles of Approach', *Sequence*, no. 2, Winter 1947, p. 9.
13 Jeffrey Richards, 'Our American Cousins', *Britain Can Take It*, op. cit., pp. 277–98, provides a useful analysis of *The Way to the Stars* and also quotes from Lejeune's review, *Observer*, 10 June 1945.
14 According to a letter quoted by Jeffrey Richards, Giudice assured Jack

Beddington, head of the MOI Films Division, that: 'It is the policy of this company not to make any films whether on subjects connected directly with the war or not without the approval of the Ministry of Information.' Richards, 'Naval Cavalcade', op. cit., pp. 198–9.

15 See Vincent Porter and Chaim Litewski, 'The Way Ahead: Case History of a Propaganda Film', *Sight and Sound*, Spring 1981.

16 *Tendencies to Monopoly in the Cinematograph Film Industry: Report of a Committee Appointed by the Cinematograph Films Council*; Chairman Albert Palache, London, 1944, p. 6.

17 See Vincent Porter, 'The Context of Creativity: Ealing Studios and Hammer Films', in Vincent Porter and James Curran (eds), *British Cinema History*, London, 1983, pp. 182–92, for Balcon's dominant personality.

18 Palache, op. cit., p. 11.

19 Ibid.

20 Ibid.

21 Rank had assets of around $200 million, MGM around $190 million.

22 See Allen Eyles, 'Universal and International', *Focus on Film* 30, June 1978; and Robert Murphy, 'Rank's Attempt on the American Market' in Porter and Curran, op. cit., for more detail.

5 Great Expectations

1 J. L. Hodson, *The Sea and the Land*, quoted by Paul Addison in *The Road to 1945*, London, 1977, p. 19.

2 Addison, op. cit., p. 14.

3 Angus Calder, *The People's War*, London, 1971, p. 677.

4 Elizabeth Sussex, *The Rise and Fall of British Documentary*, Berkeley and London, 1975, p. 167.

5 Ambitious plans were also made for the film industry. Helmut Junge (the son of the art director Alfred Junge) proposed to build a network of new studios, and living quarters for those who would work in them, which would bridge the gap between Pinewood and Denham and become a real British equivalent to Hollywood. Helmut Junge, *Plan for Film Studios*, London, 1945.

6 See Susan Cooper, 'Snoek Piquante', in Michael Sissons and Philip French (eds), *The Age of Austerity*, Oxford, 1986, p. 32, for the squatters.

7 Harry Hopkins, *The New Look*, London, 1963, p. 97.

8 Charles Barr, *Ealing Studios*, London and Newton Abbot, 1977, p. 50.

9 See Raymond Durgnat, 'Two On A Tandem', *Films and Filming*, July 1966, for an assessment of the achievements of Dearden and Relph.

10 Barr, op. cit., p. 72.

11 Raymond Durgnat, *A Mirror for England*, London, 1970, p. 65.

12 Tom Harrisson, *Living Through the Blitz*, London, 1976, p. 318.

13 Sydney Box, WPN, 27 June 1952, Sydney Box Microfiche held in the British Film Institute Library, London.

14 Interview with Lady Gardiner, Sue Aspinall and Robert Murphy (eds), *Gainsborough Melodrama*, p 65.

15 *Daily Worker*, 22 November 1947; *Observer*, 23 November 1947.

16 The best scenes are those shot at a holiday camp – the location for a bigger budget picture in which Pat Roc makes a guest appearance as herself.

17 *The People*, 16 March 1947.

18 George Orwell, *Collected Essays, Journalism and Letters*, vol. 4, Harmondsworth, 1971, p. 128.
19 *Observer*, 2 November 1948.
20 *Kinematograph Weekly*, 27 May 1948, p. 18.
21 Alan Wood, *Mr Rank*, London, 1952, p. 244.
22 Durgnat, op. cit., p. 67; see Tony Aldgate, 'Lest We Forget' in Tony Aldgate and Jeffrey Richards, *Best of British*, Oxford, 1983, pp. 75–86.
23 See Jeffrey Richards, 'Old School Ties' in Aldgate and Richards, op. cit., pp. 87–97.
24 Lindsay Anderson, 'Get Out and Push!' in Tom Maschler (ed.) *Declaration*, London, 1957.
25 In 1948 Anderson dismissed the possibility of making films for 'the moronic mass audience' and declared that 'What is required is a cinema in which people can make films with as much freedom as if they were writing poems, painting pictures or composing string quartets.' 'A Possible Solution', *Sequence*, no. 3, Spring 1948, p. 9
26 Quoted by Geoff Brown, 'Which Way to the Way Ahead?', *Sight and Sound*, Autumn 1978, p. 242.
27 Sidney Bernstein, *Film and International Relations*, London, 1945, p. 7.
28 Geoff Brown, 'Which Way to the Way Ahead?', op. cit., p. 243.

6 Passionate Friends?

1 Herbert Lom as Dr Larsen the psychiatrist in *The Seventh Veil*.
2 Catherine de la Roche, 'That "Feminine Angle"', *Penguin Film Review* 8, January 1949, p. 34.
3 Peter Lewis, *A People's War*, London, 1986, p. 133.
4 Ellen Wilkinson quoted by Denise Riley, 'The Free Mothers', *History Workshop Journal* 11, Spring, p. 81.
5 Anne Scott-James, 'Why Women Don't Have Babies', *Picture Post*, 13 November 1943.
6 Elizabeth Wilson, *Women and the Welfare State*, London, 1977, p. 154.
7 Ibid.
8 Anne Scott-James, op. cit.
9 Lewis, op. cit., p. 147.
10 Catherine de la Roche, 'The Mask of Realism', *Penguin Film Review* 7, September 1948, pp. 37–8.
11 Sue Aspinall, 'Women, Realism and Reality in British Films 1943–53', in Vincent Porter and James Curran, *British Cinema History*, London, 1983, p. 282.
12 Lewis, op. cit., p. 151.
13 Eric Newby, *Something Wholesale*, London 1985, p. 195.
14 Pearson Phillips, 'The New Look', in Philip French and Michael Sissons, *The Age of Austerity*, Oxford, 1986, p. 132.
15 Catherine de la Roche, 'That "Feminine Angle"', op. cit., p. 27.
16 E. Arnot Robertson, 'Woman and the Film', *Penguin Film Review* 3, August 1947, p. 32.
17 *Evening Standard*, 30 April 1948.
18 Martha Wolfenstein and Nathan Leites, *Movies: A Psychological Study*, Glencoe, Illinois, 1950, p. 236.

19 *Kinematograph Weekly*, 13 February 1947.
20 Pam Cook, 'Melodrama and the Woman's Picture', Sue Aspinall and Robert Murphy (eds), *Gainsborough Melodrama*, London, 1983, p. 26.
21 Muriel Box, *Odd Woman Out*, London, 1974, p. 184.
22 *The Listener*, 29 November 1945.
23 Aspinall, 'Women, Realism and Reality', op. cit., p. 274.
24 Andre Bazin, 'Bicycle Thieves', *What Is Cinema*, vol. 2, Berkeley, 1971, p. 49. Bazin later had second thoughts and re-assessed his high opinion of *Brief Encounter*.
25 See John Ellis, 'Watching Death at Work' in Ian Christie (ed.), *Powell, Pressburger and Others*; and Christie's *Arrows of Desire*, London, 1985, for a more sustained analysis of the film.

7 Exotic Dreams

1 M.R. Booth, *English Melodrama*, London, 1965, p. 14.
2 Rachael Low, *The History of the British Film 1906–14*, London, p. 95.
3 MGM's mean-mindedness in collecting up all the old prints of the British version and destroying them perpetuated a myth that Dickinson's film is the superior of the two. In fact both are excellent. The American film (retitled *The Murder in Thornton Square* in Britain), is more complex, and more psychologically convincing – a good Hollywood thriller. But Dickinson's film with its fluttering upper class heroine (Diana Wynyard), its kindly, avuncular policeman and its black-hearted villain (Anton Walbrook), is a very satisfying melodrama. See Jeffrey Richards, *Thorold Dickinson*, London, 1986, pp. 72–82, for a detailed analysis of *Gaslight* and a judicious comparison with the MGM film.
4 A. E. Wilson, *East End Entertainment*, London, 1954, p. 134.
5 M. R. Booth, op. cit., p. 14.
6 Interview with Phyllis Calvert in Sue Aspinall and Robert Murphy (eds), *Gainsborough Melodrama*, London, 1983, p. 61.
7 Arthur Vesselo, 'Films of the Quarter', *Sight and Sound*, Summer 1947, p. 76.
8 *Daily Graphic*, 9 May 1947.
9 *Sunday Chronicle*, 17 August 1947.
10 *Daily Telegraph*, 20 June 1949.
11 Muriel Box, *Odd Woman Out*, London, 1974, p. 197.
12 Interview with Lady Gardiner in Aspinall and Murphy, op. cit., p. 64.
13 *The Spectator*, 1 April 1949.
14 Charles Barr, *Ealing Studios*, London and Newton Abbot, 1977, p. 61.
15 *The Times*, 13 September 1948.
16 Richard Winnington, 'Critical Survey', *Penguin Film Review* 2 January 1947, p. 16.
17 Arthur Vesselo, 'Films of the Quarter', *Sight and Sound*, Autumn 1948, p. 143.
18 Linda Wood, *The Commercial Imperative in the British Film Industry; Maurice Elvey, A Case Study*, London, 1987, pp. 30, 55.
19 Quoted by Jeffrey Richards, op. cit., pp. 142–3. Richards gives a detailed analysis of *The Queen of Spades* and an account of its production history.
20 Jeffrey Richards, 'Gainsborough: Maniac in the Cellar', *Monthly Film Bulletin*, September 1985, p. 293.

8 The Spiv Cycle

1 Billy Hill, *Boss of Britain's Underworld*, London, 1955, pp. 75–6.
2 Edward Smithies, *Crime in Wartime*, London, 1982, p. 58.
3 Ibid., pp. 87–8; Fred Barnes – Romford Food Officer – interviewed on 'A People's War', transmitted Channel 4, November 1986.
4 Smithies, op. cit., p. 52.
5 Geoff Brown, *Launder and Gilliat*, London, 1977, p. 105.
6 David Hughes, 'The Spivs' in Philip French and Michael Sissons (eds), *The Age of Austerity*, Oxford, 1986, pp. 87–8.
7 See, for example, Philip Carr, 'Licit or Illicit', *The Spectator*, 28 December 1945, p. 617.
8 Hughes, op. cit., p. 105.
9 The *People*, 9 March 1947, p. 2.
10 *News Chronicle*, 13 January 1945.
11 *New Statesman*, 17 January 1945; *Manchester Guardian*, 13 January 1945.
12 *New Statesman*, 2 November 1946.
13 The BBFC considered it 'undesirable and extremely unlikely to obtain our certificate'. *British Board of Film Censors Annual Report*, 1933, p. 246.
14 *New Statesman*, 16 August 1947.
15 Arthur Vesselo, 'Films of the Quarter', *Sight and Sound*, Autumn 1947, p. 120.
16 *Observer*, 20 November 1947.
17 See Charles Barr, *Ealing Studios*, London and Newton Abbot, 1977, p. 70; and the essays by Sheila Whitaker and Gerry Turvey in *Framework* no. 9, Winter 1978–9.
18 *Sunday Chronicle*, 30 November 1947.
19 Arthur Vesselo, 'Films of the Quarter', *Sight and Sound*, Winter 1947–8, p. 137.
20 Richard Winnington, *Film Criticism and Caricatures*. ed. Paul Rotha, London, 1975, p. 72.
21 *Reynold's News*, 11 January 1948.
22 *Sunday Times*, 18 June 1950.

9 Morbid Burrowings

1 Arthur Helliwell, the *People*, 23 March 1947.
2 Arthur Vesselo, 'Films of the Quarter', *Sight and Sound*, Autumn 1947.
3 *Kinematograph Weekly*, 18 December 1947, p. 18.
4 British critics who have attempted to explore the 'underside' of British cinema include Geoff Brown in his article 'Which Way to the Way Ahead?', *Sight and Sound*, Autumn 1978; Raymond Durgnat in *A Mirror for England*, London, 1970, and more recently, Julian Petley in his article 'The Lost Continent' in *All Our Yesterdays*, Charles Barr (ed.), London, 1986.
5 Frank Motteshaw, *The Life of Charles Peace*, and William Haggar. *Charles Peace*.
6 R. Broad and S. Fleming, *Nella Last's War*, Bristol, 1981, p. 57.
7 *Documentary Newsletter*, April/May 1947, p. 84.
8 Ibid., pp. 84–5.
9 Ibid., p. 85.
10 George Orwell, 'Decline of the English Murder', *Collected Essays, Journalism and Letters*, vol. 4, Harmondsworth, 1980, pp. 124–8.

11 Martha Wolfenstein and Nathan Leites, *Movies: A Psychological Study*, Glencoe, Illinois, 1950, p. 23.
12 Arthur Vesselo, 'Films of the Quarter', *Sight and Sound*, Summer 1947.
13 George Orwell, 'Raffles and Miss Blandish', *Collected Essays, Journalism and Letters*, vol. 3, pp. 256, 259.

10 Nothing to Laugh at at All

1 Herbert Wilcox, *Twenty-Five Thousand Sunsets*, London, 1967, p. 88.
2 Gracie Fields' last British film was *Shipyard Sally*, which was released in July 1939. However she remained tremendously popular in Britain as a live entertainer.
3 Quoted in Jeffrey Richards, *The Age of the Dream Palace*, London, 1984, p. 198.
4 Basil Dean, *Mind's Eye*, London, 1973, p. 213.
5 Quoted by Alan Randall and Ray Seaton, *George Formby*, London, 1974, p. 85.
6 According to his biographer, John M. East, 'Max's screen career was financially successful but artistically it was a disaster. He did not photograph well: he had a round face, a large nose and a small cranium. He was no good as a romantic lead. Without his byplay with an audience, he ceased to amuse people. His raucous voice and his speed of delivery often rendered him unintelligible.' *Max Miller*, London, 1977, p. 132.
7 Quoted Randall and Seaton, op. cit., pp. 16–17.
8 Jeffrey Richards, op. cit., p. 192.
9 All the Formby films released in the forties, with the exception of *Come on George* (Anthony Kimmins) and *Spare a Copper* (John Paddy Carstairs), were, directed by Marcel Varnel.
10 J. B. Priestley, *English Journey*, Harmondsworth, 1979, p. 375.
11 Arthur Askey, *Before Your Very Eyes*, London 1975, p. 98.
12 Ibid., p. 99.
13 George Orwell, 'The Lion and the Unicorn', in *Collected Essays, Journalism and Letters*, vol. 2, Harmondsworth, 1980, pp. 78–79.
14 Jeff Nuttall, *King Twist*, London, 1978, p. 52.
15 Leslie Halliwell, *Halliwell's Film Guide*, London, 1986, p. 905.
16 Julian Poole, 'British Cinema Attendance in Wartime', *Historical Journal of Film, Radio and Television*, vol. 7, no. 1, 1987, pp. 15–34.
17 Quoted by Jeff Nuttall, op. cit., p. 68.
18 I am indebted to Tony Coldwell's postgraduate research on Mancunian Studios at the University of East Anglia.
19 To be fair, the lack of cohesion I found in *When You Come Home* might be due to the missing chunk out of the version of the film I have seen.
20 For Old Mother Riley see John Fisher, *Funny Way to be a Hero*, London, 1976, pp. 72–81, and Jeffrey Richards, op. cit., pp. 298–9. Flanagan and Allen's films have yet to find a champion; *Dreaming*, the only one of the four I have seen is not one of Baxter's best, but the episode where Goebbels comes to England in person to sabotage Bud Flanagan's super de luxe Service canteen/dance hall is bizarre enough to deserve attention.
21 Ealing was not a studio which looked favourably on stars. See Stewart Granger's account of the frosty reception afforded him when he came to Ealing to work on *Saraband for Dead Lovers*; in *Sparks Fly Upwards*, London, 1981, pp. 110–13.
22 Gainsborough didn't have a similar faith in Margaret Lockwood's singing

powers and her voice was dubbed for the songs in *I'll be Your Sweetheart*, though ironically she was allowed to sing them live when touring the country promoting the film. See Margaret Lockwood, *Lucky Star*, London, 1955, p. 111.

23 Andy Medhurst, 'Music Hall and British Cinema' in *All Our Yesterdays*, Charles Barr (ed.), London, 1986, p. 181.

24 George Orwell, 'The Lion and the Unicorn', op. cit., p. 88.

25 J.B. Priestley, op. cit., p. 372.

26 Charles Barr puts forward a convincing case for *Cheer Boys Cheer*, also directed by Walter Forde, as a precursor of the Ealing comedy proper. Charles Barr, *Ealing Studios*, London and Newton Abbot, 1977, p. 5.

27 For Will Hay, see Allen Eyles, 'Will Hay and Co.', *Focus on Film*, no. 34, December 1979, pp. 5–18, and Ray Seaton and Roy Martin, *Good Morning Boys*, London, 1978.

28 With the possible exception of Launder and Gilliat's *Green for Danger*, almost too much of a thriller to qualify as a comedy, and Sydney Box's suburban middle-class sex comedy *29 Acacia Avenue*, none of the films of 1945 or 1946 did much to indicate future trends.

29 Michael Balcon, *A Lifetime of Films*, London, 1969, p. 159.

30 Charles Barr, op. cit., where most of the important Ealing comedies are analysed in perceptive detail.

31 See Colin Ward and Dennis Hardy, *Goodnight Campers*, London, 1986, for the popularity of holiday camps.

32 Henry Cass, a former theatre director who had been brought into films by Sydney Box to direct *29 Acacia Avenue*, presumably knew Priestley through his stage work.

11 Challenge to Hollywood

1 J. Arthur Rank speaking on 'Challenge to Hollywood', a *March of Time* programme released December 1945.

2 Quoted in Alan Sked and Chris Cook, *Post-War Britain*, Harmondsworth, 1980, p. 29.

3 *Variety*, 6 March 1946, p. 5.

4 Ibid., 30 October 1946, p. 3.

5 Ibid., 11 June 1947, p. 1.

6 *Kinematograph Weekly*, 2 October 1947, British Studio Supplement, p. iv.

7 Board of Trade minute quoted by Paul Swann, *The Hollywood Feature Film in Postwar Britain*, London, 1987, p. 128.

8 According to the PEP Report, *The British Film Industry*, London, 1952, p. 95, thirty-two of the sixty-three feature films registered for quota in 1947–8 came from the Rank companies.

9 See, for example, *Economist*, 20 November 1947, p. 1041.

10 *Variety*, 9 June 1948, p. 3.

11 Ibid., 27 October 1948, p. 3.

12 Ibid., 2 March 1949, p. 15.

13 Ibid., 6 October 1948, p. 18. The figures were: an average of $2,348 per week for British films, $2,264 for American films.

14 Ibid., 17 November 1948, p. 3. For a more detailed account of how British films fared in the American market, see Robert Murphy, 'Rank's Attempt on the American Market' in James Curran and Vincent Porter (eds), *British Cinema History*, London, 1983.

15 *Economist*, 12 November 1949, p. 1076, analysed Rank's accounts and concluded: 'The Odeon group, then, is stripped and bare. It has emerged from a disastrous year only by pulling out reserves and bringing in special credits on the grand scale. It will not be able to repeat those devices in a second year.'

16 PEP, op. cit., p. 109.

17 Geoff Brown, *Launder and Gilliat*, London, 1977, p. 124.

18 *Kinematograph Weekly*, 6 February 1947, p. 20.

19 PEP, op. cit., p. 118.

20 According to Sarah Street and Margaret Dickinson, even the government-backed Finance Corporation for Industry refused to get involved, turning down a request from Korda for a loan of £1,000,000 in February 1948. *Cinema and State*, London, 1985, p. 212.

21 PEP, op. cit., p. 258.

22 Sarah Street and Margaret Dickinson, op. cit., p. 222.

23 *The Crisis of British Films*, Film Industry Employees Council, London, 1951, p. 3.

24 The high price paid for cinemas by the Ostrer brothers and John Maxwell when they were building up their Gaumont-British and ABC circuits, and the speed with which exhibitors installed expensive American sound equipment could be cited as evidence of this prosperity, though it would have to be balanced against the long hours and low wages of cinema employees.

25 Sarah Street and Margaret Dickinson, op. cit., p. 209.

26 *The Crisis of British Films*, op. cit., p. 3.

Conclusion

1 J.P. Mayer, *British Cinemas and their Audiences*, London, 1948, document 28A, twenty-two-year-old male Jack of all trades, p. 202.

2 J.P. Mayer, *Sociology of Film*, London, 1946, p. 25.

3 Mayer, *British Cinemas and their Audiences*, document 17A, eighteen-year-old female aspiring drama student, p. 188.

4 Mayer, *Sociology of Film*, p. 182, for Deanna Durbin's suitor.

5 Ibid., pp. 278–9.

6 Mayer, *British Cinemas and their Audiences*, p. 249.

7 Lindsay Anderson, 'A Possible Solution', *Sequence*, Spring 1948, p. 9.

Chronology

1 At the end of each year Josh Billings the *Kine Weekly* reviewer compiled what he called his 'book of form', an assessment of the box-office performance of the year's films. His calculations were not based on actual attendance figures and should not be taken as infallible, but his contacts in the industry were extensive and his results seem to have been generally accepted as fair and accurate. Two important points should be borne in mind however. First, that Billings often includes among his successes films like *Major Barbara* and *London Town* which were made on such large budgets that what they brought in at the box-office failed to cover their costs, and conversely he ignores films like *Next of Kin* where an economical budget combined with modest box-office success to make for very healthy profits. Second, Billings' assessments are based on how well a film was received on its general, country-wide, release and consequently films like *In*

Which We Serve, The Wicked Lady, Green for Danger, and *It Always Rains On Sunday,* shown in the West End at the end of a particular year are included in the next year's results.

2 I have chosen to calculate the number of films released in a year as those films of sixty minutes or over listed by Denis Gifford in *The British Film Catalogue 1895–1985.* The cut-off point of sixty minutes might seem arbitrary, particularly in dealing with the large number of featurettes released from 1947 onwards, but it has the virtue of simplicity. Gifford's catalogue is solely devoted to fiction films, but during the war feature-length drama documentaries and newsreel reconstruction films played too important a part to be ignored and I have included: *Target for Tonight* (1941), *Coastal Command* (1942), *Fires Were Started* (1943), *Desert Victory* (1943), *Close Quarters* (1943), *Tunisian Victory* (1944), *The True Glory* (1945), *Western Approaches* (1945), and *Theirs Was the Glory* (1945), in the number of films released between 1940–45.

Bibliography

Addison, Paul, *Now the War is Over*, London, Jonathan Cape, 1985.

Addison, Paul, *The Road to 1945*, London, Quartet Books, 1977.

Aldgate, Tony and Richards, Jeffrey, *Best of British*, Oxford, Basil Blackwell, 1983.

Aldgate, Tony and Richards, Jeffrey, *Britain Can Take It*, Oxford, Basil Blackwell, 1986.

Anderson, Lindsay, 'Angle of Approach', *Sequence 2*, Winter 1947.

Anderson, Lindsay, 'British Cinema: The Descending Spiral', *Sequence 7*, Spring 1949.

Anderson, Lindsay, 'Only Connect: Some Aspects of the Work of Humphrey Jennings', *Sight and Sound*, April/June 1954.

Anderson, Lindsay, 'A Possible Solution', *Sequence 3*, Spring 1948.

Anstey, Edgar, Hardy, Forsyth, Lindgren, Ernest, and Manvell, Roger (eds), *Shots in the Dark*, London, Allan Wingate, 1951.

Armes, Roy, *A Critical History of the British Cinema*, London, Secker & Warburg, 1978.

Askey, Arthur, *Before Your Very Eyes*, London, Woburn Press, 1975.

Aspinall, Sue and Murphy, Robert (eds), *Gainsborough Melodrama*, London, British Film Institute, 1983.

Balcon, Michael, *Michael Balcon Presents . . . A Lifetime of Films*, London, Hutchinson, 1969.

Balcon, Michael, *Realism and Tinsel*, London, Workers Film Association, 1944.

Balcon, Michael, Hardy, Forsyth, Lindgren, Ernest, and Manvell, Roger, *Twenty Years of British Films*, London, Falcon Press, 1947.

Barr, Charles, *Ealing Studios*, London and Newton Abbott, Cameron & Tayleur/David & Charles, 1977.

Barr, Charles (ed.), *All Our Yesterdays*, London, British Film Institute, 1986.

Barsacq, Leon, *Caligari's Cabinet and Other Grand Illusions*, New York, New American Library, 1978.

Bernstein, Sidney, *The Film and International Relations*, London, Workers Film Association, 1945.

Betts, Ernest, *The Film Business*, London, Allen & Unwin, 1973.

Bogarde, Dirk, *Snakes and Ladders*, London, Chatto & Windus, 1978.

Bond, Ralph, *Monopoly: The Future of British Film*, London, Association of Cine Technicians, 1946.

Booth, M.R., *English Melodrama*, London, Herbert Jenkins, 1965.

Box, K., *The Cinema and the Public*, London, Central Office of Information, 1947.

Box, K. and Moss, L., *The Cinema Audience*, London, Ministry of Information, 1943.

Box, Muriel, *Odd Woman Out*, London, Leslie Frewin, 1974.

Braun, Eric, *Deborah Kerr*, London, W. H. Allen, 1977.

Braun, Eric, 'Images in a Chocolate Box', *Films and Filming*, November 1973.

Braun, Eric, 'The Indestructibles', *Films and Filming*, September 1973.

Braun, Eric, 'Rank's Young Generation', *Films and Filming*, October 1973.

British Film Academy, *The Film Industry in Great Britain: Some Facts and Figures*, London, British Film Academy, 1950.

Broad, R. and Fleming, S. (eds), *Nella Last's War: A Mother's Diary*, Bristol, Falling Wall Press, 1981.

Brown, Geoff, 'Ealing Your Ealing', *Sight and Sound*, Summer 1977.

Brown, Geoff, *Launder and Gilliat*, London, British Film Institute, 1977.

Brown, Geoff, *Walter Forde*, London, British Film Institute, 1977.

Brown, Geoff, 'Which Way to the Way Ahead?', *Sight and Sound*, Autumn 1978.

Brunel, Adrian, *Nice Work*, London, Forbes Robertson, 1949.

Busby, Roy, *British Music Hall – An Illustrated Who's Who from 1850 to the Present Day*, London, Paul Elek, 1976.

Calder, Angus, *The People's War*, London, Granada, 1971.

Carrick, Edward, *Art and Design in the British Film*, London, Dobson, 1948.

Cavalcanti, Alberto, Interview with Alan Lovell, Jim Hillier, and Sam Rohdie, *Screen* 13/2, Summer 1972.

Christie, Ian, *Arrows of Desire*, London, Waterstone, 1985.

Christie, Ian (ed.), *Powell, Pressburger and Others*, London, British Film Institute, 1973.

Clark, Kenneth, *The Other Half*, London, John Murray, 1977.

Clarke, T.E.B., *This is Where I Came In*, London, Michael Joseph, 1974.

Collier, John W., *A Film in the Making: It Always Rains On Sunday*, London, World Film Publications, 1947.

Cook, Chris and Sked, Alan, *Post-War Britain: A Political History*, Harmondsworth, Penguin, 1980.

Costello, John, *Love, Sex and War*, London, Pan Books, 1985.

Crow, Duncan (uncredited), *P.E.P. Report: The British Film Industry*, London, Political and Economic Planning, 1952.

Crow, Duncan, 'The Protected Industry' (in five parts), *Sight and Sound*, December 1950–April 1951.

Curran, James and Porter, Vincent (eds), *British Cinema History*, London, Weidenfeld & Nicolson, 1983.

Dalton, Hugh, *High Tide and After*, London, Frederick Muller, 1962.

Danischewsky, Monja, *White Russian, Red Face*, London, Victor Gollancz, 1966.

Darlow, Michael and Hodson, Gillian, *Terence Rattigan: The Man and His Work*, London, Quartet Books, 1979.

Davenport, Nicholas, *Memoirs of a City Radical*, London, Weidenfeld & Nicolson, 1974.

Davenport, Nicholas and Winnington, Richard, *Crisis in the Studios* (pamphlet), London, News Chronicle, 1950.

Dean, Basil, *Mind's Eye*, London, Hutchinson, 1973.

De La Roche, Catherine, 'That "Feminine Angle"', *Penguin Film Review* 8, January 1949.

De La Roche, Catherine, 'The Mask of Realism', *Penguin Film Review* 7, September 1948.

Denison, Michael, *Overture and Beginners*, London, Victor Gollancz, 1973.

Dickinson, Margaret and Street, Sarah, *Cinema and State: The Film Industry and the Government 1927–84*, London, British Film Institute, 1985.

Durgnat, Raymond, *A Mirror For England*, London, Faber & Faber, 1970.

Durgnat, Raymond, 'The Great British Phantasmagoria', *Film Comment*, May/June 1977.

Durgnat, Raymond (as O.O Green), 'Michael Powell', *Movie* 14, Autumn 1965.

Durgnat, Raymond, 'Two on a Tandem', *Films and Filming*, July 1966.

East, John M., *Max Miller*, London, W.H. Allen, 1977.

Ellis, John, 'Art, Culture and Quality – terms for a Cinema in the Forties and Seventies', *Screen* 19/3, Autumn 1978.

Everson, William K., 'Arthur Askey', *Films in Review*, March 1986.

Eyles, Allen, 'Universal and International', *Focus on Film* 30, June 1978.

Eyles, Allen, 'Will Hay and Co.', *Focus on Film* 34, December 1979.

Farrar, David, *No Royal Road*, Eastbourne, Mortimer Publications, 1948.

Fisher, John, *Funny Way to Be a Hero*, London, Frederick Muller, 1973.

Fisher, John, *George Formby*, London, Woburn-Futura, 1975.

Fisher, John, *What a Performance: A Life of Sid Field*, London, Seeley Service, 1975.

Foot, Paul, *The Politics of Harold Wilson*, Harmondsworth, Penguin, 1968.

French, Philip and Sissons, Michael (eds), *The Age of Austerity*, Oxford, Oxford University Press, 1986.

Gater, G.H. (Chairman), *Report of the Working Party on Film Production Costs*, London, HMSO, 1949.

Gibson, Monk, *The Red Shoes Ballet: A Critical Study*, London, Saturn Press, 1967.

Gifford, Denis, *The British Film Catalogue 1895–1985*, Newton Abbot and London, David & Charles, 1986.

Granger, Stewart, *Sparks Fly Upwards*, London, Granada, 1981.

Griffiths, Richard, 'Where Are the Dollars?' (in three parts), *Sight and Sound*, December 1949, January and March 1950.

Grigg, John, *1943: The Victory That Never Was*, London, Methuen, 1985.

Guback, Thomas, *The International Film Industry*, Bloomington, Indiana University Press, 1969.

Guinness, Alec, *Blessings in Disguise*, London, Fontana, 1986.

Halliwell, Leslie, *Halliwell's Film Guide*, London, Granada, 1985.

Hardy, Dennis and Ward, Colin, *Goodnight Campers*, London and New York, Mansell, 1986.

Harper, Sue, 'History With Frills', *Red Letters* 14, Winter 1982–3.

Harrisson, Tom, *Living Through the Blitz*, London, Collins, 1976.

Hewison, Robert, *In Anger: Culture in the Cold War 1945–60*, London, Weidenfeld & Nicolson, 1981.

Hewison, Robert, *Under Siege: Literary Life in London 1939–45*, London, Quartet Books, 1979.

Hillier, Jim and Lovell, Alan, *Studies in Documentary*, London, Secker & Warburg, 1972.

Hodson, J.L., *The Sea and the Land*, London, Victor Gollancz, 1945.

Hopkins, Harry, *The New Look*, London, Secker & Warburg, 1963.

Humphries, Steve and Taylor, John, *The Making of Modern London 1945–1985*, London, Sidgwick & Jackson, 1986.

Huntley, John, *British Film Music*, London, Skelton Robinson, 1947.

Huntley, John, *British Technicolor Films*, London, Skelton Robinson, 1948.

Hurd, Geoff (ed.), *National Fictions*, London, British Film Institute, 1984.

Hurst, Brian Desmond, 'The Lady Vanishes', *Sight and Sound*, August 1950.

Jennings, Mary-Lou (ed.), *Humphrey Jennings: Film-maker, Painter, Poet*, London, British Film Institute, 1982.

Junge, Helmut, *Plan for Film Studios*, London, Focal Press, 1945.

Katz, Ephraim, *The International Film Encyclopedia*, London, Macmillan, 1982.

Korda, Michael, *Charmed Lives*, London, Allen Lane, 1980.

Kulik, Karol, *Alexander Korda: The Man Who Could Work Miracles*, London, W.H. Allen, 1975.

Labour Party, *Proposals for Improvement in the British Film Industry. Report of the Film Sub-Committee of the Trade and Industry Group of the Labour Party*, London, Labour Party, 1946.

Lambert, Gavin, 'British Films. 1947: Survey and Prospect', *Sequence* 2, Winter 1947/8

Lee, Norman, *Log of a Film Director*, London, Quality Press, 1949.

Lewis, Peter, *A People's War*, London, Thames Methuen, 1986.

Litewski, Chaim and Porter, Vincent, *'The Way Ahead:* Case History of a Propaganda Film', *Sight and Sound*, Spring 1981.

Lockwood, Margaret, *Lucky Star*, London, Odhams, 1955.

Longmate, Norman, *The G.I.s: The Americans in Britain 1942–1945*, London, Hutchinson, 1975.

Longmate, Norman, *How We Lived Then*, London, Hutchinson, 1971.

Low, Rachael, *Film Making in 1930s Britain*, London, Allen & Unwin, 1985.

Low, Rachael, 'The Implications Behind the Social Survey', *Penguin Film Review* 7, September 1948.

McCallum, John, *Life With Googie*, London, Heinemann, 1979.

Manvell, Roger (ed.), *The Years Work in Film (1949)*, London, Longmans Green, 1950.

Manvell, Roger (ed.), *The Years Work in Film (1950)*, London, Longmans Green, 1951.

Martin, Roy and Seaton, Ray, *Good Morning Boys: Will Hay, Master of Comedy*, London, Barrie & Jenkins, 1978.

Martin, Roy and Seaton, Ray, 'Gainsborough in the Forties', *Films and Filming*, June 1982.

Marwick, Arthur, *British Society Since 1945*, Harmondsworth, Penguin, 1982.

Mason, James, *Before I Forget*, London, Hamish Hamilton, 1981.

Mass Observation, *The Journey Home*, London, Advertising Service Guild, 1944.

Mass Observation, *Peace and the Public*, London, Longmans Green, 1947.

Mass Observation, *People in Production*, London, Advertising Service Guild, 1942.

Mass Observation, *Puzzled People*, London, Victor Gollancz, 1947.

Mass Observation, *War Begins at Home*, London, Chatto & Windus, 1940.

Mass Observation, *War Factory*, London, Victor Gollancz, 1943.

Mass Observation, 'Film and Public: *Chance of a Lifetime*', *Sight and Sound*, January 1951.

Matthews, A.E., *Matty: An Autobiography*, London, Hutchinson, 1952.

Mayer, J.P., *British Cinemas and their Audiences*, London, Dennis Dobson, 1948.

Mayer, J.P., *Sociology of Film*, London, Faber & Faber, 1946.

Millar, Daniel, 'Fires Were Started', *Sight and Sound*, Spring 1969.

Mills, John, *Up in the Clouds, Gentlemen, Please*, London, Weidenfeld & Nicolson, 1980.

Minney, R.J., *Puffin Asquith*, London, Leslie Frewin, 1973.

Minns, Raynes, *Bombers and Mash: The Domestic Front 1939–45*, London, Virago, 1980

Monaghan, J.P., *The Authorized Biography of James Mason*, London, World Film Publications, 1947.

Montgomery, John, *Comedy Films*, London, Allen & Unwin, 1954.

Moorehead, Caroline, *Lord Bernstein*, London, Jonathan Cape, 1984.

Morgan, Guy, *Red Roses Every Night*, London, Quality Press, 1948.

Morley, Sheridan, *A Talent to Amuse: A Biography of Noel Coward*, London, Heinemann, 1969.

Morley, Sheridan, *Tales from the Hollywood Raj*, New York, Viking Press, 1984.

Mullally, Frederick, *Films – An Alternative to Rank*, London, Socialist Book Centre, 1946.

Neagle, Anna, *There's Always Tomorrow*, London, W.H. Allen, 1974.

Nuttall, Jeff, *King Twist: A Portrait of Frank Randle*, London, Routledge & Kegan Paul, 1978.

Oakley, C.A., *Where We Came In*, London, Allen & Unwin, 1964.

Orwell, George, *Collected Essays, Journalism and Letters* (four volumes), Harmondsworth, Penguin, 1971.

Orwell, George, *The Road to Wigan Pier*, Harmondsworth, Penguin, 1979.

Palache, Albert (Chairman), *Tendencies to Monopoly in the Cinematograph Film Industry. Report of a Committee Appointed by the Cinematograph Films Council*, London, HMSO, 1944.

Palmer, Scott, *A Who's Who of British Film Actors*, Metuchen, New Jersey, Scarecrow Press, 1981.

Pascal, Valerie, *The Devil and his Disciple*, London, Michael Joseph, 1971.

Perry, George, *Forever Ealing*, London, Pavilion/Michael Joseph, 1981.

Perry, George, *The Great British Picture Show*, London, Pavilion Books, 1985.

Perry, George, *Movies from the Mansion: A History of Pinewood Studios*, London, Elm Tree Books/Hamish Hamilton, 1976.

Pirie, David, *A Heritage of Horror*, London, Gordon Fraser, 1973.

Plant, Sir Arnold (Chairman), *Report of the Committee of Inquiry into the Distribution and Exhibition of Cinematograph Films*, London, HMSO, 1949.

Poole, Julian, 'British Cinema Attendance in Wartime: Audience Preference at the Majestic, Macclesfield, 1939–1946', *Historical Journal of Film, Radio and Television*, vol. 7 no. 1, 1987.

Powell, Dilys, *Films Since 1939*, London, Longmans Green, 1947.

Powell, Michael, *A Life in Movies*, London, Heinemann, 1986.

Pronay, Nicholas and Spring, D.W. (eds), *Propaganda, Politics and Film 1918–45*, London, Macmillan, 1982.

Pronay, Nicholas and Thorpe, Frances, *British Official Films in the Second World War*, Oxford, Clio Press, 1980.

Quinlan, David, *British Sound Films*, London, B.T. Batsford, 1984.

Randall, Alan and Seaton, Ray, *George Formby*, London, W.H. Allen, 1974.

Raynor, Henry, 'Nothing to Laugh at', *Sight and Sound*, April 1950.

Redgrave, Michael, *In My Mind's Eye*, London, Weidenfeld & Nicolson, 1983.

Redgrave, Michael, *Mask or Face: Reflections in an Actor's Mirror*, London, Heinemann, 1958.

Richards, Jeffrey, *The Age of the Dream Palace*, London, Routledge & Kegan Paul, 1984.

Richards, Jeffrey, *Thorold Dickinson*, London, Croom Helm, 1986.

Richards, Jeffrey, 'Maniac in the Cellar', *Monthly Film Bulletin*, September 1985.

Richards, Jeffrey, 'Wartime British Cinema Audiences and the Class System: the Case of *Ships With Wings* (1941), *Historical Journal of Film, Radio and Television*, vol. 7 no. 2, 1987.

Riley, Denise, 'The Free Mothers: Pronatalism and Working Women in Industry at the End of the Last War in Britain', *History Workshop Journal* 11, Spring 1981.

Robertson, E. Arnot, 'Woman and the Film', *Penguin Film Review* 3, August 1947.

Robertson, James, *The British Board of Film Censors: Film Censorship in Britain 1896–1950*, London, Croom Helm, 1985.

Robson, E.W. and M.M., *The Shame and Disgrace of Colonel Blimp*, London, Sidneyan Society, 1943.

Robson, E.W. and M.M., *The World is My Cinema*, London, Sidneyan Society, 1947.

Rotha, Paul, *Rotha on the Film*, London, Faber & Faber, 1958.

Short, K.R.M., *Feature Films as History*, London, Croom Helm, 1981.

Smithies, Edward, *Crime in Wartime*, London, Allen & Unwin, 1982.

Speakman, W.J., 'Audience Reaction', *Film Appreciation and Visual Education*, London, British Film Institute, 1944.

Sussex, Elizabeth, *The Rise and Fall of British Documentary*, Berkeley and London, University of California Press, 1975.

Swann, Paul, *The Hollywood Feature Film in Postwar Britain*, London, Croom Helm, 1987.

Taylor, A.J.P., *English History 1914–45*, Harmondsworth, Penguin, 1976.

Taylor, John Russell, *Alec Guinness – A Celebration*, London, Pavilion/Michael Joseph, 1984.

Todd, Ann, *The Eighth Veil*, London, William Kimber, 1980.

Trewin, J.C., *Robert Donat: A Biography*, London, Heinemann, 1968.

Truby, Jeffrey (ed.), *British Films of 1947*, London, Winchester Publications, 1948.

Truby, Jeffrey (ed.), *Daily Mail Film Award Annual 1948*, London, Winchester Publications, 1948.

Truby, Jeffrey (ed.), *British Film Annual 1949*, London, Winchester Publications, 1949.

Ustinov, Peter, *Dear Me*, London, Heinemann, 1977.

Vaughan, Dai, *Portrait of an Invisible Man*, London, British Film Institute, 1983.

Vargas, A.L., 'British Films and Their Audience', *Penguin Film Review* 8, January 1949.

Voight, Michael, 'Pictures of Innocence: Sir Carol Reed', *Focus on Film* 17, Spring 1974.

Watt, Harry, *Don't Look at the Camera*, London, Paul Elek, 1974.

West, Rebecca, *A Train of Powder*, London, Virago, 1984.

Wilcox, Herbert, *Twenty-Five Thousand Sunsets*, London, Bodley Head, 1967.

Wilding, Michael, *Apple Sauce*, London, Allen & Unwin, 1982.

Wilson, Elizabeth, *Only Halfway to Paradise*, London, Tavistock, 1980.

Wilson, Elizabeth, *Women and the Welfare State*, London, Tavistock, 1977.

Wilson, Harold, Interview with Margaret Dickinson and Simon Hartog, *Screen* 22/3, 1981.

Winnington, Richard, *Film Criticism and Caricatures 1943–53*, London, Paul Elek, 1975.

Wolfenstein, Martha and Leites, Nathan, *Movies: A Psychological Study*, Glencoe, Illinois, Free Press, 1950.

Wood, Alan, *The Groundnut Affair*, London, Bodley Head, 1950.

Wood, Alan, *Mr Rank*, London, Hodder & Stoughton, 1952.

Wood, Linda, *British Films 1927–1939*, London, British Film Institute, 1986.

Wood, Linda, *The Commercial Imperative in the British Film Industry; Maurice Elvey, a Case Study*, London, British Film Institute, 1987.

Index of Film Titles

General Index